T0385445

HARVARD EARLY MODERN AND
MODERN GREEK LIBRARY

SELECTED POEMS

NIKOS ENGONOPOULOS

HEMMGL III

HARVARD EARLY MODERN AND MODERN GREEK LIBRARY

Series Editors: Panagiotis Roilos, Dimitrios Yatromanolakis

Harvard Early Modern and Modern Greek Library makes accessible to scholars and general readers, through both original text and English translation, major works of Greek literature and thought produced in the last millennium, from vernacular Greek texts of the late eleventh century to the present.

Advisory Board

NIKOS ENGONOPOULOS

SELECTED POEMS

TRANSLATED WITH AN INTRODUCTION BY

DAVID CONNOLLY

HARVARD EARLY MODERN AND MODERN GREEK LIBRARY
HARVARD UNIVERSITY
DEPARTMENT OF THE CLASSICS
DISTRIBUTED BY HARVARD UNIVERSITY PRESS
CAMBRIDGE, MASSACHUSETTS
2016

Library of Congress Cataloging-in-Publication Data

Names: Engonopoulos, Nikos, 1907-1985, author. | Connolly, David, 1954-
translator, writer of introduction.
Title: Selected poems / Nikos Engonopoulos ; translated with an introduction
by David Connolly.
Description: Cambridge, Massachusetts : Harvard University, Department of the
Classics ; Distributed by Harvard University Press, 2016. | Series:
Harvard early modern and modern Greek library ; III | Includes
bibliographical references and index.
Identifiers: LCCN 2016045715 | ISBN 9780674063440 (hardcover : alk. paper)
Subjects: LCSH: Engonopoulos, Nikos, 1907-1985--Translations into English.
Classification: LCC PA5610.E5 A2 2016 | DDC 889.1/32--dc23
LC record available at https://lccn.loc.gov/2016045715

Ἡ ἀγάπη εἶναι ὁ μόνος τρόπος κάτι νὰ γνωρίσουμε
Love is the only way for us to know something

Nikos Engonopoulos

Acknowledgements

Earlier versions of translations in this selection have previously been published in *Modern Greek Studies Yearbook, Poetry Greece, Modern Greek Writing, Atlanta Review, A Century of Greek Poetry 1900–2, The Greek Poets. Homer to the Present* and in a bilingual edition Ὡραῖος σὰν Ἕλληνας / *The Beauty of a Greek.*

Contents

· CONTENTS ·

Foreword

Harvard Early Modern and Modern Greek Library makes accessible to scholars and general readers, through both original text and English translation, major works of Greek literature and thought produced in the last millennium, from vernacular Greek texts of the late eleventh century to the present. Each volume offers a reliable Greek text together with an accurate and literate English translation on facing pages. The editors/translators provide wide-ranging introductions as well as explanatory notes and selective bibliographies. This series presents current scholarship in a convenient and elegant format, aiming to make this substantial component of postclassical European literature available to researchers and students from a broad range of disciplines.

The present volume includes important works by Nikos Engonopoulos, one of the most prominent representatives of Greek Surrealist poetry and painting. Closely associated with Andreas Embeirikos, the "patriarch" of Surrealism in Greece, and with Nicolas Calas, an influential figure of the European and American avant-garde, Engonopoulos developed highly experimental pictorial and poetic aesthetics. Both in his paintings and poems, he engaged in a critical, often ironic dialogue with Greek history and cultural traditions and their ideological appropriations in established cultural and political discourses. His overall approach to the Greek past, informed as it was by the socioaesthetic principles of French Surrealism, constitutes one of the most ingenious and provocative cases of artistic *mythogenesis* in the European avant-garde (see Yatromanolakis 2012). Remaining a nonconformist artist and thinker throughout his life, Engonopoulos was arguably the keenest advocate of Surrealist black humor and irony in Greece. His poetic language, not unlike that of Embeirikos but in a distinctively personal fashion, combined lexical and morphological forms of simple or elevated puristic Greek with demotic ones and with elements of the Constantinopolitan dialect.

Engonopoulos's best-known work is the long poem *Bolivar*, which was written in the winter of 1942–1943 and circulated in handwritten copies before its publication in 1944. Inspired by the feats of the homonymous Latin American hero and by the Greek historical past and present, that work was received by Engonopoulos's readers as an emblematic act of resistance against the Nazis and their allies (Italians and Bulgarians) who had occupied Greece in 1941.

Panagiotis Roilos
Dimitrios Yatromanolakis

Introduction

I. "The Marvel of Elbasan and of the Bosphorus..."

Στὸν ὑπερρεαλισμό δὲν προσεχώρησα ποτέ. Τὸν ὑπερρεαλισμό τὸν εἶχα μέσα μου...
I never went over to surrealism. I always had surrealism in me...
Nikos Engonopoulos

1. General

Nikos Engonopoulos was born in Athens in 1907, with family roots in Constantinople on his father's side and in Hydra on his mother's side. In 1914, following the outbreak of the First World War, his family moved to Constantinople where he attended a private school. He continued his education in Paris as a boarder at high school from 1919 to 1927. This cosmopolitan upbringing perhaps accounts for his wide-ranging knowledge of foreign languages and literatures in addition to his deep knowledge of the Greek language and tradition in all its phases. After returning to Athens and completing his national service, he enrolled in the School of Fine Arts in 1932 and studied under the renowned Greek painter, Konstantinos Parthenis. At the same time, he worked as an apprentice in the studio of the equally renowned painter and iconographer, Fotis Kontoglou. His first appearance in Greek letters came in February 1938 with the publication of his translations of poetry by Tristan Tzara and others. In March of the same year, he published three of his own poems in the literary magazine, *O Kyklos*, and, in June, his first collection, *Do Not Distract the Driver*. With Greece's entry into the Second World War in 1941, he was enlisted and served on the Albanian front. He was taken prisoner by the Germans, escaped and walked half the length of Greece to return to Athens. In 1945, he was seconded from a minor post in the Ministry of Public Works to teach in the School of Architecture in the National Technical University of Athens, eventually becoming a tenured lecturer there in 1956 and professor in 1969. As a painter, he held many individual and group exhibitions both in Greece and abroad and represented Greece at the Biennale in Venice in 1954. He also designed the sets and costumes for numerous theatrical productions. He was awarded the National Prize for Poetry in 1958 for his collection, *In the Flourishing Greek Tongue*, and again in 1979 for his collection, *In the Vale of Roseries*. He married twice, acquiring a son from his first and a daughter from his second marriage. He died in 1985.

Derided and maligned more than any other Greek artist for his innovative and, at the time, often incomprehensible modernist experiments, Engonopoulos is today justifiably regarded as one of the leading and most original artists of his generation and as a unique figure in Greek letters. Though he considered himself first a painter and only afterwards a poet, his poetry is widely read and appreciated, with more and more critical studies appearing in the last twenty years or so[1] and with a growing recognition of the dynamism of his work and its creative use of the Greek tradition and Greek language. He enriched post-war Greek poetry with a host of poetic expressions,

[1] Writing in 1978, Argyriou notes that although Engonopoulos' work is praiseworthy, it has still not been critically appraised (Alexandros Argyriou, *Διαδοχικές ἀναγνώσεις Ἑλλήνων ὑπερρεαλιστῶν*, Athens 1983: 170).

figures and images[2] that have come to constitute part of the Greek poetic consciousness and it is no exaggeration to say that many of these have now become, as Abatzopoulou says, "incorporated into our daily lives."[3] In both his painting and poetry, he created a peculiarly Greek surrealism, a blending of the Dionysian and Apollonian, though always in keeping with basic surrealist tenets[4], and, as such, his work can be considered a substantial and original contribution to western art and poetry.

2. The "surrealist scandal"

His recognition today would have been impossible to imagine in 1938, given the outcry following the publication of his first collection, *Do Not Distract the Driver*. The reaction in literary circles and in the press to this collection and to the first works by his fellow surrealist poets came to be known as the "Surrealist Scandal."[5] It is note-

---

[2] For example, expressions such as: "...the beauty of a Greek," "This is no playground: / This is the Balkans" and "Art and poetry do not help us to live / art and poetry help us to die"; figures such as: "Guillaume Tsitzes" and "Jef, the Great Automaton"; images such as: "the blind lighthouse-keeper" and "the secret of the well."

[3] Frangiski Abatzopoulou, *...δὲν ἄνθισαν ματαίως. Ἀνθολογία ὑπερρεαλισμοῦ*, Athens 1980: 367.

[4] Surrealism, according to Engonopoulos, means "...confronting life with passion. Confronting all the phenomena of life, even in its most extreme metaphysical implications. Since every single thing contains life, the aim of surrealism is to make that life evident. This is why it makes use of astonishing and unexpected combinations, which provoke hilarity in the uninitiated. This disparate juxtaposition is employed in order to release every element in the combination, because of the difference between them, and thus reveal in a striking manner what the artist wants to present. [...] If sometimes there is something absurd in a work, what person in good faith would not accept that life too has its absurdities?" (Nikos Engonopoulos, *οἱ ἄγγελοι στὸν παράδεισο μιλοῦν ἑλληνικὰ... Συνεντεύξεις, Σχόλια καὶ Γνῶμες*, ed. Yorgos Kendrotis, Athens 1999: 19).

[5] For a full account of this, see Sotiris Trivizas, *Τὸ σουρεαλιστικό σκάνδαλο. Χρονικὸ τῆς ὑποδοχῆς τοῦ ὑπερρεαλιστικοῦ κινήματος στὴν Ἑλλάδα*, Athens 1996.

worthy that it was Engonopoulos who bore the brunt of these attacks in comparison to his fellow poet and friend, Andreas Embirikos, who had published his own first collection, entitled Ὑψικάμινος [Blast Furnace] in March 1935. This was the first genuinely surrealist work to appear in Greece. Two months earlier, Embirikos had delivered in Athens his now famous lecture on Surrealism, but this apparently did not prove sufficient to prepare the ground for the reception of the first surrealist works in Greece.[6] The initial bewilderment following the publication of *Blast Furnace* was soon followed by polemic, which, in turn, gave way to a series of libelous texts. According to Trivizas: "People of every social class and educational level, from random journalists to eminent scholars of the period, took it upon themselves to ridicule and hurl abuse at the movement. Ignorance of the basic tenets of Surrealism on the part of its critics excluded the possibility of the dialogue taking place on a theoretical level, with the result that the main weapon of the opponents of the movement was lampooning and crude witticisms."[7]

Engonopoulos' first public association with the surrealist movement in Greece[8] came with the publication in February 1938 of his translations of poems by Éluard, Crevel, Breton, Dali, Péret, Prasinos, Rosey, Tzara and Hugnet in the volume Ὑπερρεαλισμός Α ΄ [Surrealism I], which was the first and only collective appearance of

---

[6] Elytis recalls that the lecture: "…took place in the presence of a few grim-faced bourgeois who, to their visible annoyance, heard that apart from Kondylis and Tsaldaris, there were other people of note in the world, whose names were Freud or Breton…" (Odysseus Elytis, Ἀνοιχτὰ Χαρτιά, Athens 1974: 279).

[7] Sotiris Trivizas, Τὸ σουρεαλιστικό σκάνδαλο. Χρονικὸ τῆς ὑποδοχῆς τοῦ ὑπερρεαλιστικοῦ κινήματος στὴν Ἑλλάδα, Athens 1996: 21.

[8] It is sometimes questioned whether the term "movement" is appropriate in the case of the appearance of surrealism in Greece. According to Nanos Valaoritis, a subsequent and leading exponent of surrealist poetry, there was perhaps no other surrealist group in the world (with the exception of France) that was more active or exercised more influence. The only thing missing, he says, were collective manifestos. (See Nanos Valaoritis and Andreas Pagoulatos, "Ἕνας διάλογος γιὰ τὸν ἑλληνικὸ ὑπερρεαλισμό," in *Synteleia* 4–5 (1991): 112).

Greek surrealist poets in the interwar years.[9] In March of the same
year, Engonopoulos's first poems appear in the literary magazine Ὁ
Κύκλος[10] followed in June by the publication of his first collection.
The hostility on the part of both the press and critics was unprec-
edented in Greek literary history. According to Karandonis: "The
book helped make the surrealist movement in Greece more well-
known, and at the same time it set off a wave of public hostility
against its exponents. Not only did the book attract public attention,
but it also became the object of every kind of negative reaction and
denigration on the part of both the critics and the general public.
It eventually attracted also the attention of music-hall writers and
book reviewers who made it the target of their hurt sensibilities and
outrage."[11] In the notes that he appended to the republication of his
first two collections some thirty years later, Engonopoulos recalls:
"We had already had intimations of what was to come with the
publication of the magazine. When the book appeared, however, the
'scandal' that was caused not only exceeded anything that had ever
before been seen in Greek letters, but went beyond the bounds of the
wildest imagination. […] Magazines, newspapers, le premier *chien
coiffé venu*, parodied and derisively quoted my poems. In fact, one of
the larger newspapers, I no longer recall which one, brazenly ignoring
all idea of intellectual property, went so far as to re-publish the entire
book in two installments! Accompanied, each time, with scornful
and malicious, not to say superficial, comments."[12] But the "scandal"
provoked by his first collection was not sufficient to deter the poet
and, in September of the following year (1939), he published his
second collection Τὰ Κλειδοκύμβαλα τῆς Σιωπῆς (The Clavicembalos

---

[9] The volume contains works by Embirikos, Kanellis, Karapanos, Elytis, Ritoridis
and Kalamaris.
[10] "Do Not Distract the Driver" [Three Poems: "There," "The Secret Poet,"
"Nocturnal Maria"], Ὁ Κύκλος 4,4 (March 1938): 116–119.
[11] Andreas Karandonis, "Two Greek Surrealist Poets. A. Embiricos—N.
Engonopoulos," (Tr: Theodore Sampson), in *Greek Letters* 1 (1982): 262.
[12] Nikos Engonopoulos, Ποιήματα, Athens 1999: 328–329.

of Silence), which met with the same, if not worse, reception by the "intellectual" circles in Athens.[13]

It is surprising, given the express aims of surrealism to provoke and scandalize, that this reaction should have so upset both poets.[14] Though perhaps their protest at this reaction, voiced in their later writings and interviews, was not so much at the reaction itself, but at the way it was expressed. Discussing the reception of *Blast Furnace*, Embirikos talks of "ridicule," "derision" and "malice."[15] While Engonopoulos, who devotes most of his "Notes" accompanying the republication of his first two collections to this scandal, says: "I can't say that the scandal created and the ensuing outcry against me did not deeply upset me. Such vehement abuse in response to a genuine contribution is, if nothing else, cruelly unfair."[16] In these same notes, he expresses his gratitude to Embirikos, who, he says, "was the first who, when the scandal broke, bravely raised his voice and protested against my unjust persecution."[17]

The question arises as to why the outcry was so vehement and protracted in the case of Engonopoulos.[18] As noted above,

---

[13] Mimika Kranaki talks of "waves of hysteria" (see Nikos Engonopoulos, Ποιήματα, Athens 1999: 330 and 332).

[14] Sachtouris talks of Engonopoulos' extreme sensitivity and how he was unable to work all day if someone had said a harsh word to him (see Miltos Sachtouris, "Νίκος Ἐγγονόπουλος," in *Hartis* 25–26 (November 1988): 21).

[15] Andreas Embirikos, "Συνέντευξη στὴν Ἀνδρομάχη Σκαρπαλέζου," in *Iridanos* 4 [February-March 1976]: 15.

[16] Nikos Engonopoulos, Ποιήματα, Athens 1999: 328.

[17] Nikos Engonopoulos, Ποιήματα, Athens 1999: 335. In 1945, Embirikos had published his essay "Νικόλαος Ἐγγονόπουλος ἤ τὸ θαῦμα τοῦ Ἐλμπασάν καί τοῦ Βοσπόρου" [Nikolaos Engonopoulos or the Marvel of Elbasan and of the Bosphorus], in which he expresses his respect and admiration for Engonopoulos and his work and encourages him to continue because he is "a truly great poet, and let others say what they like" (in Frangiski Abatzopoulou, ... δὲν ἄνθισαν ματαίως. Ἀνθολογία ὑπερρεαλισμοῦ, Athens 1980: 331–334).

[18] In his notes, Engonopoulos quotes a well-known critic on the period under discussion as saying: "[...] Yet whereas the work of others gradually came to gain

Engonopoulos bore the brunt of the attacks on the new poetry, more so than Embirikos or any other of his surrealist colleagues. It has been suggested that Embirikos' financial position (he was from a wealthy family of ship owners) and his social position (he was a psychiatrist by profession) tempered the criticism leveled at him.[19] This may or may not be so, however, there is no doubt that Engonopoulos was, of all the Greek surrealist poets, the most provocative and uncompromising. As Robinson puts it: "If Embirikos was the father of Greek surrealism, Engonopoulos was undoubtedly its *enfant terrible*."[20] Similarly, writing in 1963, Argyriou notes: "… If in Embirikos surrealism was deliriousness, dream and the coincidental, in Elytis, magic, intoxication and the illusory, with Engonopoulos comes all the subversive current of the surrealist revolution…."[21] Also making a comparison between the two poets, Friar concludes: "Surrealism in the early Embiricos was almost clinical, liberating, didactic, whereas in Engonopoulos's two first books […], it was explosive, daring and revolutionary."[22]

3. The nature of his poetry

What, then, was the nature of Engonopoulos' "subversive" and "revolutionary" poetry? It might quite reasonably be supposed from such characterizations that the outcry was due, in part, to the concomi-

---

acceptance 'in small doses' as original and new poetry, no pardon was granted to Engonopoulos, and his name was placed in the most inaccessible region of our literature as explicitly prohibited…" (Nikos Engonopoulos, Ποιήματα, Athens 1999: 331).

[19] See Sotiris Trivizas, Τὸ σουρεαλιστικό σκάνδαλο. Χρονικὸ τῆς ὑποδοχῆς τοῦ ὑπερρεαλιστικοῦ κινήματος στὴν Ἑλλάδα, Athens 1996: 55. See, too, Argyriou, who also asserts that Engonopoulos did not enjoy the same social protection as Embirikos and so remained defenseless against the attacks (Alex. Argyriou, Διαδοχικές ἀναγνώσεις Ἑλλήνων ὑπερρεαλιστῶν, Athens 1983: 156).

[20] Christopher Robinson, "The Greekness of Modern Greek Surrealism," in *Byzantine and Modern Greek Studies* 7 (1981): 124.

[21] Alex. Argyriou, Διαδοχικές ἀναγνώσεις Ἑλλήνων ὑπερρεαλιστῶν, Athens 1983: 32.

[22] Kimon Friar, *Modern Greek Poetry. From Cavafis to Elytis*, New York 1973: 76.

tant political views he and his fellow surrealist poets held, as was the case, for example, in France. However, Greek surrealism in general had nothing of the political dimension of French surrealism, nor was there any link between the surrealist poets in Greece and the program of a particular political party.[23] It limited and focused its attention on the revolutionary aspect of surrealism that concerned the renewal of the artistic tradition. So the question remains, if surrealist poetry in Greece consisted simply of an adaptation of the tenets of international surrealism to the Greek context, with a view to renewing the tradition, then why was Engonopoulos' poetry (far more so than that of his fellow surrealist poets) singled out by the critics and press for such derision and mockery?

It has been said that the French surrealist movement in poetry remains more impressive as a collective phenomenon than as a series of separate, individual achievements.[24] The same could not be said of surrealist poetry in Greece. The diversity of its reception in Greece and its adaptation by Greek poets is singularly impressive. Elytis notes: "Every one of our so-called surrealist poets has done something altogether different with surrealism: Embiricos, Engonopoulos, Gatsos, Sachtouris have all done something different, and I have done something else...."[25] If surrealism proved fruitful in Greece, this was because the Greek poets did not imitate the French, but adapted surrealism to the Greek reality.[26] What we find in the work of these

[23] For a fuller discussion, see Takis Kayalis, "Modernism and the Avant-Garde: The Politics of 'Greek Surrealism,'" in Dimitris Tziovas (ed.) *Greek Modernism and Beyond*, Maryland 1997: 95–110.

[24] See W.D. Howarth, H.M. Peyre, and J. Cruikshank, *French Literature from 1600 to the Present*, London 1974: 124.

[25] Odysseus Elytis, "Odysseus Elytis on his Poetry. From an Interview with Ivar Ivask," *Books Abroad* Vol. 49, Number 4 (Autumn 1975): 631.

[26] That it was fruitful is generally agreed. Its success can be measured by the extent to which it has become an integral part of contemporary Greek poetry. See, e.g., Beaton: "[...] the legacy of surrealism had been assimilated by many writers of the younger generation. One reason for this lasting effect of the Surrealist experiment in Greece [...] may be that Embirikos and his fellow Surrealist, the painter and poet

poets are not the complexes of the subconscious but the ecstasy. Greek surrealist poetry, in general, is characterized by what Valaoritis refers to as "ἑλληνομαγεία" [the Greek spell], consisting of things sensuous, intoxicating, legendary, commonplace, of flowers, birds, insects, angels, perfumes, place names mythological heroes and sun—a particularly Greek reality, where, it might be added, the irrationality inherent in surrealism is more a way of life than a neurosis.[27] According to Elytis, it was precisely this anti-rationalistic aspect of surrealism that appealed to the Greek poets. He explains that surrealism contained a kind of supernatural element that enabled them to form a kind of alphabet out of purely Greek elements with which to express themselves.[28]

This is certainly true in Engonopoulos's case. He created his own unique and personal idiom (unlike anything else in Greek letters) through which he converses with Greek tradition using the tenets of surrealism. Speaking in 1954, he says: "Personally, I don't believe in surrealism as a school. Yet it suits me. What I tried to do was to renew it with Greek elements. To add to it Greek metaphysics, to elevate it beyond a simple mannerism, which is where it stops abroad."[29] The elements he uses to create his poetic alphabet belong, thematically and linguistically, to the historical Greek consciousness even if they are filtered through his own highly idiosyncratic and personal consciousness. In the same way, many poems of purely personal

---

Nikos Engonopoulos [...], used the theoretical principles of Surrealism to draw upon and emphasize traits already present in the Greek literary tradition" (Roderick Beaton, *An Introduction to Modern Greek Literature*, Oxford 1994: 164).

[27] Nanos Valaoritis and Andreas Pagoulatos, "Ἕνας διάλογος γιὰ τὸν ἑλληνικὸ ὑπερρεαλισμό," in *Synteleia* 4–5 (1991): 116. See also Ploritis, who quotes Breton as once having said: "We don't have to import Surrealism into Greece. The land itself is surrealistic" (Marios Ploritis, "Σουρεαλισμοί," in *To Vima tis Kyriakis* 2004: 93).

[28] Odysseus Elytis, "Odysseus Elytis on his Poetry. From an Interview with Ivar Ivask," *Books Abroad* Vol. 49, Number 4 (Autumn 1975): 631.

[29] Nikos Engonopoulos, *οἱ ἄγγελοι στὸν παράδεισο μιλοῦν ἑλληνικὰ... Συνεντεύξεις, Σχόλια καὶ Γνῶμες* (ed. Yorgos Kendrotis), Athens 1999: 23.

fantasy are interspersed with overt or covert references to all historical phases of the Greek tradition. Robinson gives the example of Engonopoulos's poem "Hydra" where, he says, "after the simplicity of the poem's opening, the verse violently shifts into a deliberately discordant series of "shocking" images, presenting the synthesis of present and past via the personality of the poet, the evocation of the familiar landscape of Hydra, with its tall flights of stairs offering a glimpse of the sea, the violent introduction of Hector and Hecuba, heroic but tragic losers...." In Engonopoulos, Robinson concludes, "the elements are thrown together in one serial image, a synthesis of inner and outer, real and mythical, that does not function as a symbol, but represents the poet's new perception of Greekness."[30]

Zamarou reveals a network of relationships between Engonopoulos's often personal and highly idiosyncratic poetry and the Greek tradition that is even closer than would appear at first sight, contradicting those who believe that the idea of modernism is incompatible with elements of a national tradition. "In Engonopoulos," she says, "tradition and the avant-garde come together in a way that is both enchanting and ingenious. Tradition motivates and infuses personal poetry, while, at the same time, the traditional material (on the level of language and subject matter) is highlighted and rejuvenated in the light of the personal and avant-garde art of the young poet."[31] Greek mythology and tradition constitutes the basis for his subject themes, but not in the sense of a nostalgic return to the roots of the Greek consciousness. In both his painting and poetry, Engonopoulos presents his own version of tradition, personalizing, reshaping and transforming it. One of his primary aims as painter and poet is to express this tradition in modernist terms. Zamarou gives the example of his poem "Eleonora," where, she says, "the descrip-

[30] Christopher Robinson, "The Greekness of Modern Greek Surrealism," *Byzantine and Modern Greek Studies* 7 (1981): 125–126.

[31] Rena Zamarou, Ὁ ποιητής Νίκος Ἐγγονόπουλος. Ἐπίσκεψη τόπων καί προσώπων, Athens 1993: 7.

tion of the body of the beloved woman, which appears to embody Engonopoulos's very own art, reveals in a concise way his debt to tradition and at same time programmatically sets out the way in which his poetry makes use of old material...."[32] Yet his ability to reshape and transform is not limited to the elements of tradition. He has the ability, common to great artists and poets, to create myth out of the mundane and insignificant.[33] His mythopoeia enables him to reveal in the most commonplace and disparate objects and events in everyday life and in the simplest coincidences, combinations that are magic and unique, that without any longer having a connection with reality (that are *irrational*), nevertheless come to constitute a new reality of their own. This is particularly well expressed by Abatzopoulou, who writes: "Man becomes again a creator and reconstructs his world anew from all the elements surrounding him, from nature and machines, houses and factories, the ancient marble and Byzantine churches, old and new words; everything has its special place in this world of marvel. And this marvel is love, which collects them all together indiscriminately and refashions them in a world that is poetical and notional, and above all real."[34] The realization of this new reality, however, may baffle and irritate precisely because it subverts accepted notions of reality, by using not the unfamiliar and odd, but the familiar and traditional. This is perhaps what differentiates him from other poets of his generation and what unsettled and outraged his uninitiated critics and public.

In many ways, Engonopoulos is the most orthodox surrealist of his generation, as one might expect from someone who said of himself:

---

[32] Rena Zamarou, Ὁ ποιητής Νίκος Ἐγγονόπουλος. Ἐπίσκεψη τόπων καί προσώπων, Athens 1993: 10–11. See also Engonopoulos's note to the poem for the sources of his inspiration (in Nikos Engonopoulos, Ποιήματα, Athens 1999: 339).

[33] Like Elytis, who kept the method of myth-making but not the figures of mythology (see Odysseus Elytis, "Odysseus Elytis on his Poetry. From an Interview with Ivar Ivask," *Books Abroad* Vol. 49, Number 4 (Autumn 1975): 639).

[34] Frangiski Abatzopoulou, ... δὲν ἄνθισαν ματαίως. Ἀνθολογία ὑπερρεαλισμοῦ, Athens 1980: 367.

"I never went over to surrealism, I always had surrealism in me."[35] Yet, as one perspicacious critic and contemporary poet has pointed out, surrealism fits him like an "uncomfortable corset."[36] The difference between his poetry and painting and that of the orthodox French and other Surrealists is that whereas they used irrationality to sever the bonds with tradition, he used it as a "connecting link," as a means of inventing a convincing continuity that would revitalize and unite the scattered fragments of a distant cultural past. And this is perhaps the source of the intellectual strain noted by many in his work. Though, for example, his poetic images clearly well up out of the subconscious, it is equally clear, as Friar remarks, that "they flow into the control of a highly conscious will."[37] However, this should not be seen as a denial of the basic tenets of surrealism; if anything, it is, as Robinson says, "a moving closer to the famous definition by Breton in his second manifesto, a definition which Engonopoulos uses as the epigraph to *The Clavicembalos of Silence* ...."[38] One cannot ignore, however, what Engonopoulos says in the notes to accompany the republication in 1966 of his first two collections, where he refers to Breton as: "...a person both important and notable of course, but to whom I also attached overly much importance at that time concerning surrealism and poetry."[39] What can be said with certainty is that, regardless of how orthodox a surrealist he was, or of how conscious his surrealism was, his work constitutes an original and creative use, rather than a mere imitation, of surrealist tenets.

[35]   Nikos Engonopoulos *Πεζά κείμενα*, Athens 1987: 41.

[36]   Yannis Varveris, "Ὁ ἄφιλτρος καπνιστής," in *i lexi* 179 (January-March 2004): 99.

[37]   Kimon Friar, *Modern Greek Poetry. From Cavafis to Elytis*, New York 1973: 77. See also Valaoritis, who characterizes Engonopoulos's surrealist work as "a conscious surrealism" Nanos Valaoritis ("Γιὰ τὸν θερμαστὴ τοῦ ὡραίου στοὺς κοιτῶνες τῶν ἐνδόξων ὀνομάτων," in *Hartis* 25–26 (November 1988): 89).

[38]   Christopher Robinson, "The Greekness of Modern Greek Surrealism," *Byzantine and Modern Greek Studies* 7 (1981): 124.

[39]   See Nikos Engonopoulos *Ποιήματα*, Athens 1999: 338.

4. His "mixed" language

If it was Engonopoulos's irreverent and subversive use of Greek tradition, of the historical rather than the individual consciousness, that upset and led him to be singled out by the critics, it was also his provocative and subversive use of the Greek language. Again, in this, he was not unique among Greek surrealist poets. One of the first reactions to the tenets of surrealism on the part of Greek poets such as Embirikos and Engonopoulos is connected with the use of both katharevousa, the purist language, and demotic, the colloquial language, which constituted the peculiarly Greek diglossia.[40] It should be noted, however, that the Greek surrealist poets did not simply make use of this diglossia but, as Beaton says: "by mixing elements of katharevousa and demotic, of accepted poetic diction with journalese and the language of officialdom, the Surrealists targeted the conventions of diglossia by flagrantly violating them. This practice of juxtaposing linguistic styles conventionally seen as separate is clearly part of the Surrealist programme of challenging all artificial and rational constraints on the free operation of the unconscious."[41] To put it another way, in poetry which is characterized by automatic writing, or which flows unchecked (to whatever degree) from the subconscious, it would be unreasonable to exclude katharevousa as being a part of the Greek consciousness and, most likely, of the Greek subconscious. Just as Greek surrealism gave the same weight to the

[40]   When the Greek State was established following the 1821 War of Independence, one of the burning questions concerned what the language of the new State should be. Opinions were divided between supporters of the existing spoken language (demotic) and supporters of a return to ancient attic Greek. Katharevousa, an artificial language purified of foreign (mainly Turkish) words, represented something of a compromise between these two tendencies and was eventually adopted as the standard form of written Greek, though demotic remained as the everyday spoken language. Katharevousa remained the official language of the Greek State until 1976.
[41]   Roderick Beaton, *An Introduction to Modern Greek Literature*, Oxford 1994: 344–5.

logical and the absurd, the significant and the insignificant, it could not ignore either demotic or katharevousa (or any other historical phases of the Greek language for that matter).

What characterizes Engonopoulos's poetic diction, however, is not just the use of katharevousa but the creative juxtaposition of disparate and often conflicting linguistic elements (as with the content of his poetry, so also with the diction). His idiosyncratic language[42] is astonishingly diverse and colorful, deceptively simple yet composite. It does not only alternate between demotic and katharevousa, but draws on the byzantine and post-byzantine period and is embellished with dialectical and sociolectical forms and with loan words and foreign words (Turkish, Albanian, French, Italian, Latin), often within the same poem. The way that he combines heterogeneous linguistic elements in the text recalls the technique that we recognize in his paintings. He applies layers of language to his text just as he does layers of paint to his canvas. As a poetic technique it focuses the attention of the reader on the linguistic medium itself. Perhaps this is why his first collections were the subject of such critical attacks in comparison with Embirikos's works, written in more standard katharevousa, in that Engonopoulos's linguistic deviations are more daring and more disturbing.[43] Through his mixing of linguistic idioms, he becomes, according to Valaoritis, "a transgressor of the common social and esthetic use of language."[44] This is language which offers

[42] On Engonopoulos' language, Varveris writes: "I don't know of any other Greek literary language that could be compared with his. It appears simple, plain, innocent; it appears to spring out, without make-up, unadorned, from his studio onto the road—onto the paper. And yet it is a language as Montesquieu would say in his Persian Letters 'd'une desinvolture habillement calculée,' of a calculated casualness" (Yannis Varveris, "Ὁ ἄφιλτρος καπνιστής," in i lexi 179 (January-March 2004): 99).

[43] On his singular and characteristic idiom, see Giorgis Giatromanolakis, "Προκαταρκτικά στὴ γλῶσσα τοῦ Νίκου Ἐγγονόπουλου," in Diavazo 381 (January 1998): 141–146.

[44] Nanos Valaoritis, "Γιὰ τὸν θερμαστὴ τοῦ ὡραίου στοὺς κοιτῶνες τῶν ἐνδόξων ὀνομάτων," in Hartis 25–26 (November 1988): 79.

a different way of organizing the world in the reader's conscious-
ness and also of organizing that consciousness itself and is, naturally,
baffling and unnerving to those who see language as no more than a
means of expression and communication.[45]

Engonopoulos himself has on more than one occasion explained
that his "mixed" language is the language he speaks and that the only
legitimate language for poets is the Greek language in all its aspects.
Again in the appended "Notes" to the republication of his first two
collections, he says: "I will confine myself to just a few lines about
the language I use, and which has often been characterized, in the
form of a reproach, as being "mixed." I have to say that, very simply,
this is the language I speak. And besides, is not the prime importance
to be understood by those who really do wish to understand? The
legitimate language, for us, is the Greek language. Those fanatic views
concerning a "mixed," "purist" or "popular" language have absolutely
no meaning whatsoever. [...] I came to realize that there is only one
Greek language. And that it is more a lack of prudence that leads one
to stubbornly become devoted to one single form of it, to scorn that
unimaginable wealth, that horde of treasure at one's disposal, instead
of drawing on it freely, with respect and care of course, so as to adorn
one's verse and reinforce one's meaning."[46] And elsewhere, he states:
"The Greek language is *one*. It would be foolish not to avail ourselves
of this, to disregard its enormous treasures, all its forms: ancient, anti-
quated, contemporary, popular and dialectical ... ."[47]

[45] See Nanos Valaoritis, "Γιὰ τὸν θερμαστὴ τοῦ ὡραίου στοὺς κοιτώνες τῶν ἐνδόξων
ὀνομάτων," in *Hartis* 25–26 (November 1988): 81. "Through his puzzling, enigmatic
formulation, the surrealist poet signifies anew, like the Pythia at Delphi. However the
message of the poetic discourse in the magic power of the sacred discourse scares,
irritates, often panics those who pride themselves on their grey matter."

[46] Nikos Engonopoulos *Ποιήματα*, Athens 1999: 336–337.

[47] See Nikos Engonopoulos, *οἱ ἄγγελοι στὸν παράδεισο μιλοῦν ἑλληνικά... Συνεντεύξεις,
Σχόλια καὶ Γνῶμες* (ed. Yorgos Kendrotis.), Athens 1999: 192–3. Vistonitis also
notes: "The purely formalistic view sees the main exponents of surrealism in our
country using katharevousa because it provides the possibilities for a 'social'

Be this as it may, the same is true of Engonopoulos's poetic diction as is true of his poetic images. In other words, the disparate linguistic features characterizing his poetic diction flow through the same "highly conscious will" as the disparate objects that characterize his poetic images. As with the perceptible rational strain in the content of his poetry, so too, as many have pointed out[48], his language is far from the spontaneous outpouring of the subconscious mind advocated by the French surrealists. I think, that is, that his statement that the language he uses is quite simply the language he speaks should not be accepted unreservedly. Firstly, it should not be forgotten that he made this statement as a reply to the reproach accompanying the characterization of his language as "mixed." And secondly, it might be concluded from what he says elsewhere about how he worked and reworked his poems until they achieved the form he wished. Engonopoulos himself explains in an interview that "… many of my poems were never worked into their final form, with the result that I have forgotten them… Others occupy me for a long time, until I give them the most perfect form that I am able."[49]

---

exoticism, the opportunity to ridicule rationalism and the established literature by means of the most 'established' linguistic form. However, Engonopoulos most certainly does not use katharevousa as a dead language. The dispute between the supporters of katharevousa and demotic didn't interest him. By avoiding taking sides in the dispute he may be idiomatic and extreme, but based on personal choice, not by following linguistic formalities, since he sees language in a way that is unifying, that is visionary and transformative" (Anastassis Vistonitis, "Γιὰ τὸν Ἐγγονόπουλο καὶ τὸν ὑπερρεαλισμό," in *Hartis* 25–26 (November 1988): 176).

[48] As, e.g., Karandonis notes: "Engonopoulos's use of automatic writing is a very conscious and intellectual operation which does not involve his subconscious mind in the least; therefore, regardless of how spontaneously written his texts may seem to be, they give the distinct impression of the 'fabricated' or the consciously 'made.'" (Andreas Karandonis, "Two Greek Surrealist Poets. A. Embiricos—N. Engonopoulos," (Tr.: Theodore Sampson), *Greek Letters* 1 (1982): 264).

[49] Nikos Engonopoulos, *οἱ ἄγγελοι στὸν παράδεισο μιλοῦν ἑλληνικὰ... Συνεντεύξεις, Σχόλια καὶ Γνῶμες* (ed. Yorgos Kendrotis), Athens 1999: 191.

5. His subsequent works

The hostility towards his work continued for several years until the time of the publication of *Bolivar*. This poem, Engonopoulos informs us, was liked by the youth of the time and, very gradually, the situation began to ease.[50] *Bolivar*, first published in September 1944, is very different from Engonopoulos's two previous collections of explicitly surrealist poetry. Though infused with a surrealist sensibility, there is none of the willful provocation of his earlier collections, and the language is simpler and more immediate, with little embellishment or affectation, and with far fewer elements of katharevousa. It is much less irrational in tone with little of the outrageous yoking together of disparate elements as in the first two collections. The poem was not greeted with the uproar and ridicule of his first two collections. Written in the Winter of 1942–43 (after Engonopoulos had endured five months' hard labor in captivity on the Albanian Front), *Bolivar* first circulated in handwritten copies and was read at resistance gatherings.[51] It may be seen as a surrealist poet's response to those years of war and Nazi occupation, in other words, an imaginative response to the harsh reality of the time. The underlying and unifying theme is the struggle for liberty, thinly disguised beneath references to the Greek War of Independence and the exploits of the South-American revolutionary hero, Simon Bolivar. It is, according to Karandonis, "the surrealist *Hymn to Liberty*."[52]

---

[50] Nikos Engonopoulos, Ποιήματα, Athens 1999: 332.

[51] See Nikos Engonopopulos, Ποιήματα, Athens 1999: 342.

[52] Andreas Karandonis, "Two Greek Surrealist Poets. A. Embiricos—N. Engonopoulos," (Translation: Theodore Sampson), *Greek Letters* 1 (1982): 271. The "Hymn to Liberty," written in 1823 by Dionysios Solomos, who is regarded as the Greek National Poet. The first verses of the Hymn, set to music by Nikolaos Mantzaros, constitute the Greek National Anthem. Engonopoulos said of Solomos that he was "the first great Surrealist; the first to make an opening to the irrational and to madness." (in Nikos Engonopoulos, οἱ ἄγγελοι στὸν παράδεισο μιλοῦν ἑλληνικὰ... Συνεντεύξεις, Σχόλια καὶ Γνῶμες (ed. Yorgos Kendrotis), Athens 1999: 149).

The impact of the poem and its overall effect is achieved by remaining close to the Greek world of the senses, in other words, close to the physical elements and place names that constitute the core of the Greek consciousness—the Aegean Sea, Attica, Hydra, Macedonia, Phanar, etc.—and by recalling heroic Greek figures—Constantine Palaeologus, Rigas Ferraios, Odysseus Androutsos, etc.—while, at the same time, being interfused with place names from South America, thus creating a poetic mosaic unified by the shadow of the heroic revolutionary figure of Simon Bolivar, who stands for the universal symbol of liberty and freedom. The Greekness, therefore, of Engonopoulos's poem is not the result of folkloric, descriptive or picturesque references to Greek traditions, geography and history, but is a surrealistic refashioning of these elements in the world of poetry. The flouting of the logical conventions in Engonopoulos's work (which testifies to its surrealist character), means that Bolivar *is* Greek; he is not a foreign element imposed on another (Greek) world, but exclusively on the world of heroism, freedom, and the hope for liberation. The poet does not simply sing the praises of the hero, the particular landscape or any specific struggle; he uses these elements, as explained earlier, as a form of alphabet to express himself in the Greek context. Bolivar is not only the liberator of South American democracies but is also all the heroes of the Greek War of Independence and, in the final analysis, Engonopoulos himself: "One thing alone is sure," says the poet, "that I am your son."

It is perhaps worth commenting, here, on this last verse. According to his first wife, Nelli Andrikopoulou, "All his life, Engonopoulos inevitably and exclusively painted himself, overtly or deceptively." It is, she says, "this constant living presence of his that marks his work."[53] It is safe to assume, I think, that this is also true of his poetry. In general, Engonopoulos avoided talking about himself, believing, it seems, in the words of Paul Cezanne, that: "Certes, l'artiste désire d' élever, …mais l'homme doit rester obscure," which he uses as

---

[53] Nelli Andrikopoulou, Ἐπὶ τὰ ἴχνη τοῦ Νίκου Ἐγγονόπουλου, Athens 2003: 23.

the epigraph to his most autobiographical poem "On Elevation."[54] Perhaps this is why he makes his presence felt so strongly throughout his work, in various ways, sometimes using a persona, sometimes wearing a fairly transparent mask, sometimes in person. Zamarou notes: "… Throughout his work, there appears the wish on his part to give shape to and construct his own face and, at the same time, show his kinship with older poets and with tradition. Also throughout his work, one can see the various aspects of this face. Sometimes the poet is anonymous, secret or archetypical, sometimes the stage is given to some well-known person, some mask of an older poet (used as a persona), and at other times Engonopoulos appears in person, portrays and introduces himself straight out."[55]

In *Bolivar*, it is the poet in person who is ever-present in the first-person narrative, with some overt personal references to the reception of his previous collections, as in "And shall I now despair that to this very day no one has understood, has wanted, has been able to understand what I say? / Shall the fate then be the same for what I say now of Bolivar…." In subsequent poems, he uses personas, to a greater or lesser degree transparent. In "Noble and Sentimental Dance," he finally admits to being himself "the great poet Kalfoglous," about whom he has been talking. In "On Elevation," the clearly autobiographical content of the poem leaves no doubt that he is the "Italian pyrotechnist." And in "Belisarius," an equally strongly autobiographical poem, we can again easily identify the poet in the youthful Belisarius who "set out in the company of Andreas Embirikos."

After the less surrealistic "parenthesis" of *Bolivar*, in his next collection, *The Return of the Birds* (1946), Engonopoulos returns, as the title suggests, to the themes and techniques of his early poems,

[54] Interestingly, Argyriou suggests that the reader should begin reading Engonopoulos's work from this poem and then go back to the beginning and read the poems in chronological order (Alex. Argyriou. Διαδοχικές ἀναγνώσεις Ἑλλήνων ὑπερρεαλιστῶν, Athens 1983: 173–174).

[55] Rena Zamarou, Ὁ ποιητής Νίκος Ἐγγονόπουλος. Ἐπίσκεψη τόπων καί προσώπων, Athens 1993: 12–13.

though perhaps with less provocative intent.[56] This collection, together with two more published in the following decade (*Eleusis,* 1948, and *In the Flourishing Greek Tongue,* 1957), contain many of his most well-known and well-liked poems, revealing the voice of an "essentially lyric poet."[57] Engonopoulos may have claimed to have always had surrealism in him, but his work goes beyond surrealism. Over and above its surrealist elements, what distinguishes his poetry is a dramatic dimension that puts the—by definition—optimistic vision of surrealism on a more human level. His poems and paintings are all dramatically "staged" down to the minutest detail. One always has the feeling that everything is premeditated in terms of the result and the impression that it is intended to have on the reader or viewer. His poems and paintings often serve as a stage for the absurd, for dream and also for nightmare. On this stage, whether on canvass or the page, move faceless bodies or bodies with masks for faces. Phantoms from the Greek past, alienated contemporary man, personas of the poet. It is not without significance that, throughout his life, for financial reasons, Engonopoulos designed stage sets and costumes for the theatre.

This ever-present dramatic aspect in his work is, however, often tempered and, indeed, subverted by his wry, sardonic humor.[58] He is a poet who is "always on the border between humor and tragic romanticism."[59] Of course, humor is also one of the most effective

---

[56] This is not to suggest that Engonopoulos's work does not develop from collection to collection, nevertheless his poetic style and inspiration remain constant from his first collections and it would be difficult to talk of distinguishable periods in his work. On this, see Alex. Argyriou Διαδοχικές ἀναγνώσεις Ἑλλήνων ὑπερρεαλιστῶν, Athens 1983: 170–171.

[57] Andreas Karandonis, "Two Greek Surrealist Poets. A. Embiricos—N. Engonopoulos," (Tr.: Theodore Sampson), *Greek Letters* 1 (1982): 262.

[58] On Engonopoulos's humor, see Nanos Valaoritis, "Τὸ χιοῦμορ στὸν ἑλληνικὸ ὑπερρεαλισμό," in *Diavazo* 120 (1985): 23–32 and Sefanos Dialismas, "Τὸ χιοῦμορ τοῦ Εγγονόπουλου," in *I Kathimerini/Epta Imeres* [Special issue on Engonopoulos] (25 May 1997): 26–27.

[59] See Nanos Valaoritis, "Τὸ χιοῦμορ στὸν ἑλληνικὸ ὑπερρεαλισμό," in *Diavazo* 120

ways of achieving the stated surrealist aim to create a rupture with convention. It shakes established views, challenges custom, undermines convention, but also (and this is the main aim of art for Engonopoulos) it is a source of consolation and encouragement for both the poet and reader.

There is no better example of this combination of drama and humor in the poems of this period than in his long poem, *The Atlantic*. The poem was first published in the *Anglo-Hellenic Review* vol. 6 (Winter 1953–54) and in 1954 as an offprint. It is included in the standard edition of the poet's work, but was not part of any collection. What differentiates it from other works by Engonopoulos are the many and obvious rhymes, which give the impression of having been contrived in order to provoke, but above all to amuse (and which, of course, can only be approximated in English translation). The rhymes are intended to accentuate the humor in the poem, which, according to Argyriou, presents the dramatic meaning of life with mirth and merriment in Engonopoulos's customary way.[60] He interprets the last line "Now we're all on the ocean" as an expression of the absurdity of the world and man's precarious position in it. Nevertheless, the ensuing existential anxiety is softened by the tones of merriment running throughout the poem. And this interpretation is given credibility by the quotes used as an epigraph to the poem ("What are we? Where are we going?" and "Merrily we ply the ocean waves"). And true to Engonopoulos's inherent surrealism, the poem remains, as we would expect, a basically optimistic work. Giatromanolakis notes that the poem was first published with Engonopoulos's painting of Jason *en face* and explains: "It is not difficult for us to accept that the poet chose this particular painting (from 1951) to 'accompany' the poem and that this choice is not irrelevant either to the content of the painting or to the content of the poem. In short, it constitutes an

---

(1985): 23–32.

[60] Alex. Argyriou, Διαδοχικές ἀναγνώσεις Ἑλλήνων ὑπερρεαλιστῶν, Athens 1983: 164–165.

'illustration' of the poem (*outside the text*) which, whatever the case, now constitutes for us a new 'sign,' creates for us a new 'meaning.'"[61] And it is not difficult for us, I might add, to see Jason in the painting as the persona of the poet himself, alone in the ocean of life, and employing his well-known humor to offset the existential drama.

The theme of the voyage, of escape from the existing reality and of the quest for "a new land" is a motif common in Engonopoulos's poetry of this period.[62] According to Beaton: "An abiding image of Engonopoulos's later poetry is the voyage through mist and rain, a voyage which [...] has no real goal other than the space it opens up in which desire can be fulfilled in language: a voyage, quite literally, out of this world."[63] *Bolivar*, in which the quest is for liberty, opens with the call for such a departure: "with one purpose behind the voyage: ad astra." In "Binary Automatism," there is again the call to arise and leave for somewhere far, where "salvation" and "tranquility" will be found and where "freedom" will prevail once and for all. *The Atlantic*, too, is based on the image of the voyage, beyond the ocean, to unknown lands, identified throughout the poem with salvation and liberation. However, in *The Atlantic*, the poet is the rebel, who calls on others to rise up, to leave the familiar places characterized by ethos, modesty, silence... the same old ways. He is, like Jason in the painting, the seafaring hero, standing erect in the ship's prow, gazing at the horizon and the beyond. The dramatic nature of the poem lies

[61] Giorgis Giatromanolakis, "Νίκου Ἐγγονόπουλου, Ὁ Ἀτλαντικός. Μία ἀνάγνωση," in Nikos Engonopoulos, Ὡραῖος σὰν Ἕλληνας (ed. Giorgis Giatromanolakis), Athens 1996: 146.

[62] The motifs of the sea voyage, the voyager-captain, the harbor and mooring in Engonopoulos's work is discussed by Rena Zamarou, Ὁ ποιητής Νίκος Ἐγγονόπουλος. Ἐπίσκεψη τόπων καί προσώπων, Athens 1993: 73ff.. See also Vangelis Hatzivassileiou, "Ἀπὸ τὸν Μπολιβάρ (1944) στὸν Ἀτλαντικὸ (1954): Ὑπερρεαλιστικὴ Ἐξέγερση καὶ Ἧττα στὴν Ποιητικὴ Μυθολογία τοῦ Νίκου Ἐγγονόπουλου," in *i lexi* 179 (January–March 2004): 80–87.

[63] Roderick Beaton, *An Introduction to Modern Greek Literature*, Oxford 1994: 221–222.

in the fact that despite the hardships, despite the possibility of not reaching port, there is no turning back. There is the sense of solitude and futility, but also the acceptance that there is no alternative: "what if I flounder or am lost you say / or even drop anchor with delay / what else could I have done? / this is how / I was cast into the ocean."

Another constant feature of his poetry which, like humor, tempers the dramatic aspect is the underlying sensuality and eroticism found throughout his poetry.[64] Many poems and paintings take their themes from famous couples from mythology with the prime example being Orpheus and Eurydice. Mythical, symbolic and actual (being part of his personal mythology), countless female figures parade through his poetry: Eurydice, Eleonora, Polyxeni, Maria, Laura, Katerina, Adelaïs, heroic maidens, virgins sometimes white and slender, sometimes cruel and loveless, beautiful Creoles, naked women and saintly women, his future wife, Eleni; all of them mysterious and enigmatic, sensuous and erotic, inspiring and comforting, donators of longing and serenity. The theme of poet and muse, so prevalent in his painting, is equally prevalent, but in various guises in his poetry. The examples are numerous throughout his work yet the role of women in Engonopoulos's poetic world is nowhere more clearly seen than in the poem "Hymn of Praise for the Women We Love," from his collection *Eleusis* (1948). The women here are a source of inspiration: "... the women we love / impart / to us too / that / divine essence / of theirs"; a source of solace and consolation: "with their breasts they end our loneliness"; a source of happiness and serenity: "they inundate our being / with joy / with peace"; the destination and end of the voyage "the women we love are like harbors / (the one goal / the destination / of our fine / ships)."[65] They elevate the poet and are elevated by the poet. But in Engonopoulos's work, the female figure

---

[64] See Valaoritis and Pagoulatos: "His poetry is deeply sensual. It vibrates with an emotion that we also find in Cavafy…" (Nanos Valaoritis and Andreas Pagoulatos, ""Ενας διάλογος γιὰ τὸν ἑλληνικὸ ὑπερρεαλισμό," in *Synteleia* 4–5 (1991): 116).

[65] See Rena Zamarou, Ὁ ποιητὴς Νίκος Ἐγγονόπουλος. Ἐπίσκεψη τόπων καί προσώπων, Athens 1993:74.

is something more too. She becomes the symbol of a restless, exciting and often scandalous eroticism that functions in keeping with basic surrealist aims to rupture social conventions and accepted notions of propriety. She is, as Badell puts it: "…the spark that rends the boundaries of reality and life, allowing creativity to emerge and burst forth. The woman […] recreates reality. She contains a world. She is marvel, surprise and, clearly, arousal."[66]

Engonopoulos was awarded the National Prize for Poetry in 1958 for his collection, *In the Flourishing Greek Tongue*, which suggests the hostility toward his work had finally abated and he had at last achieved recognition as an established poet. In his Notes, however, Engonopoulos expresses surprise at the award: "[…] in 1958, I was awarded the 'First Prize for Poetry' by the Ministry of Education for the collection I'd published in the preceding year, but also 'for my previous poetic output.' It is the only honor I have ever received from the State. I was doubly surprised because, first of all, I had not submitted any application, nor, as is my custom, had I taken any steps to this end, and also because most of the Committee members were hostile towards my work and many continue to be so even today."[67] Another twenty years would pass between his receiving this award and the publication, of his next collection, *In the Vale of Roseries*, in 1978, for which he again received the National Prize for Poetry. It is, perhaps, questionable whether one should read anything into this long period of silence, though some critics attribute it to his dedication to painting and his other professional obligations. Beaton, for example, talks of the poetry Engonopoulos published during the 1950s "before turning almost entirely to painting."[68] McKinsey, too, suggests that because of his painting, his teaching at the Technical University of Athens and his work as a set and costume designer, "it

---

[66] Helena Badell, "Οἱ γυναῖκες ποὺ ἀγαποῦσε ὁ ποιητής Νίκος Ἐγγονόπουλος," in *i lexi* 179 (January-March 2004): 138.

[67] Nikos Engonopoulos, *Ποιήματα*, Athens 1999: 332–333.

[68] Roderick Beaton, *An Introduction to Modern Greek Literature*, Oxford 1994: 221.

was perhaps inevitable that his poetry slipped into the background."[69] Engonopoulos, in the poem "To Constantine Bakeas" gives a clear explanation of his silence: "without doubt / my 'poetic' production / of late / is essentially / non-existent / not that I've stopped / mumbling to myself / or churning out / poems / and verses / and fairytales / but as I omit / to note them on paper / I forget them / and naturally / have nothing left to show / besides no one asks me for them: / I saw what / little significance / around me / they attached / and attach to poems / for some future critic / my past poems / will be more than enough / and how eloquent / my present silence / will be."

It is true, however, that Engonopoulos had always made it clear that he considered himself first a painter and afterwards a poet, and nowhere more so than in the notes he wrote to accompany the poems he published in *In the Vale of Roseries*. Here, he expressly states: "I was never a systematic writer or systematic littérateur. The one great love of my life was painting. Whatever time I do not devote to painting is, in my view, time wasted. But of course a painting does not constantly demand the total dedication of mind and heart. There are moments, I could say, when the hand moves by itself. Yet the mind is always working. It's then that I avail myself and reflect on numerous things, or, more commonly, I make up songs. After work, if I commit these songs to paper, all well and good, otherwise I simply forget them."[70] However, and despite what he says himself, he is certainly more than just a painter who wrote poems in his spare time and I think there is more of an integral connection between his poems and paintings than is often imagined, as one might expect when both works came from the same artistic inspiration and sensibility. One has the impression, comparing these works, that the poems are often commentaries on

---

[69] Martin McKinsey in Nikos Engonopoulos, *Acropolis and Tram. Poems 1938–1978*. Edited and Translated by Martin McKinsey, København & Los Angeles 2008: 13–14.

[70] Nikos Engonopoulos, Στὴν κοιλάδα μὲ τοὺς ροδῶνες, Athens 1978: 221.

the paintings and the paintings visual depictions of the poetic images. The examples are numerous and, apart from the common titles and themes to be found throughout his paintings and poetry, it is interesting to compare chronologically the dates of the paintings with the period when the poems were written.[71]

Some random examples of figures appearing in both his paintings and poems from corresponding chronological periods are: The Great Poet Kalfoglous (1934)[72] and "Noble and Sentimental Dance" (1946), Mercurius Bouas (1953) and the poem of the same name (published 1957), Belisarius (1971) and the poem of the same name (published 1978), Adelaïs (1977) and the poem of the same name (published 1978), but there are also many self-portraits (from 1935), which might easily be connected to various narrators in his poems. To these can be added the common titles of paintings and specific poems or collections, such as: SO_4H_2 (1937) and "Pomegranates = SO_4H_2" (published 1939), Waltz Noble and Sentimental (1939) and "Noble and Sentimental Dance" (published 1946), Return of the Birds (1946) and the collection of the same name (1946). It would also be possible, without too much effort, to relate paintings even with different titles to certain poems. I have already mentioned Giatromanolakis' comments on the painting Jason (1951), which Engonopoulos used to accompany his poem *The Atlantic* (1954). Similarly, The Liberator (1940) might be related to *Bolivar* (written 1942–43), or Civil War (1948) with "Poetry 1948" (published 1948). Zamarou also suggests a connection between the poems "Eleonora" and "Tel Aviv" (in which Eleonora also appears) in his first collection and many paintings with the title Poet and Muse.[73] A similar case could easily be made for the numerous paintings and poems

---

[71] To the best of my knowledge, no one has yet done comparative research on the relationship between specific paintings and poems.

[72] The dates of the paintings are as recorded in Katherina Perpinioti-Agazir, Νίκος Ἐγγονόπουλος. Ὁ ζωγραφικὸς τοῦ κόσμος, Athens 2007.

[73] Rena Zamarou, Ὁ ποιητής Νίκος Ἐγγονόπουλος. Ἐπίσκεψη τόπων καί προσώπων, Athens 1993: 11.

on the theme of Orpheus and Eurydice. One can only conclude that there is more of a connection between his painting and poetry than Engonopoulos would have us believe. His often dismissive remarks concerning his poetry may owe something to his ever-present self-irony or, indeed, to a residue of bitterness left from its initial reception. Nevertheless, it would be impossible today to conceive of the artist Engonopoulos without the parallel dimension offered by his poetry.

All the constant themes in his poetry reappear in *In the Vale of Roseries,* though one theme stands out more than ever in this, the last collection published during his lifetime: the anthropocentric nature of his poetry. Man is at the center of both his poetry and painting, which reveals a deep respect for man, a deep sorrow at the often bitter consequences of his actions and yet the artist's need to communicate with him. As he put it himself: "... man is the yardstick for every single thing: The measure of all things... Man is the subject of Hellenism. And it is for man that we create... In order to give him an outlet for his solitude. The strength, to abolish his solitude. Communication. This is what art offers...."[74] What we have here is as clear a statement as any by Engonopoulos of the main aims of his artistic work, namely, his anthropocentric views, his concern with the essence of Hellenism[75] and his concern with art as communication, above all,

[74] Nikos Engonopoulos, *οἱ ἄγγελοι στὸν παράδεισο μιλοῦν ἑλληνικὰ... Συνεντεύξεις, Σχόλια καὶ Γνῶμες* (ed. Yorgos Kendrotis), Athens 1999: 103). That this was a constant view of his can be seen from what he says twenty-two years earlier (in 1954): "In my work he plays the biggest role. It's for man that I paint. Man is my subject-matter. He is what interests me. For in the seclusion in which I live, I live only with the wish to come into contact with my future viewer, the one who will understand me. [...] The proper thing in a work of art is for the human presence to exist..." (Nikos Engonopoulos, *οἱ ἄγγελοι στὸν παράδεισο μιλοῦν ἑλληνικὰ... Συνεντεύξεις, Σχόλια καὶ Γνῶμες* (ed. Yorgos Kendrotis), Athens 1999b: 21).

[75] His constant and deep concern with Hellenism, with the Greek tradition in all its aspects, should not be seen as having its origins in any ideas of nationalism. Attempts to characterize his work as Hellenocentric (in a nationalistic sense) are, I think, misplaced. He was too much of a surrealist to be Hellenocentric. What characterizes

with art as a source of consolation. Throughout his long career, he made numerous statements to this effect: "If my life is devoted to painting and poetry, it's because painting and poetry both comfort and beguile me."[76]; "If I devoted myself to art, I did it because life is so absurd that, if you don't have those means of escape to the selfless, it becomes unbearable.";[77] and "The aim of the work of art is precisely to overcome this solitude. [...] The aim of the art work is not, simply, to amuse us. It should console us."[78] The same concern with solitude can also be found in his poetry. In "The Hawk" (published in 1948), he writes: "... we live in a depressing solitude. [...] That terrible solitude of ours! That tragic solitude of ours! For there is not the slightest doubt, we are alone, alone, ever alone, eternally, tortuously alone. Everyone. Everyone. All of us. All of you, everyone." Whether or not, through his painting and poetry, Engonopoulos succeeded in overcoming artistic solitude and finding the consolation he sought from art is not something open to scholarly investigation. What can be said, however, is that his poetry communicates today, in a way unimaginable fifty years ago, with younger readers in Greece as much if not more so than any other poet of his generation. It is full of Dionysian ecstasy, sensuality, profanity and outrage yet also of Apollonian nobleness, tenderness, humaneness and detachment. It has all the beauty, color and light of Greece, yet remains enigmatic, ironic and often disturbing. Perhaps, above all, the appeal of his work lies in the glimpses it offers of the "secret of the well," an image that characterizes all his work. As Abatzopoulou says: "In Engonopoulos's work there is the constant appearance from 1938 to his last collec-tion, in different forms, of well (φρέαρ), crucible (χοάνη), cavity (τρούπα), casket (κιβούρι), cradle (σαρμανίτσα), trunk (κασέλλα), of

---

his work is hellenolatry, a love of all things Greek. He was "Hellenic" in the Cavafian sense (see Cavafy's poem "Epitaph of Antiochus, King of Commagene").

[76]   Nikos Engonopoulos, *Ποιήματα*, Athens 1999: 329–330.

[77]   Nikos Engonopoulos, *οἱ ἄγγελοι στὸν παράδεισο μιλοῦν ἑλληνικὰ... Συνεντεύξεις, Σχόλια καὶ Γνῶμες* (ed. Yorgos Kendrotis), Athens 1999: 148.

[78]   Nikos Engonopoulos, *Πεζά κείμενα*, Athens 1987: 38.

whatever conceals within it the mystery of human existence, of birth and death, of beginning and end, together with the mystery—the magic, the marvel—of art....”[79]

II. On Translating Engonopoulos

Ἡ μετάφρασή του [...] περιέχει πολλοὺς κινδύνους. Εἶναι, ὅπως λέμε, παρακεκινδυνευμένη.
Translation [...] involves many risks. It is, as we say, a risky business.

Nikos Engonopoulos

1. General

Like the majority of Greek surrealist poets, Engonopoulos, at least until quite recently, has been only selectively and rather randomly translated into English and generally remains unknown to the English-speaking readership.[80] As can be seen from the list of English translations (see Bibliography), only Friar[81], Goumas[82], McKinsey

---

[79] Frangiski Abatzopoulou, *Νίκος Ἐγγονόπουλος. Ἡ ποίηση στὸν καιρό "τοῦ τραβήγματος τῆς ὑψηλῆς σκάλας,"* Athens 1987: 44.

[80] Apart from the relative lack of translations, there are also other reasons, of course, which hinder the reception of his work by the English-speaking readership. As Mitropoulos observes: "Another member of the Generation of the '30s, Nikos Engonopoulos, a fine poet and painter, never made it in the English-speaking world and probably never will. Engonopoulos was poor, reclusive, influenced by French Surrealism and lacking in access to Anglo-American literary circles. Several epic poems like 'Bolivar: a Greek Poem,' written to commemorate a Latin-American revolutionary hero, hardly fit Anglo-American perceptions of modern Greek culture" (Dimitri Mitropoulos, "On the Outside Looking in: Greek Literature in the English-Speaking World," *Journal of Modern Greek Studies* 15 (2) (1997): 189).

[81] Engonopoulos himself seems to have held Friar's translations in high esteem. In an interview in 1974, he says: "I think that Kimon Friar has translated my poems in a masterly way…" (Nikos Engonopoulos, *οἱ ἄγγελοι στὸν παράδεισο μιλοῦν ἑλληνικὰ... Συνεντεύξεις, Σχόλια καὶ Γνῶμες* (ed. Yorgos Kendrotis), Athens 1999: 194).

[82] Goumas informs us that Engonopoulos considered his translations better than the originals and that this was a belief he repeated publically in press interviews

and Connolly have somewhat more systematically translated his work and only McKinsey and Connolly have discussed at any length the particular problems involved in translating this work.[83] Apart from the particular problems which I will discuss below, the difficulties facing the translator of his poetry are similar, of course, to the difficulties inherent in translating surrealist poetry in general. Engonopoulos' poetry exhibits all the common features of surrealism—startling images, contradictory and logically unconnected phrases, unexpected metaphors, a lack of similes, the exchange of properties between animate and inanimate objects, elliptical syntax, etc.—all of which contribute to the immediacy of poetic communication by attempting to eliminate any rational response. The translator's concern, then, is how and to what extent these features can be conveyed in a different language and culture so that they may function in a corresponding way for a linguistically and culturally different readership.

Yet, how are translators to reconcile their highly conscious craft with a poetry that is rooted in the subconscious, that aims at the irrational and that makes use of writing that is logically unconnected, if not wholly automatic? [84] Translators, who function as receivers in

---

(Yannis Goumas, "Νίκος Εγγονόπουλος, ή μᾶλλον ποίηση καὶ ζωγραφική," in *i lexi* 179 (January-March 2004): 95).

[83] See Martin McKinsey, "Language Questions: Diglossia, Translation and the Poetry of Nikos Engonopoulos," in *Journal of Modern Greek Studies* 8 (2) (1990): 245–261 and David Connolly, "Nikos Engonopoulos. *Bolivar*, A Greek Poem, Translated from the Modern Greek With an Introduction," in *Modern Greek Studies Yearbook*, vol. 12/13 (1996–1997): 441–472, "Greek Surrealist Poets in English Translation: Problems, parameters and possibilities," in *Κάμπος. Cambridge Papers in Modern Greek* 6 (1998): 1–18 and "Ὡραῖος σὰν Ἐγγλέζος: Ὁ ἀγγλόφωνος Ἐγγονόπουλος" in Andrianna Chachla, (ed.), *Νίκος Ἐγγονόπουλος: Ὁ ποιητής καὶ ὁ ζωγράφος*, Conference Proceedings, Athens 2010: 241–252.

[84] A fact noted by other translators of Engonopoulos. McKinsey notes: "Of course, there remains the irony that a poem formed out of materials at hand, through automatic writing perhaps in a form of oral composition [...] is being recreated in English through a sometimes laborious process of trial and error, substitutions and

one sign system and as writers in another, are involved in a particularly complex process of judgment and choice. They must possess a detailed knowledge of the source language and culture, which will allow them to determine the semantic content of the text (or, at least, arrive at some conclusion concerning the author's statement or message), be able to locate the characteristic stylistic features in the author's work and also to assess the probable effect of both the content and style on the source-text readership, then find corresponding if not similar means in order to convey the semantic content and stylistic features together with the perceived pragmatic effect[85] to the readers of the target text.

The translator's already difficult task would seem to be even more difficult, however, in the case of surrealist poetry, which contains no logically developed theme, no narrative statement or message, and where all traditional poetic forms are abandoned and (theoretically at least) aesthetic preoccupations disregarded. According to Embirikos, a surrealist poem: "[...] does not consist of one or more subjective or objective themes logically defined and developed along conscious lines, but is a poem that might consist of any elements that arise in the flow of its creation, regardless of all conventional and standard aesthetic, moral and logical constructions... [It is] a poem-happening, rather than a succession of static descriptions of certain events or feelings, described using one or another artistic style."[86] How then is the translator to deal with such poetry? What is it that has to be reproduced in the target language so that the translation might function in a corresponding way in a different language and culture and for a different readership?

---

approximation." (Martin McKinsey, "Language Questions: Diglossia, Translation and the Poetry of Nikos Engonopoulos," in *Journal of Modern Greek Studies* 8 (2) (1990): 258).

[85] By the term "pragmatic effect," I am referring to the communicative, emotive element in language and the effect this has on the readership in contrast to the purely informative or formal elements.

[86] Andreas Embirikos, *Γραπτά ή προσωπική μυθολογία*, Athens 1991: 10.

2. Linguistic problems

Automatic writing is probably the main (if not defining) feature of orthodox surrealism. Although it was soon brought into question, it is, even in the modified form used by Engonopoulos as consciously unconnected writing, a technique which, firstly, frees the poet from all rational and aesthetic constraints and the translator from all worries concerning poetry's traditional forms. Yet automatic writing, in whatever form, also means a break with normal word order, something more easily accepted in Greek (or even in French) than in English, which, being a non-inflected language, relies upon a fairly rigid word order to convey meaning. Particular care, then, must be given by the translator to the order of the words, but also to the way these words are spatially arranged. The problem of spatial arrangement is particularly important in Engonopoulos, who will often isolate a single word in a line, often no more than an article, so that its own peculiar force might be felt. As stated earlier, one of the main features of surrealist poetry is the illogical yoking together of the most disparate objects, yet, in Engonopoulos, all these disparate images have a central harmony in that they create a coherent reality of their own. So, for example, in "The Clavicembalos of Silence," we find the words of a typical surrealist image arranged in the following way: "I lose myself / in dark caverns / that conceal / in their depths / sewing machines / and fish / yellow ones / that talk / like flowers." The spatial arrangement is all-important and the translation should follow closely—even, I would argue, contravening if necessary normal target-language word order—for the reason that the spatial arrangement is itself meaningful, even if the content is not logical. The overall meaning derives from the association of the illogical elements in a seemingly logical regular structure. The meaning, then, is not *content-bound* but, rather, both the individual words and the association of ideas accumulate "meaning" as the poem is read.

Yet even Engonopoulos' choice of words presents a problem for the translator into English. As noted earlier, Greek surrealism affirms the general principles of international surrealism, but manifests its originality within the framework of Greek culture, historically and also linguistically, making full use of the Greek language in all its aspects, including its peculiar diglossia, with its mixture of demotic and katharevousa. Katharevousa simply offers to the Greek poet another linguistic key with which to play and juxtapose various layers of expression as in a collage. The use of katharevousa sometimes results in irony, sometimes humor, sometimes bombast, sometimes an air of seriousness. Such an admixture of the popular and purist, as in Engonopoulos's poetry, cannot be reproduced in English, which contains no corresponding phases in its historical evolution and no corresponding linguistic idiom for katharevousa. For example, there is no way of differentiating in English purist forms such as "εἰς τρόπον ὥστε" (in such a way that), "κανεὶς ἐξ ὑμῶν" (not one of us), "ἴσαμε καταγῆς" (down to the ground), "ὁλοῦθε" (all around), "ἐκ τῶν ἔσωθεν" (from within), "ὅστις" (who) etc., even less so entire phrases in katharevousa which stand out in the rest of the poem, such as "κατηγγέλθην ἤδη ὡς 'προσήκων σεβασμὸς'" (already I have been accused of "due respect") or "ὡδηγήθην εἰς τὸ ἰκρίωμα ὑπό αὐστηρὰς συνοδίας" (I was led to the scaffold under strict escort).

One possible solution suggested by Friar (1973: 660), one of the first translators of Engonopoulos, is "to impose, on a basic English, colorations taken from colloquial, literary, and formal usages. A note of the purist may occasionally be indicated by the use of rather stilted words or expressions derived from the Latin or Greek and which, against a general Teutonic structure and diction, may sometimes take on a formal and even exotic note."[87] Keeley disagrees with this translation strategy. On the linguistic level, he thinks that it is impossible to find a decorous equivalent and that the approach adopted by Friar of using Latinate forms in English simply results in stilted English. He considers the problem an insoluble one and explains that, in translating Cavafy, he and Sherrard decided not to try for an

---

[87] Kimon Friar, *Modern Greek Poetry. From Cavafis to Elytis*, New York 1973: 660.

equivalent of Cavafy's purist forms except where these were clearly used for purposes of irony or where he wants a character to sound pompous. And then, he says, you can use "a bit of deliberate stylistic pomposity in order to get the right tone."[88] In keeping with these two differing strategies, the translator can, therefore, either adopt a higher register, using Latinate words (as Friar suggests) or simply ignore it rather than having recourse to stilted English (as Keeley suggests). Translation strategies of this kind perhaps provide some solution to the problem on a purely stylistic level, but they rarely provide a solution on a pragmatic level. As regards the pragmatic effect of using katharevousa (irony, humor, pomposity, etc.), this can usually only be rendered by using different stylistic means. So when the intended effect is, for example, humor, the use of a coarser Anglo-Saxon idiom would perhaps be more appropriate than some form of correspondingly learned or formal register.

McKinsey considers that it is relatively easy to find parallels to the Greek situation in the English language and literature and discusses the use of legalese or liturgical archaisms.[89] The problem, however, as he himself notes, is that to use them in extraneous contexts is to confuse spheres. Like Keeley, he too suggests "translating out" the katharevousa element, translating it, that is, into standard English, at least when the katharevousa used by the author is simply an expression of the normal linguistic conventions of the time, when, in other words, the author is simply writing in the language expected by his readership, as, for example, is the case with Roidis or Vizyinos. In such cases, I agree that: "To serve up English versions that creak at the joints with archaism would be to distort the original intent."[90] However, I think that the duty of the translator is not limited solely to

[88] See Edmund Keeley, "The Translator's Voice: An Interview with Edmund Keeley," by Warren Wallace, *Translation Review* 11 (1983): 10.

[89] Martin McKinsey, "Language Questions: Diglossia, Translation and the Poetry of Nikos Engonopoulos," in *Journal of Modern Greek Studies* 8 (2) (1990): 246–247.

[90] Martin McKinsey, "Language Questions: Diglossia, Translation and the Poetry of Nikos Engonopoulos," in *Journal of Modern Greek Studies* 8 (2) (1990): 247.

the author's original intent (even if the translator were privy to this) but also to the reception of the text by the contemporary reader. For example, Cavafy's "mixed" language may have been the language he spoke and the colloquial language of the time (a fact used to justify the decision by many translators to translate his language using a contemporary colloquial idiom presumably as a form of linguistic and cultural correspondence), but his mixed language is perceived and received by the contemporary reader in a particular way, in other words, as mixed and archaic and perhaps for this reason as idiosyncratic and charming today. And without doubt this fact constitutes a major factor in the enjoyment and popularity of Cavafy's poetry in Greek and consequently constitutes an important parameter in the translation process. The same is true of Engonopoulos. Even if Engonopoulos's mixed language was simply the language he spoke (though above I have expressed my reservations concerning this), it remains a fact that it affects the contemporary reader in a certain way. It has a pragmatic effect on the contemporary reader that it did not have on the reader of sixty or seventy years ago. His language is no longer met with ridicule but rather it charms the reader just as with Cavafy's language today and the translator has to take this fact into account in the translation process if he wants Engonopoulos's text to have a similar pragmatic effect on the contemporary English-speaking reader.

How the translator is to find linguistic correspondences in the target language is, of course, another matter. We may accept that a taste of katharevousa can be given by using a more learned register (e.g., "a certain Italian gentleman answering to the name..." for "Ἰταλὸς τίς ἀκούων εἰς τὸ ὄνομα...") or using somewhat older vocabulary (e.g. "eyeglasses" or even "spectacles" instead of "glasses" for "ματογυάλια," and "necktie" instead of "tie" for "λαιμοδέτης," or "amidst" instead of "in the middle" for "ἐν μέσῳ"), though the difference in register, as noted earlier, is, unfortunately, somewhat slighter in English. However, apart from the problems that arise in rendering the linguistic register of katharevousa (and corresponding pragmatic effect), there is also the—seemingly unsurpassable—problem of rendering the various linguistic forms of katharevousa, namely, the rendering of the participles, e.g., "Ἀλβανοί χορεύοντες" (Dancing Albanians), "ἐπαγγελόμενος" (professing to be), of the verb augment, e.g. "ἐγγενήθη" (was born), "ἀνευρέθη" (was found), "ἀπεδόθη" (was attributed), of the accusative case, e.g., "τὰς ἀπογοητεύσεις" (disappointments), "εἰς τὰς θνησιγενεῖς ραπτομηχανὰς" (to the stillborn sewing-machines), of the dative, e.g., "ἐν ὥρα καταιγίδος" (in time of storm), "ἐν στιγμὴ ὀργῆς" (in a moment of rage), "τὴ συνοδεία" (to the accompaniment), of the enclitic "ν", e.g., "τὸν ἐπιδιορθωτήν" (a repairer), "σὲ [...] ραπτομηχανήν" (sewing machine), "δὲν μπορῶ καὶ ναν τὰ πῶ" (about which I can't speak), of the different syllable stress, e.g. "του ευγενεστάτου Οθωμανού" (most gracious Ottoman), "μία μακροσκελεστάτη ἐπιστολή" (a most lengthy letter), "τῶν φιλησύχων πολιτῶν" (of law-abiding citizens), etc. This is a serious problem because these linguistic forms, which are invariably lost in translation, naturally influence the rhythm of the poem. The effect of the verb augments, the enclitic "ν", and the different syllable stress is that they lend a certain musicality to the poem and we should not forget that this was a factor uppermost in Engonopoulos's mind when composing the poem. As he says: "In poetry I compose with words and with their music...."[91] And very often when reading his poetry, one has the impression that it is the words themselves, their musical tones and combinations that guide the poet more than their semantic content.[92]

It will have become clear, I hope, that the linguistic characteristics of katharevousa, particularly distinct in Greek, both optically and acoustically, cannot be successfully rendered in English translation and that the loss on the stylistic but also on the pragmatic level is

---

[91] See Nikos Engonopoulos, οἱ ἄγγελοι στὸν παράδεισο μιλοῦν ἑλληνικὰ... Συνεντεύξεις, Σχόλια καὶ Γνῶμες (ed. Yorgos Kendrotis), Athens 1999: 192.

[92] Something which should not surprise us if we take into account, as noted earlier, that he composed his poems (that he himself called "songs") orally while he was working on his paintings.

consequently great. Everything I have mentioned so far concerning the problems of rendering katharevousa in English is not limited, of course, just to Engonopoulos's poetry. Similar problems exist in translating the poetry of Cavafy or of any poet who uses a "mixed" language.[93] I discussed earlier the question of Engonopoulos's mixed language. Here, it interests me only insofar as it presents particular translation problems. His poetic language, regardless of whether it was the language he spoke or not, verges on an idiolect to the degree that it differs from any form of standard Greek. Or to put it another way, more poetically, and using Engonopoulos's own words: "He spoke another language, the peculiar dialect of a now long forgotten city, for which in any case he alone felt nostalgia." (The Lover). The question remains, however, as to how the translator might render this peculiar language in English. If, to the problems in rendering katharevousa, we also add the problems of rendering Engonopoulos's peculiar poetic diction taken from all phases of the Greek language (ancient, Byzantine, medieval, ecclesiastical[94], colloquial, dialectical, etc.) that embellish his poetry, it can be understood how difficult it is for the translator into English to give even a taste of his idiosyncratic yet extremely charming language.[95] And Engonopoulos's use of

---

[93] The comparison with Cavafy is by no means random. There are many similarities in the diction of these two poets apart from their "mixed" language, as others have noted. See, e.g., Valaoritis: "Also the mixture of learned and extreme demotic words and expressions imbue the writing [of Engonopoulos] with the eclecticism of a dandy. Here his style approaches that of Cavafy with similar roots in Constantinople" (Nanos Valaoritis, "Γιὰ τὸν θερμαστὴ τοῦ ὡραίου στοὺς κοιτώνες τῶν ἐνδόξων ὀνομάτων," in Hartis 25–26 (November 1988): 87).

[94] The rendering of biblical words and expressions does not normally present a major problem given that the translator can always have recourse to older English translations of the Bible, e.g., "τὸ κύμβαλον τὸ ἀλαλάζον τῆς ἀγάπης, ὁ χαλκὸς ὁ ἠχῶν τῆς ἀγάπης" (love's sounding brass, love's tinkling cymbal), which usually have a similar pragmatic effect on the reader.

[95] Keeley notes that: "Any modern Greek who uses certain words will bring with him in these words the Byzantine tradition and the classical tradition, and maybe the pre-classical tradition as well. [...] I do not think that we have a parallel in our

varying lexical, orthographic and also syntactical forms often within the same poem[96] only adds to the translation problems. Some characteristic examples of Engonopoulos's mixed language found in his poems are:

archaic words and expressions: "ἀμφιλύκη" (twilight), "ἵμερος" (libido), "οἰδίπους" (swollen-footed), "χαῖρε παροδῖτα" (hail, passer-by)

medieval and older words: "ἡδύγευστος" (luscious), "μπροστέλλα" (pinafore), "μυδραλλιοβόλο" (machine-gun), "περιαλγὴς" (distressed)

learned words and expressions: "ὡσαύτως" (likewise), "ψιλῶ ὀνόματι" (bare name), "νενομισμένες σπονδὲς" (due libations)

foreign loan words (mainly of Turkish and Albanian origin): "γιαβουκλού" (betrothed), "σαρμανίτσα" (cradle), "τσαρντάκια" (shacks), "τακάτι" (mettle), "σέρρα" (conservatory)

dialectical and idiomatic words: "βιάση" (haste), "μόνε" (only), "μουντέρνω" (lunge), "προβέλνω" (proceed), "στρατοκόποι" (wayfarers), "σφυρώ" (whistle), "ωραιοτική" (fairest)

---

language. I do not think you could say that a modern poet might bring into his diction, without some degree of obscurity, an Anglo-Saxon connotation that is still fully natural in our everyday language. He might bring in Elizabethan connotations that are still accessible, but he will rarely go much farther back than that. The echoes in Greek go back naturally to Homer. It is a tremendous advantage to the Greek poet, a tremendous disadvantage to the translator of Greek poetry" (Edmund Keeley, "The Translator's Voice: An Interview with Edmund Keeley," by Warren Wallace, *Translation Review* 11 (1983): 6).

[96] See Giorgis Giatromanolakis, "Προκαταρκτικά στὴ γλῶσσα τοῦ Νίκου Ἐγγονόπουλου," in *Diavazo* 381 (January 1998): 144–145. See also the introduction by Giatromanolakis to Adamantios Koumbis, *Πίνακας λέξεων τῶν ποιημάτων τοῦ Νίκου Ἐγγονόπουλου*, Herakleion 1999, pp. xxi-xxv, for lists and classifications of the varying words and forms used by Engonopoulos.

alternative spellings: "ἀνάφτω" (light), "ἔμορφα" (lovely), "σερτάρι" (drawer), "ἔτζι" (thus)

What we observe in most English translations is that the linguistic tapestry characterizing Engonopoulos's poetry is to a greater or lesser degree absent and is, of necessity, replaced by a uniform standard English, thus giving a misleading image of Engonopoulos's poetic diction. In itself, the removal of his peculiar poetic diction is a serious disadvantage in presenting his work to an English-speaking readership, yet this diction is much more than a simple stylistic choice. As he himself says in one of his poems: "Mark well these words. They have as many obvious as hidden meanings" (in "The Moment Midnight Strikes, Jef the Great Automaton"). A number of scholars[97] have pointed out the attempt by Engonopoulos and also other surrealist poets through language to open the doors of perception to another reality or, to put it in the poet's own terms, to reveal "the secret of the well." I do not intend to develop this theme here, but simply to note that in terms of translating his work the loss of his diction in English translation is not limited only to the stylistic level, but also has serious consequences on the pragmatic level.

I have spoken only of the difficulties and loss in translating Engonopoulos's poetic diction into English. What can be saved? As McKinsey writes: "In translating such a distinctive poetic idiom, one must work down to the foundations of the subject-poet's language [...], then engineer a way back via one's own language and literature."[98] This, then, is the double labyrinth that the translator has to navigate: first he has to be bold enough to embark on the arduous and risky

---

[97] See, e.g., David Connolly, "Odysseus Elytis: Metalingual Poetry and Obscure Verbs," in Dimitris Tziovas (ed.) *Greek Modernism and Beyond*, Maryland 1997, pp. 121–132, Yannis Karavidas, "Surrealism and the Early Poetry of Nikos Engonopoulos," in *Journal of Modern Greek Studies* 5 (1987): 39–40, and Nanos Valaoritis, "Γιὰ τὸν θερμαστὴ τοῦ ὡραίου στοὺς κοιτῶνες τῶν ἐνδόξων ὀνομάτων," in *Hartis* 25–26 (November 1988): 79.

[98] Martin McKinsey, "Language Questions: Diglossia, Translation and the Poetry of Nikos Engonopoulos," in *Journal of Modern Greek Studies* 8 (2) (1990): 256.

journey into the foundations of the poet's work in order to discover the "secret of the well," and then to attempt the equally arduous and risky return using a different path (linguistic expression) and with a different destination (foreign culture and readership). As a result of this conscious and analytical translation process, it goes without saying that a large part of the spontaneity, charm and music stemming from the fortuitous lexical choices of the original will be lost.

3. Cultural problems

Just as with his poetic diction, often insurmountable translation problems are encountered in Engonopoulos' poetry in his references to Greek culturally-specific elements. Translation, it should be remembered, is concerned not just with transfer between languages but also with transfer between cultures and with transfer for a different cultural readership. Apart, therefore, from the usual semantic and stylistic factors involved in the translation process, culturally-specific references, which, due to the connotations and associations they conjure in the mind of the source-text (ST) reader, have a pragmatic effect on the reader, constitute one of the most difficult factors to account for in the process of transferring the text for a different linguistic and cultural readership. The translator's task is to adequately render these elements in another language so that the poem may have a corresponding or, at least similar, pragmatic effect on the target-text (TT) readership.

From antiquity, the many and varying strategies for dealing with cultural references can be divided into two basic categories: domesticating and foreignizing. A translation, that is, may be made to conform to values currently dominating the target-language (TL) culture, taking an assimilationist approach to the foreign ST, appropriating it in accordance with domestic values and norms. Alternatively, a translation may be motivated by an impulse to preserve the linguistic and cultural differences of the foreign ST by deviating from prevailing domestic values and norms. The inherent danger in adopting a foreignizing approach is that it often hinders the reader's comprehension and this may explain why, historically, most translating tends to be of the domesticating kind. In the case of Engonopoulos, it might be argued that a foreignizing strategy, which registers the linguistic and cultural otherness of the foreign text, is preferable even if this results in sometimes baffling the readers and provoking in them a reassessment of linguistic norms and cultural values, as such an effect is precisely in keeping with the aims and intentions of surrealist poetry. A domesticating strategy making use of culturally corresponding TL equivalents in the translated text would to be to deprive Engonopoulos's poetry of its peculiar Greekness, which constitutes one of its main characteristic features.

For cultural references consisting of Greek proper names and place names, of which there are a proliferation in Engonopoulos's poetry, the most reasonable procedure is transliteration and transference, that is, conversional conventions are used to alter the phonic and graphic form of a ST name so that it comes more into line with TL patterns of pronunciation and spelling. How the name is transliterated will depend on established conversion standards (ELOT, ISO, US Library of Congress, British Library, etc.), but also on cultural and historical conventions. So "Καραμανλάκης" ("Nocturnal Maria") and "Κάλφογλους" ("Noble and Sentimental Dance") may be transferred using a phonetically-based transliteration in keeping with the conversion standards mentioned as "Karamanlakis" and "Kalfoglous" respectively. In the case of a name like "Κωνσταντίνος" this may become "Konstantinos" or "Konstandinos" or "Konstadinos" depending on the conversion standards used, but "Κωνσταντίνος Παλαιολόγος" (who appears in *Bolivar*) must, I would argue, be transliterated in its Latinized form as "Constantine Palaeologus" due to historical considerations and established TL conventions. The same applies to ancient names such as "Ευρυδίκη" or "Ορφέας," and historical names such as "Βελισάριος." They would have to be transferred in their historically established TL equivalents as "Eurydice" (not "Evrydiki"), "Orpheus" (not "Orfeas") and "Belisarius" (not "Velisarios").

The problem for the translator is not so much with the transliteration of these names as with their culturally-specific associations. Whereas the translator may safely assume that the English-speaking reader is familiar with the myths surrounding such ancient figures as "Eurydice" and "Pandora" and the connotative significance of these names in the poetic text, the same is not true for the connotative significance associated with proper names such as "Constantine Palaeologus" and "Odysseus Androutsos" and with place names such as "Hydra" and "Leskovik," which rely on the connotations created in the mind of the ST reader to produce a pragmatic effect. This is the aspect of cultural reference that is perhaps the most difficult to deal with. All texts have connotations; ideas and feelings suggested by words and phrases. Even words ostensibly simple to translate, such as "sun," "bread," "olive," etc. often carry different connotations for the Greek and English reader. The problems are far greater, of course, with proper names and place names, which are culturally-specific and carry specific connotations. The connotative aspect of a poem like *Bolivar* (and the need to account for this in the translation in order to avoid pragmatic loss) is of particular importance as the whole conceptual framework of the poem is based to a large extent on allusions and associations for the reasons mentioned earlier relating to the historical context (Nazi Occupation and Greek Resistance) in which it was written. Subtitled "A Greek Poem," its Greekness is to be found in the cultural and historical associations and in the poem's allusions to the theme of liberty and relies on the ST reader's assumed ability to recognize and interpret these associations and allusions. For this reason, in the discussion that follows, most of the examples used have been taken from *Bolivar*.

So, the transliteration of the name "Κωνσταντῖνος Παλαιολόγος" is fairly easily dealt with, but not so the connotations arising from cultural references such as "The myriad forms assumed and successively discarded by Constantine Palaeologus." The problem for the TT reader is: who is Constantine Palaeologus and what are these "myriad forms" he assumed and discarded? The translator naturally cannot assume that the TT reader will be aware of the legend surrounding the last Byzantine Emperor, namely that he was not killed in the fall of Constantinople, but remains in hiding until the time comes when Constantinople will be retaken. A similar and culturally-equivalent legend in the English-speaking world surrounds King Arthur. The easiest and obvious solution to problems of this type is to use an explanatory note. In this specific example, it is somewhat surprising, given that most educated Greek readers would be aware of the legend, to observe that Engonopoulos himself added a note of explanation concerning Constantine Palaeologus in the subsequent republication of the poem.[99]

Similar connotative problems arise with the numerous other proper names in *Bolivar*. So what of "the figures, austere and magnificent, of Odysseus Androutsos and Simon Bolivar"? What associations do these names have for the English reader? We may expect an educated English reader to know something about Bolívar, but not about Androutsos. (An entry for Bolivar can be found in any standard English dictionary; one for Androutsos, needless to say, cannot). A

---

[99] It is a matter of discussion why Engonopoulos later added almost nine pages of notes to the poem in the standard edition of his work. It is true that some of the allusions incomprehensible to the TT reader are equally obscure for the ST reader, but one would not expect the educated Greek reader to require notes on Constantine Palaeologus or, indeed, on Odysseus Androutsos. Beaton states that these notes were "provided by the poet for a French translation [by Robert Levesque] some years after the poem's first publication" (Roderick Beaton, *An Introduction to Modern Greek Literature*, Oxford 1994: 185). Presumably they were then added by Engonopoulos to the subsequent republication of the work in Greek. This can be inferred to some extent from Engonopoulos's introduction to the notes. It also seems, however, that some of these notes were not written by the poet but by his translator and were then translated into Greek and added to Greek original. See, for example, the note to Androutsos, where the poet is referred to in the third person, as also he is in the note referring to Phanar, Mouchlio and Constantine Palaeologus. See also the final note concerning the poet's grandfather, which is openly attributed to Robert Levesque.

short explanatory note on Androutsos (most likely taken from the French translation) can be found in the notes later added in the standard edition of the poem, yet even without any explanatory note, the poem itself informs us that Androutsos, *like* Bolivar, was "a figure austere and magnificent," that they were both heroes "for their countries, their nations, their people," that "they remained throughout the ages, both of them, alone always, and free, great, brave, and strong," and that "it's no easy thing for figures of the importance of Androutsos and Bolivar to be so quickly understood." There are many instances where Engonopoulos—almost anticipating the translation problems caused by the culturally-specific associations—includes contextual information and explanations within the text of the poem. This is, in fact, a useful translation strategy for dealing with such problems. The addition of a word or two of contextualization in the text of the work constitutes a slight concession to the TT reader and helps to avoid too many copious notes, while reducing the inevitable pragmatic loss. McKinsey, for example, quite reasonably adds the word "Emperor" to the name "Constantine Palaeologus," while Friar translates "Μιὰ καντήλα στὸ Μουχλιὸ" as "a candle from the church of Mouhlio," adding the word "church" to the text and so explaining for the TT reader that the district is famous for its church. In general, however, the pragmatic loss resulting from the connotations arising from the use of place names or proper names in a poem can only be dealt with through translator's notes.[100]

A further example is provided by the isle of Hydra ("Υδρα), with which the poet had family connections and which appears several times in his work. First of all, the place name, for conventional

[100]   It was a conscious decision on my part in this selection not to provide explanatory or any other form of notes in order to "facilitate" the English-speaking reader in his or her understanding. Given the aims and nature of Engonopoulos's poetry, such notes, I believe, are counterproductive as they not only distract the reader's attention but also constantly bring him or her back into the world of conventional reality. The notes to the poems included in this selection were written by Engonopoulos himself to accompany subsequent editions of his collections.

reasons, is more acceptably transliterated as "Hydra" rather than the strictly phonetically-based "Ydra." But the translation problems stem more from the island's associations, which have to do with its tradition as the birthplace of notable naval commanders and with its historic and heroic role in the Greek War of Independence. So, for example, in the poem of the same name, the sudden appearance of the names "Miaoulis, Kanaris, Tombazis, Lazaros Kountouriotis" will have no meaning for the TT reader, without the explanatory note that these people were renowned naval commanders from Hydra. As one might expect, Engonopoulos himself provides no note to this early poem. He does provide a note, however, explaining the island's heroic associations when the island reappears in *Bolivar*, in the line "…on Hydra's seven shores," adding further credence to the assumption that these notes were originally composed with the non-Greek (French?) reader in mind, regardless of whether or not they were subsequently added to the standard edition of the work in Greek. In the second instance, then, the translation problem is solved simply by including Engonopoulos's own note in order to explain the island's connotations for the TT reader. In the other cases where Hydra appears, the translator can add a word of contextualization such as "the heroic isle of Hydra," if this is necessary to understanding the poem, or simply leave it as an exotic name offering local color and atmosphere. Such exoticism is, in any case, wholly in keeping with the surrealist aim to startle and bewilder, thereby distorting the usual rational processes in the reader.

Apart from the associations stemming from place names and proper names, the connotations stemming from references to culturally-specific customs and traditions again have to be carefully considered if pragmatic loss is to be reduced in the translated text. Take, for example, the reference in *Bolivar* to the lakeside town "Kastoria" and "the icons that creak there." The fact that this event usually signifies impending evil would be lost for the TT reader. The translator can transfer the reference and provide a note or culturally transpose the reference by finding some approximate cultural equivalent in the target culture for the creaking icons, such as weeping statues, which is a similar though not exactly corresponding phenomenon in the Catholic West. Though a cultural equivalent as a solution is more concise and reduces pragmatic loss, the inherent disadvantage, of course, is that of incongruity when dealing with culturally-specific references to traditions and customs peculiar to Greece.

So, references such as "And they came and painted you in the ways of Indian braves, / With wash, half white, half blue so you'd appear like a lonely chapel on one of Attica's shores," have to be explained—with a note—for the TT reader. Why should being painted with "wash, half white, half blue" make Bolivar resemble a deserted chapel on the shores of Attica, unless it is known that, in Greece, it is customary at times of religious festivals to paint the exterior of the church or the churchyard wall with whitewash and bluing? It may be obvious to the ST reader but it certainly is not to the TT reader. Other culturally-specific words, however, can be dealt with in the translation in a number of ways. For example, the word "κουμπαράς," which, as the poet informs even the ST reader in his notes, means "a hand grenade in the slang of the 1821 Revolution." To avoid pragmatic loss, a similar slang word for hand grenade should, if possible, be found in the TL. "Pineapple," used in military slang to mean "grenade," is perhaps a solution. The important point here is that, in such cases, the use of a *culturally equivalent* word is undoubtedly valid. The literal translation of "κουμπαράς" as "piggybank" would be meaningless, and Friar's and McKinsey's translation as "grenade" is referentially correct, but the pragmatic loss is total. "Pineapple" for "κουμπαράς" is an example of an approximate *cultural equivalent* which has a greater pragmatic impact than the culturally neutral "grenade." On the whole, I am not in favor of the substitution of cultural equivalents of the type "weeping statues" for "creaking icons," but what of expressions such as "Μὴν ὁμιλεῖτε εἰς τὸν ὁδηγὸν" (the title of Engonopoulos's first collection)? In terms of pragmatic effect, should this be translated literally as "Don't talk to the driver" or by the culturally corresponding expression in the TL culture, which may or may not be expressed in the same words? So, for example, the corresponding sign found on a bus or tram in the target culture would be "Don't distract the driver." This is a different category of cultural reference from the reference to "wash, half white, half blue so you'd appear like a lonely chapel on one of Attica's shores." The latter is culturally specific, the former culturally universal. The first category is more likely to require literal translation with an explanatory note; the second can be more concisely translated using the culturally equivalent expression.

In cases where there is no cultural equivalent, the translator can always have recourse to other types of equivalence. For example, the poet explains in the notes he subsequently added that the culturally specific word "ντολάπια" in the phrase "Πόσα ντολάπια καὶ δὲν σοῦ' στησαν," means "traps in the slang of the [Greek] Struggle." Here, no cultural equivalent is immediately obvious but the translator can still use the *functional equivalent* "traps," in other words, a culturally-free word that explains its use, even though the pragmatic loss is greater than with a cultural equivalent, just as in the case of "grenade" for "κουμπαράς." Similarly, in the case of the culturally-specific word "καντήλι," the translator can only have recourse to a *descriptive equivalent* such as "oil lamp" or "candle," i.e. a culture-free word that explains what the object looks like, accepting the pragmatic loss relating to its almost exclusive use in Greece in a religious context.

An example of a further category of culturally-specific word, for which, however, there is no cultural, functional or descriptive equivalent, is provided by the word "παλληκαρά" in the phrase "On the crown of your head, παλληκαρά, run unbroken stallions and wild cattle." Such words: "παλληκάρι," "φιλότιμο," "λεβεντιά," etc. are often, though wrongly, classed as being untranslatable. Every word can be translated, or, at least, accounted for in translation, and the easiest method is by translating it into its various component qualities (i.e. using componential analysis). In other words, the translation is based on a component common to both the SL and the TL. So, here, the component qualities of being a "παλλικάρι" include being handsome, young, valiant, etc. Friar translates as "O gallant youth," while

McKinsey uses the word "warrior." There is another solution, namely to keep the culturally-specific loan word "palikar," contained in standard English dictionaries and defined as "a Greek soldier in the war of independence against Turkey" (CED). Normally, I would, like Friar, use some form of componential analysis, but here, the poet is using the word in a culturally-specific way for a particular reason, to once again liken Bolivar to a Greek. Hence the need to retain the Greek word, perhaps qualifying it with the adjective "brave" or "valiant" as a slight concession to the TT reader. For the same reason, I retain the culturally-specific word "fustanella" in the poem "A Journey to Elbasan," rather than using the approximately cultural equivalent "kilt" or the descriptive equivalent "skirt." The word is contained in standard English dictionaries and is defined as "a white, knee-length plaited skirt worn by men in Greece and Albania" (CED). Retaining the Greek word in such cases introduces an element of exoticism into the text and signals cultural foreignness. As such, the pragmatic effect on the TT reader will be different than for the ST reader, for whom the word has no such foreign or exotic impact. However, as discussed earlier, an overall foreignizing strategy is more closely in keeping with the aims of surrealist poetry.

4. Conclusions

We have to accept that there will always be loss in the translation of a literary text on both a linguistic and cultural level. The question is: where is this loss avoidable and where unavoidable (or, better, where can it be reduced and where not), and what strategies are available to the translator for dealing with the problems that arise? Any solution will almost inevitably be a compromise, but the compromise should be the result of deliberate decisions by the translator based on the latitude afforded by the SL and TL and all the other relative factors, including the nature of the ST and its intended effect on the ST readers, the purpose of the translation and the putative TT readership. The translator should not overlook or underestimate the active role played by the reader in the success of a translation. "One doesn't "write" poems, one lives them," says Engonopoulos.[101] The same may be said of someone who reads poems. Engonopoulos's poetry presupposes an emotive and intuitive rather than a rational response on the part of the reader. It appeals emotively, through sets of related if elliptical images, to subconscious responses in the reader, with the aim of giving the reader a new vision of his integration in the world around him. As such, the translator should assume an intelligent, sensitive TT reader who will counterbalance some of the linguistic loss and bridge some of the cultural gaps by intuitive leaps of the imagination, which, in any case, is a basic requirement for reading poetry in translation.

The standard edition of Engonopoulos's early work together with his later collections, *In the Vale of Roseries* and *Man: The Measure*, contain a total of 176 poems (ten of which were written in French). The present volume contains over seventy poems in English translation including representative selections from each of his collections and the whole of his long poems *Bolivar* and *The Atlantic*. It should be remembered, of course, that the translator's criteria for selection are not quite the same as those of the literary critic, given that, despite the relative merits of individual poems, some poems lend themselves to translation, others do not. Engonopoulos, as a translator himself[102], would no doubt have been aware of the difficulties involved in the task and the inevitable loss. However, he also seems

---

[101]   Nikos Engonopoulos, *Ποιήματα*, Athens 1999: 329.

[102]   It is worth noting that although Engonopoulos was never a systematic translator, his first appearance in Greek letters was with a selection of his translations published, as mentioned earlier, in *Surrealism I* (1938) and his last published work during his lifetime (*In the Vale of Roseries*, 1978) ends with a selection of some fifteen translations from the work of, among others, Lautréamont, Charles Baudelaire, Federico Garcia Lorca, John Donne, Dante Alighieri and Vladimir Mayakovski. Regarding his translation work, he says: "Sometimes, while I'm at work, I recite both Greek and foreign poems to myself; those, that is, that I like a lot and have read often and know by heart. I put some of the foreign ones into Greek by playing around with them. Here [i.e. in *In The Vale of Roseries*], I include a number of those that I

to have been aware of the relative rewards. Writing in 1954, he says: "...many of my poems have been translated into foreign languages. For me this is a great reward; and I'm happy."[103] And, from the point of view of the translator, if the aim of the artwork, as Engonopoulos maintains, is to overcome solitude, then the aim of the translator is to overcome the artwork's linguistic and cultural solitude. And this was precisely my aim with this bilingual selection from the work of a unique Greek poet.

---

consider reasonably successful and that I noted down" (see Nikos Engonopoulos, Στὴν κοιλάδα μὲ τοὺς ροδῶνες, Athens 1978: 221).

[103] Nikos Engonopoulos, οἱ ἄγγελοι στὸν παράδεισο μιλοῦν ἑλληνικὰ... Συνεντεύξεις, Σχόλια καὶ Γνῶμες (ed. Yorgos Kendrotis), Athens 1999: 24.

Bibliography

Works by Engonopoulos

1938. *Μὴν ὁμιλεῖτε εἰς τὸν ὁδηγὸν* [Do Not Distract the Driver], Athens.

1939. *Τὰ Κλειδοκύμβαλα τῆς Σιωπῆς* [The Clavicembalos of Silence], Athens.

1944. *Μπολιβάρ* [Bolivar], Athens.

1946. *Ἡ ἐπιστροφὴ τῶν πουλιῶν* [The Return of the Birds], Athens.

1948. *Ἔλευσις* [Eleusis], Athens.

1954. *Ὁ Ἀτλαντικός* [The Atlantic], Athens.

1957. *Ἐν Ἀνθηρῷ Ἕλληνι Λόγῳ* [In the Flourishing Greek Tongue], Athens.

1978. *Στὴν κοιλάδα μὲ τοὺς ροδῶνες* [In the Vale of Roseries], Athens.

Works Published Posthumously

1987. *Πεζά κείμενα* [Prose Texts], Athens.

1994. *"...καὶ σ' ἀγαπῶ παράφορα"* ["... And I Love You Passionately"], (Letters to Lena), Dimitris Daskalopoulos (ed.), Athens.

1996. *Ἑλληνικὰ σπίτια* [Hellenic Houses], Athens.

1996. *Σχέδια καὶ χρώματα / Sketches and Colours* (English translation: David Connolly), Athens.

1999. *"Οἱ ἄγγελοι στὸν παράδεισο μιλοῦν ἑλληνικὰ..."* ["The Angels in Heaven Speak Greek"], (Interviews, Comments and Views), Yorgos Kendrotis (ed.), Athens.

2005. *Τὸ μέτρον: ὁ ἄνθρωπος, Πέντε ποιήματα καὶ δέκα πίνακες* [Man the Measure: Five Poems and Ten Paintings], Athens.

2006. *Μυθολογία* [Mythology], Introduction and Texts: Katerina Perpinioti-Agazir, Athens.

English Translations of His Work

1951. "Bolivar" (tr. Kimon Friar). *New Directions* 13, New York: Norfolk, Conn.

1955. "Poetry 1948" (tr. Kimon Friar). *The Atlantic Monthly* 195 (6): 148.

1968. "Osiris"; "The Ship of the Woods"; "Sinbad the Sailor"; "Guard and Vulture"; "The Clavichords of Silence"; "Morning Song"; "The Hydra of Birds"; "Early in the Morning"; "News of the Death of the Spanish Poet, Federico Garcia Lorca, on August 19, 1936, in a Ditch at Camino de la Fuente" (tr. John A. Goumas). *Nine Greek Poets*, Athens, pp. 67–85.

1969. "Mercurias Bouas"; "Psychoanalysis of Phantoms"; "Poetry 1948" (tr. Kimon Friar). Mary P. Gianos, *Introduction to Modern Greek Literature. An Anthology of Fiction, Drama and Poetry*, New York, pp. 530–534.

1969. "Poems" (tr. Thanasis Maskaleris). *Poems and Translations*, San Francisco.

1970. "Poems" (tr. John Richmond and Bryan McCarthy). *The Singing Cells. Modern Greek Poems*, Montreal.

1970. "Ballad of the Tall Ladder" or "An Episode from the Life of the Painter Theofilos"; "Supplication"; "On Boeotian Lands"; "Memory"; "The Lover"; "The Kindness of Man; "Orpheus Xenophobe"; "Reality"; "Nocturnal Maria"; "Ten and Four Themes for a Painting"; "Eleonora" (tr. Kimon Friar). *Contemporary Literature in Translation* 9: 13–18.

1973. "Vulture and Guard"; "Mercurius Bouas"; "Psychoanalysis of Phantoms" (tr. Yannis Goumas). *Contemporary Literature in Translation* 14: 18–19.

1973. "Eleonora"; "Ten and Four Themes for a Painting"; "The Hýdra of Birds"; "Bolívar, A Greek Poem"; "The Apprentice of Sorrow"; "Souvenir of Constantinople"; "The Last Appearance of Judas Iscariot"; "The Golden Plateaus"; "Poetry 1948"; "Mercurius Bouas"; "News About the Death of the Spanish Poet Federico Garcia Lorca on the Nineteenth of August 1936 in the Ditch of the Camino De La Fuente"; "On Boeotian Roads" (tr. Kimon Friar). Kimon Friar, *Modern Greek Poetry. From Cavafis to Elytis.* New York, pp. 570–589.

1977. "Four Poems" (tr. Martin McKinsey). *The Paris Review* 69: 124–128.

1977. "Gardens in the Blazing Sun" (tr. Nanos Valaoritis); "News about the Death of the Spanish Poet Federico Garcia Lorca on the 19th of August 1936 in a Ditch of Caminonte La

Fuente" (tr. Thanasis Maskaleris); "For Rent" (tr. Kimon Friar). *The Coffeehouse* 5: 8–13.

1977. "Vulture and Guard" (tr. M. Byron Raizis). M. Byron Raizis, *Greek Poetry Translations*, Athens, pp. 76–77.

1996. "Flight Model" (tr. Nanos Valaoritis); "News about the Death of the Spanish Poet Federico Garcia Lorca on the 19th of August 1936 in a Ditch of Caminonte La Fuente" (tr. Thanasis Maskaleris). *London Magazine* 36 (1/2): 108–109.

1996/97. "Bolivar. A Greek Poem" (tr. David Connolly). *Modern Greek Studies Yearbook* 12/13: 441–472.

1997. "The Trumpet" (tr. Martin McKinsey). *Dialogos* 4 (1997): 19–20.

2. "The Hydra of Birds"; "Early in the Morning" (tr. Yannis Goumas). *Hellenic Quarterly* No. 6 (Autumn 2): 68–69.

2. "Ship of the Forest"; "Nocturnal Maria"; "A Journey to Elbasan" (tr. David Connolly). *Poetry Greece* 3 (Winter 2–2001): 3–5.

2001. "A Hymn of Glory to the Women We Love" (tr. Maria Thanassa). *Poetry Greece* 5 (Autumn 2001): 32–37.

2003. "Bolivar" (tr. by David Connolly). *Modern Greek Writing* (ed. David Ricks), London, pp. 290–296.

2004. "Do Not Distract the Driver I, II"; "Poetry 1948" (tr. David Connolly). *Atlanta Review* X: 2 (Spring/Summer 2004): 42–43.

2004. "Eleonora"; "Hymn of Praise for the Women We Love" (tr. David Connolly); "On the Byways of Life" (tr. Martin McKinsey). *A Century of Greek Poetry 1900–2* (eds Peter Bien, Peter Constantine, Edmund Keeley, Karen Van Dyck), New Jersey: Cosmos Publishing, pp. 234–249.

2007. Ὡραῖος σὰν Ἕλληνας. Ποιήματα / *The Beauty of a Greek. Poems*, Selected and Translated by David Connolly, Athens.

2008. *Acropolis and Tram. Poems 1938–1978.* Edited and Translated by Martin McKinsey, København & Los Angeles.

2010. "Eleonora" (tr. David Connolly); "On the Byways of Life"; "Aubade"; "City of Light" (tr. Martin McKinsey). *The Greek Poets. Homer to the Present* (eds Peter Constantine, Rachel Hadas, Edmund Keeley, Karen Van Dyck), New York/London, pp. 519–524.

2011. *The Collected Works of Nikos Engonopoulos.* Translated by Philip Ramp. Introduction by Giorgis Giatromanolakis. Springfield, OR.

Selected Studies

In English

Connolly, David, "Nikos Engonopoulos. *Bolivar*, A Greek Poem, Translated from the Modern Greek With an Introduction," *Modern Greek Studies Yearbook*, vol. 12/13 (1996–1997), pp. 441–472.

———, "Greek Surrealist Poets in English Translation: Problems, parameters and possibilities," *Κάμπος. Cambridge Papers in Modern Greek* 6 (1998): 1–18.

Karandonis, Andreas, "Two Greek Surrealist Poets. A. Embiricos —N. Engonopoulos," (Translation: Theodore Sampson), *Greek Letters* 1 (1982): 255–271.

Karavidas, Yannis, "Surrealism and the Early Poetry of Nikos Engonopoulos," *Journal of Modern Greek Studies* 5 (1987): 33–46.

Kayalis, Takis, "Modernism and the Avant-Garde: The Politics of 'Greek Surrealism,'" in Dimitris Tziovas (ed.) *Greek Modernism and Beyond*, Maryland 1997, pp. 95–110.

McKinsey, Martin, "Language Questions: Diglossia, Translation and the Poetry of Nikos Engonopoulos," *Journal of Modern Greek Studies* 8 (2) (1990): 245–261.

Robinson, Christopher, "The Greekness of Modern Greek Surrealism," *Byzantine and Modern Greek Studies* 7 (1981): 119–137.

Yatromanolakis, Dimitrios, *Greek Mythologies: Antiquity and Surrealism*, Cambridge, Mass. 2012.

In Greek (book-length)

Abatzopoulou, Frangiski, *Νίκος Ἐγγονόπουλος. Ἡ ποίηση στὸν καιρό "τοῦ τραβήγματος τῆς ὑψηλῆς σκάλας,"* Athens 1987.

Andrikopoulou, Nelli, *Ἐπὶ τὰ ἴχνη τοῦ Νίκου Ἐγγονόπουλου*, Athens 2003.

Argyriou, Alex. *Διαδοχικές ἀναγνώσεις Ἑλλήνων ὑπερρεαλιστῶν*, Athens 1983.

Chachla, Andriana (ed.), *Νίκος Ἐγγονόπουλος: Ὁ ποιητής καὶ ὁ ζωγράφος*, Conference Proceedings, Athens 2010.

Engonopoulos, Nikos, *Ὡραῖος σὰν Ἕλληνας*, (ed. Giorgis Giatromanolakis), Athens 1996.

Koumbis, Adamantios, *Πίνακας λέξεων τῶν ποιημάτων τοῦ Νίκου Ἐγγονόπουλου*, (ed. and intro. Giorgis Giatromanolakis), Herakleion 1999.

Perpinioti-Agazir, Katherina, *Νίκος Ἐγγονόπουλος. Ὁ ζωγραφικὸς τοῦ κόσμος*, Athens 2007.

Trivizas, Sotiris, *Τὸ σουρεαλιστικό σκάνδαλο. Χρονικὸ τῆς ὑποδοχῆς τοῦ ὑπερρεαλιστικοῦ κινήματος στὴν Ἑλλάδα*, Athens 1996.

Zamarou, Rena, *Ὁ ποιητής Νίκος Ἐγγονόπουλος. Ἐπίσκεψη τόπων καί προσώπων*, Athens 1993.

POEMS

ΜΗΝ ΟΜΙΛΕΙΤΕ ΕΙΣ ΤΟΝ ΟΔΗΓΟΝ

… la voix surréaliste, celle qui continue à prêcher
à la veille de la mort et au-dessus des orages.
ANDRÉ BRETON: *"Manifeste du Surréalisme"*

ΤΡΑΜ ΚΑΙ ΑΚΡΟΠΟΛΙΣ

le soleil me brûle et me rend lumineux

μέσ' στή μονότονη βροχή
τίς λάσπες
τήν τεφρήν ἀτμόσφαιρα
τά τράμ περνοῦνε
καί μέσ' ἀπό τήν ἔρημη ἀγορά
– πού νέκρωσε ἡ βροχή –
πηγαίνουν πρός
τά
τέρματα

ἡ σκέψη μου
γιομάτη συγκίνηση
τ' ἀκολουθεῖ στοργικά ὥσπου
νά φθάσουν
ἐκεῖ π' ἀρχίζουν τά χωράφια
πού πνίγει ἡ βροχή
στά τέρματα

τί θλίψη θά ἤτανε – Θέ μου –
τί θλίψη
ἄν δέ μέ παρηγοροῦσε τήν καρδιά
ἡ ἐλπίδα τῶν μαρμάρων
κι' ἡ προσδοκία μιᾶς λαμπρῆς ἀχτίδας
πού θά δώση νέα ζωή
στά ὑπέροχα ἐρείπια

From: *DO NOT DISTRACT THE DRIVER* (1938)

*… la voix surréaliste, celle qui continue à prêcher
à la veille de la mort et au-dessus des orages.*
ANDRÉ BRETON: "Manifeste du Surréalisme"

TRAMS AND ACROPOLIS

le soleil me brûle et me rend lumineux

in the monotonous rain
the mud
the ashen atmosphere
the trams pass
and cross the deserted marketplace
– made lifeless by the rain –
heading towards
the
terminus

filled with emotion
my thoughts
fondly follow them till
they arrive
at the terminus
where swamped by the rain
the fields begin

how sad it would be – dear God –
how sad
if my heart were not consoled
by the hope of the marbles
and the expectation of a bright ray
to give new life
to the splendid ruins

ἀπαράλλαχτα ὅπως
ἕνα κόκκινο λουλούδι
μέσ' σέ πράσινα φύλλα

identical to
a red flower
amidst green leaves

ΜΗΝ ΟΜΙΛΕΙΤΕ ΕΙΣ ΤΟΝ ΟΔΗΓΟΝ

I

Άλβανοί χορεύοντες σκέπτονται νά στρέψουν πρός νέες διευθύνσεις τίς ἐνέργειές τους, εἰς τρόπον ὥστε τά παιδιά νά μήν καταλάβουν τίποτες ἀπό τίς πικρίες καί τάς ἀπογοητεύσεις τῆς ζωῆς. Νά μήν καταλάβουν τίποτες πρίν ἀπό τόν καιρό τους. Πάντως οἱ σκέψεις αὐτῶν τῶν Ἀλβανῶν δέν περνοῦν πέρα ἀπό τούς σκαρμούς τῶν παραθύρων. Κι' αὐτό διότι Ἰταλός τις, ἀκούων εἰς τό ὄνομα Γιουλιέλμος Τσίτζης, καί ἐπαγγελλόμενος τόν ἐπιδιορθωτήν πνευστῶν ὀργάνων, προσπαθεῖ νά ἐξαπατήσῃ τούς μελλονύμφους, ἐφαρμόζων σέ παλαιοῦ συστήματος ραπτομηχανήν Σίγγερ τέσσερα χουνιά, ἐκ τῶν ὁποίων τά δύο γυάλινα καί τ' ἄλλα δύο καμωμένα ἀπό ἕνα ὁποιονδήποτε μέταλλο. Νά μήν ταραχθῆ κανείς: ἡ εἰκών αὕτη εἶναι ἡ μόνη πού ἐβοήθησε τόν ἀποθανόντα ἀόμματο φαροφύλακα νά ἀνακαλύψῃ τό μυστικόν τοῦ φρέατος.

II

(περί ἀνέμων καί ὑδάτων)

Αἰωνία ἡ μνήμη τοῦ εὐγενεστάτου Ὀθωμανοῦ Ἀλῆ Χαντζάρ ἐφένδη, ποτέ ἀνωτάτου ὑπαλλήλου τῆς Αὐτοκρατορίας, ὅστις μεγάλως εὐεργέτησε τήν ἀνθρωπότητα, βοηθούμενος ἀπό Ἰταλόν τινα, Γουλιέλμο Τσίτζη λεγάμενο. Αὐτῆς ἄλλωστε τῆς γνώμης εἶναι καί ἡ κυρία Ἄρτεμις. Τῆς «κυρία Ἄρτεμις» ἡ βεβαίωσις γαληνεύει τίς ἀνήσυχες ψυχές, καί συνεισφέρει μεγάλως εἰς τήν προσπάθειαν γάλλων ποιητῶν τοῦ Χΐου αἰῶνος νά συμπήξουν νέαν σχολήν ὑπό τήν ἐπωνυμίαν «Πλειάδα». Ἄλλωστε κανείς ἐξ ὑμῶν δέν λησμονεῖ ὅτι ὁ μοναχός Σβάρτς ἀνεκάλυψε τήν πυρίτιδα. Καί ἔτζι διά τά ἄλλα...

DO NOT DISTRACT THE DRIVER

I

Dancing Albanians think of giving new turns to their activities, in a way such that children will not understand anything of life's sorrows and disappointments. Not understand anything before their time. Yet the thoughts of these Albanians go no further than the windows' swivel locks. And all because a certain Italian, answering to the name of Guillaume Tsitzes, and professing to be a repairer of wind instruments, attempts to deceive the bridal couple, attaching to an old-fashioned Singer sewing machine four horns, two of which are crystal and the other two fashioned from any old metal. Let no one be alarmed: this is the one image that helped the blind lighthouse-keeper now deceased to discover the secret of the well.

II

(on everything under the sun)

Blessed be the memory of Alí Hadjár, most gracious Ottoman effendi, never a high official in the Empire, who most greatly benefitted mankind, assisted by a certain Italian, Guillaume Tsitzes by name. Of this opinion moreover is mistress Artemis. The assurance of "mistress Artemis" calms troubled souls, and contributes most greatly to the endeavors of 16th century French poets to found a new school under the name of "Pléiade." Moreover, not one of us can forget that it was the monk Schwartz who invented gunpowder. And thus for the rest…

ΤΕΛ-ΑΒΙΒ

ἡ Ἐλεωνόρα
ἡ χρυσή κόρη
ἔπαιζε ἄρπα
μέ τά ὡραῖα
λευκά της
χέρια

ἀπό τήν ἄρπα
ὅμως

δέν ἀκουγότανε
ἦχος κανείς

ὅλη ἡ μουσική
ἤτανε
μέσα
στά ἔμορφά της μάτια
ἀνάμεσα
στά πράσινά της τά μαλλιά

ἀπό τήν ἄρπα
ὅμως
βγῆκαν
τό ἕνα κατόπιν τοῦ ἄλλου
ἕνα πουλί
μιά πλάκα πράσινο σαπούνι
κι' ἕνα
σίδερο
τοῦ σιδερώματος
– ἀπό τά κοινότατα –
αὐτά ἀκριβῶς
πού οἱ Ζυγιῶται
ὀνομάζουν
ἐν ὥρᾳ καταιγίδος
Ars Amantis   8

TEL AVIV

Eleonora
precious girl
was playing the harp
with her lovely
white
hands

from the harp
though
no sound
was heard

all the music
was
within
her beautiful eyes
amidst
her green hair

from the harp
though
emerged
one after the other
a bird
a bar of green soap
and an
iron
for ironing
– of the commonest kind –
the very same
that the Zygiots
in time of storm
call
Ars Amantis

ΟΣΙΡΙΣ

Ἀργά χτές τήν νύκτα, στούς ἀπάνω μαχαλάδες, ἄγριοι κι᾽ αἱμοβόροι ἀλβανοί, ἑπτά τόν ἀριθμόν, ἔσφαξαν ἀλύπητα, μέσα στό ἴδιο του τό κρεβάτι, τόν κυνοκέφαλο ἐραστή τῆς λησμονημένης Ἱππολύτης. Οἱ ἀπαίσιοι κακοῦργοι μπῆκαν, χωρίς νάν τούς καταλάβη κανείς, μέσα στό δωμάτιο τοῦ στυγεροῦ ἐγκλήματος. Ἀφοῦ ἔψαλαν, τῇ συνοδείᾳ πλαγιαύλου, δύο ἄγνωστους – τουλάχιστον εἰς ἐμέ – ὕμνους πρός τούς τσαλαπετεινούς, ἐτοποθέτησαν προσεκτικώτατα κάτω ἀπό ἕνα ποτήρι, περιέχον ἐλαφράν διάλυσιν ψαρόκολλας ἐντός ἐλαχίστης ποσότητος νιτρογλυκερίνης, ἕνα χαρτί. Τό χαρτί αὐτό ἦταν ἕνα φύλλο κοινοτάτου χάρτου ἀλληλογραφίας, ἐπί τοῦ ὁποίου ἦσαν γραμμέναι αἱ λέξεις: «Χρυσή κολώνα». Κατόπιν τούτου οἱ δολοφόνοι ἐξῆλθον καί πάλιν ἀνενόχλητοι. Ὁ κυνοκέφαλος ἐραστής – ἄς τόν ποῦμε ἔτσι, διότι τό ὄνομά του Ἰσίδωρος μᾶς εἶναι ἄγνωστον – ἐξῆλθε πολύ ἀργότερα τοῦ τραγικοῦ δωματίου. Ἐφόρει φαιόχρουν ἀδιάβροχον καί ὀμματοϋάλια.

OSIRIS

Late last night, in the upper districts, brutal and bloodthirsty Albanians, seven in number, mercilessly slew, in his very own bed, the cynocephalus lover of long-forgotten Hippolyta. The foul fiends entered the room of the heinous crime without anyone hearing them. After having sung, to a flute accompaniment, two unknown – at least to me – hymns to the hoopoes, they very carefully placed a piece of paper beneath a glass containing a weak solution of fish glue in a tiny amount of nitroglycerine. The paper was a sheet of common writing paper, on which were written the words: "Golden column." Following this the murderers left again undisturbed. The cynocephalus lover – let's call him that, for his name, Isidorus, is unknown to us – left the tragic room much later. He was wearing a grey-colored raincoat and spectacles.

ΤΟ ΚΑΡΑΒΙ ΤΟΥ ΔΑΣΟΥΣ

ξέρω ὅτι
ἄν εἶχα
μιά φορεσιά
– ἕνα φράκο –
χρώματος πράσινο ἀνοιχτό
μέ μεγάλα κόκκινα σκοτεινά λουλούδια

ἄν στή θέση τῆς
ἀόρατης
αἰολικῆς ἅρπας πού μοῦ χρησιμεύει
γιά κεφάλι
εἶχα μιά τετράγωνη πλάκα
πράσινο σαπούνι
ἔτσι πού ν' ἀκουμπᾶ
ἁπαλά
ἡ μιά της ἄκρη
ἀνάμεσα στούς δύο μου ὤμους

ἄν ἤτανε δυνατό
ν' ἀντικαταστήσω
τά ἱερά σάβανα
τῆς φωνῆς μου
μέ τήν ἀγάπη
πού ἔχει
μιά μεταφυσική μουσική κόρη
γιά τίς μαῦρες ὀμπρέλλες τῆς βροχῆς

ἴσως τότες
μόνο τότες
θά μποροῦσα νά πῶ
τά φευγαλέα ὁράματα
τῆς χαρᾶς

SHIP OF THE FOREST

I know that
if I had
a suit of clothes
– a dress coat –
pale green in color
with big red gloomy flowers

if in place of the
invisible
aeolian harp that serves me
for a head
I had a square bar
of green soap
so that its one end
rested
lightly
between my two shoulders

if I were able
to replace
the sacred shrouds
of my voice
with the love
felt by
a metaphysical musical maiden
for the rain's black umbrellas

perhaps then
and only then
I would be able to relate
the fleeting visions
of joy

πού εἶδα κάποτες
– σάν ἤμουνα παιδί –
κυττάζοντας
εὐλαβικά
μέσα στά στρογγυλά
μάτια
τῶν πουλιῶν

I once saw
– as a child –
when staring
devoutly
into the round
eyes
of birds

ΟΔΟΣΤΡΩΤΗΡΕΣ

Ἡ καρδιά μου εἶναι ἕνα ἀντικείμενο ἀπό λάστιχο συμπαγές. Ἔχει μέσα δύο ὀδυνηρά ἀνάξια γυάλινα καρφιά. Παίρνω αὐτό τ' ἀντικείμενο, κι' ἐνῶ μ' ἀντιστέκεται μέ χέρια καί πόδια, κατορθώνω, μόλις καί μέ βία, νάν τό κρύψω μέσα στό σερτάρι ὅπου φυλάω, κρυφά, λόγια κι' ἱστορίες ἀπό τό χωριό τῶν ποδηλάτων. Δέν φοβοῦμαι οὔτε τή φαλλοφόρο παρθένο οὔτε τόν ἄνθρωπο μέ τά γούνινα μάτια π' ἀνεβοκατεβαίνει τή σκοτεινή σκάλα. Γνωρίζω ἀπό παιδί τόν καθρέφτη τῶν λουλουδιῶν. Τραγουδῶ τίς δόξες τῶν ὀδοστρωτήρων, λέω τούς ἀγνούς ψαλμούς τῶν μπουκαλιῶν, ἐνῶ ἡ χάρτινη κουκουβάγια μοῦ λέει ἴσια μέσα στ' αὐτί – με το χουνί της – τή λέξη «ξένη».

STEAMROLLERS

My heart is an object of solid rubber. Inside it has two painful worthless glass nails. I take this object, and though it resists me tooth and nail, I manage, albeit with a struggle, to hide it in the drawer where I secretly keep words and tales from the bicycles' village. I fear neither the phallus-bearing virgin nor the man with the furry eyes walking up and down the dark stairs. Since childhood I have known the flowers' mirror. I sing the steamrollers' praises, chant the bottles' innocent psalms, while – through its horn – the paper owl says right into my ear the word "stranger."

ΕΛΕΟΝΩΡΑ

for hands she hath non, nor eyes, nor feet, nor golden Treasure of hair.

(προσθία ὄψις)

τά μαλλιά της εἶναι σάν χαρτόνι
καί σάν ψάρι
τά δύο της μάτια εἶναι
σάν ἕνα περιστέρι
τό στόμα της
εἶναι σάν τόν ἐμφύλιο πόλεμο
(στήν Ἱσπανία)
ὁ λαιμός της εἶναι ἕνα κόκκινο
ἄλογο
τά χέρια της
εἶναι
σάν τή φωνή
τοῦ πυκνοῦ
δάσους
τά δυό της στήθη εἶναι
σάν τή ζωγραφική μου
ἡ κοιλιά της εἶναι
ἡ ἱστορία
τοῦ Βέλθανδρου καί τῆς Χρυσάντζας
ἡ ἱστορία
τοῦ Τωβία
ἡ ἱστορία
τοῦ
γαϊδάρου
τοῦ λύκου καί τῆς ἀλωποῦς
τό φῦλο της
εἶναι
ὀξέα σφυρίγματα

ELEONORA

for hands she hath non, nor eyes, nor feet, nor golden Treasure of hair.

(*front view*)

her hair is like cardboard
and like a fish
her two eyes are
like a dove
her mouth
is like civil war
(in Spain)
her neck is a red
horse
her hands
are
like the voice
of the dense
forest
her two breasts are
like my painting
her belly is
the tale
of Bélthandros and Chrysántza
the tale
of Tobias
the tale
of
the ass
the wolf and the fox
her sex
is
shrill whistling

μέσα στή γαλήνη
τοῦ μεσημεριοῦ
οἱ μηροί της εἶναι
οἱ τελευταῖες
ἀναλαμπές
τῆς σεμνῆς χαρᾶς
τῶν ὁδοστρωτήρων
τά δυό της γόνατα
ὁ Ἀγαμέμνων
τά δυό της λατρευτά
μικρά
πόδια
εἶναι τό πράσινο
τηλέφω-
νο μέ τά κόκκινα
μάτια

(ὀπισθία ὄψις)

τά μαλλιά της
εἶναι
μιά λάμπα τοῦ πετρελαίου
πού καίει
τό πρωΐ
οἱ ὦμοι της
εἶναι
τό σφυρί
τῶν πόθων
μου
ἡ πλάτη της
εἶναι τά
ματογυάλια
τῆς θάλασσας
τό ἄροτρο

in the calm
of midday
her thighs are
the last
flickers
of the modest joy
of steam-rollers
her two knees
Agamemnon
her two adorable
tiny
feet
are the green
tele-
phone with the red
eyes

(*rear view*)

her hair
is
an oil lamp
that burns
in the morning
her shoulders
are
the hammer
of
my desires
her back
is the
sea's
eyeglass
the plough

τῶν ἀπατηλῶν
ἰδεογραμμάτων
σφυράει
θλιμμένα
στή μέση της
οἱ γλουτοί της
ψαρόκολλα εἶναι
οἱ μηροί της
εἶναι
σάν
ἀστροπελέκι
οἱ μικρές της φτέρνες
φωτίζουν
τά
πρωϊνά
κακά
ὄνειρα

καί τελικά
εἶναι
μιά γυναῖκα
μισή
ἱπποκάμπη
καί μισή
περιδέραιο
ἴσως ἀκόμη
νά εἶναι
ἐν μέρει πεῦκο
καί ἐν μέρει
ἀνελκυστήρ

of deceptive
ideograms
whirs
sorrowfully
at her waist
her buttocks
are
fish-glue
her thighs
are
like
a thunderbolt
her tiny heels
light
the
morning's
bad
dreams

and after all
she is
a woman
half
hippocampus
and half
necklace
perhaps
she's even
part pine
and part
elevator

ΠΑΡΑΔΟΣΙΣ

Emplissez de noix la besace du héros.

G. APOLLINAIRE: "Le larron"

Ἕνας λύκος οὐρλιάζει πένθιμα στή γωνιά τῆς σκάλας. Κι' εἶμαι ἐγώ ὁ ἴδιος, ἤ μᾶλλον εἶναι ἡ καρδιά μου, πού προσμένει, χρόνια τώρα, τόν ἐρχομό τοῦ Σαρδανάπαλου, ὑπό μορφήν εἴτε φυσιγγίου δυναμίτιδος, εἴτε ἄνθους χαρίτων. Διασκεδάζω τήν ἀνία μου διαβάζοντας τά κεφάλαια «τῶν ψαριῶν» μέσα στά σεξουαλικά συναξάρια τῶν λωτοφάγων. Κι' ὅμως αἰσθάνομαι γύρω μου νά ὀγκοῦται ἡ ἀγανάκτησις κι' ἡ ἐχθρότης τοῦ πλήθους τῶν ἱερέων. Κατηγγέλθην ἤδη ὡς «προσήκων σεβασμός» ὑπό ὁμάδος ἀλλοπροσάλλων παμφάγων ἐρυθροδέρμων ἁλιέων. Ὁμογενεῖς ἐφοπλισταί καί ἀντισφαιρισταί τῶν δύο φύλων μ' ἐστιγμάτισαν ὡς «ποδήλατον ἐγκέφαλον» τῶν Χετταίων. Μοῦ προσήφθη ἀσυστόλως τό ἔγκλημα ὅτι ἐλάκτισα, ἐν στιγμῇ ὀργῆς, τό ἱερόν ὀστοῦν τῶν δεινοσαύρων. Ἐγώ ὅμως μένω ἤρεμος. Γαλήνη κι' ἀταραξία βασιλεύουν μέσ' στήν ψυχή μου, ἐνῶ βρέχει συνεχῶς ἀπό τό πρωΐ. Ὅλοι μοῦ φωνάζουν:

παραδόσου!

Ἀλλά ἐγώ δέν παραδίδομαι. Ἀρκοῦμαι νά παραδίδω μαθήματα Ἀγγλικῆς γλώσσης δίς, ἤ καί τρίς ἀκόμη τῆς ἑβδομάδος, εἰς τάς θνησιγενεῖς ραπτομηχανάς τῶν ἐπάλξεων. Ὅλοι μοῦ φωνάζουν:

παραδόσου!

Ὄχι. Θά παραδώσω μόνον τίς ἑξάγωνες φωτοβολίδες τῶν λαιμητόμων στό μαρμαρωμένο βασιλιά. Ὅλοι μοῦ φωνάζουν:

παραδόσου!

Καλά... Νά παραδοθῶ... Ἔστω. Ἀλλ' ὅμως γιατί; Εἶμαι ἤ δέν εἶμαι ὁ συμμέτοχος τοῦ νυκτερινοῦ ἐγκλήματος; Εἶμαι ἤ δέν εἶμαι τό ἀλαλάζον ἄροτρον, ὁ κροκόδειλος-βενζίνη; Εἶμαι ἤ δέν εἶμαι ἡ πύρινη περικεφαλαία τοῦ σκυτοτόμου, ὁ πολέμιος τῶν ἀστραπῶν; Καθώς καταλαβαίνω μολαταῦτα πώς ἡ ζωή μου ἤτανε τό φυτίλι τῆς λάμπας, ἤτανε, μέ μιά λέξη, ὁ ἠλεκτρικός διακόπτης τῶν ἀραμαϊκῶν κλειδοκυμβάλων τῆς σιωπῆς, γι' αὐτό,

παραδίδομαι!

SURRENDER

Emplissez de noix la besace du héros.
G. APOLLINAIRE: "Le larron"

A wolf howls dolefully at the corner of the stairs. And it is me, or rather it is my heart that, for years now, has been awaiting the coming of Sardanapulus in the form of either a cartridge of dynamite or the bloom of graces. I alleviate my ennui by reading the chapters "on fish" in the lotus-eaters' sexual legendaries. Yet, all around me, I sense the growing resentment and hostility of the multitude of priests. Already I have been accused of "due respect" by a group of fickle omnivorous redskin fishermen. Expatriate shipowners and tennis players of both sexes have branded me "bicycle brain" of the Hittites. I have been shamelessly charged with the crime that, in a moment of rage, I kicked the dinosaurs' sacred bone. I, however, remain calm. Peace and serenity prevail in my soul, though it has been raining since the morning. Everyone shouts to me:

surrender!

But I do not surrender. I am content to render English lessons twice or even thrice a week to the battlements' doomed sewing-machines. Everyone shouts to me:

surrender!

No. I will render only the guillotines' hexagonal flares to the petrified king. Everyone shouts to me:

surrender!

All right... I'll surrender... So be it. Yet why? Am I or am I not the accomplice to the nocturnal crime? Am I or am I not the tinkling plough, the crocodile-petrol? Am I or am I not the leatherer's fiery helmet, the lightning's adversary? Nonetheless since I realize that my life was the lamp's wick, was, in a word, the electric switch of the Aramaic clavichords of silence, I therefore

surrender!

ΑΓΑΠΗ

Φεύγουμε. Ἀλλά προτοῦ ν' ἀποχωριστοῦμε, ἄς ποῦμε ὅλοι μαζί τό τραγούδι τοῦ πέτρινου αὐτοκίνητου. Κι' ὅταν λέω «πέτρινο» νά ἐννοούμεθα: ἔχει πέτρες μόνο στίς γωνιές, τό ὑπόλοιπο εἶναι καμωμένο, ὡς συνήθως, μέ τοῦβλα καί σανίδες, κι' οἱ ρόδες εἶναι ἀπό βάμμα ἰωδίου. Ἄς πάρουμε μαζί μας τήν ἀνάμνηση τῶν ἀκτινωτῶν δαιδάλων καί τά ἑτεροθαλῆ χαλίκια τῶν ἐμπρηστικῶν κουτιῶν. Ὅπως πάντα, κατεύθυνση δεξιά, πρός τά φωτεινά ξυλάρμενα τῆς ἀγάπης μας. Θύμησις καί θέλησις ἀσφάλτου: ὁ Ποσειδῶν. Γιά μένα, ἕνα ἄστρο θά λέη μέσ' στό σερτάρι τό τραγούδι τῆς χαρᾶς μου μ' ἕνα πριόνι. Ἄς μή μ' ἀκολουθῆ κανείς. Ὅλοι μας, σάν μυθολογικοί πολυέλαιοι καί σάν ἀλεξικέραυνα ἐλάσματα, ἄς ἀναπαυθοῦμε. Μαζί μέ τά πουλιά, μ' ἕνα πουλί, μέ δυό πουλιά.

26

LOVE

We are leaving. Yet before we go our different ways, let us all together sing the song of the stone automobile. And when I say "stone," I mean: it has stones only at the corners, the rest is, as usual, made of bricks and boards, and the wheels are of iodine tincture. Let us take with us the memory of the radial mazes and the incendiary boxes' sibling pebbles. As always, veering right, towards our love's bright unrigged vessels. Recollection and will of the asphalt: Poseidon. For me, a star in the drawer will sing the song of my joy with a saw. Let no one follow me. Like mythological chandeliers and lightning conductors, let us all repose. Together with the birds, with one bird, with two birds.

EKEI

τά δικτυωτά ἀνύπαρκτα ριπίδια
τῆς λησμονιᾶς
ἦταν ἡ μόνη
παρηγοριά
μέσα στά αἵματα μιᾶς
παρθένου
πού δέν εἶπε ποτέ τ᾽ ὄνομά της
μέσ᾽ στά τραγούδια
τῆς τεφρῆς οὐσίας
μέσα στούς κόκκινους λεπτομερεῖς ἀνέμους

κι᾽ ὅμως ἤτανε γραφτό
ἀνάμεσ᾽ ἀπ᾽ τούς κρίκους
τίς ρόδες
τίς σοῦστες
καί τά κλάματα
τῆς φαλαινίδος
νά φυτρώση ἔτσι
ἕνας
φῦκος
πού ἦταν τό μόνο στολίδι
τῆς πτωχῆς αἰθούσης

φωνές
καί τά ξέστρωτα τραγικά κρεβάτια
σπασμῶν

THERE

The non-existent net fans
of forgetting
was the sole
consolation
amid the blood of a
virgin
who never said her name
amid the songs
of ashen substance
amid the red elaborate winds

and yet it was writ that
between the rings
the wheels
the springs
and the sobs
of the she-whale
thus would sprout
a
rubber plant
that was the sole decoration
in the seedy room

cries
and the unmade tragic beds
of convulsions

Ο ΜΥΣΤΙΚΟΣ ΠΟΙΗΤΗΣ

hommage à raveL

ή σκιά τῆς λίμνης
ἁπλώνονταν μέσ' στό δωμάτιο
καί κάτω ἀπό κάθε καρέκλα
κι' ἀκόμη κάτω ἀπ' τό τραπέζι
καί πίσω ἀπ' τά βιβλία
καί μέσ' στά σκοτεινά βλέμματα
τῶν γύψινων προπλασμάτων
ἀκούγονταν σάν ψίθυρος
τό τραγούδι τῆς
μυστικῆς ὀρχήστρας
τοῦ νεκροῦ ποιητῆ

καί τότε μπῆκε ἡ γυναῖκα πού περίμενα
τόσον καιρό
ὁλόγυμνη
μέσ' στ' ἄσπρα ντυμένη
κάτω ἀπ' τό φῶς τοῦ φεγγαριοῦ
μέ τά μαλλιά λυμένα
μέ κάτι μακριά πράσινα χορτάρια μέσα στά μάτια
πού κυματίζανε ἀργά
ὡσάν τίς ὑποσχέσεις
πού δέν δοθήκανε ποτές
σέ μακρινές ἄγνωστες πόλεις
καί σ' ἄδεια
ἐρειπωμένα
ἐργοστάσια

κι' ἔλεγα νά χαθῶ κι' ἐγώ
σάν τό νεκρό ποιητή
μέσα στά μακριά

THE SECRET POET

hommage à raveL

the lake's shadow
spread through the room
and under every chair
even under the table
behind the books
and in the dark gazes
of the plaster models
and heard like a whisper
was the song of
the dead poet's
secret orchestra

then entered the woman I'd been waiting for
so long
stark naked
dressed all in white
in the moonlight
with hair let down
with long green grass blades in her eyes
that slowly swayed
like promises
never made
in distant unknown cities
and empty
derelict
factories

and I considered vanishing too
like the dead poet
into her long

μαλλιά της
μέ κάτι λουλούδια
π' ἀνοίγουν τό
βράδυ
καί
κλείνουν
τό πρωΐ
μέ κάτι ψάρια ξερά
πού κρέμασαν
μ' ἕνα σπάγγο
ψηλά
στήν καρβουναποθήκη

κι' ἔτσι νά φύγω
μακριά
ἀπ' τήν ὀχλαγωγή
καί τό θόρυβο
τοῦ σκοπευτηρίου
νά φύγω μακριά
μέσ' στά σπασμένα
τζάμια
καί νά ζήσω
αἰώνια
πάνω στό ταβάνι
ἔχοντας ὅμως
πάντα
μέσα στά μάτια
τά μυστικά τραγούδια
τῆς νεκρῆς ὀρχήστρας
τοῦ
ποιητῆ

hair
with some flowers
that open at
night
and
close
in the morning
with some dried fish
hung
with string
high
in the coal shed

and so I would go
faraway
from the bustle
and din
of the rifle-range
I would go faraway
through the broken
panes
and live
eternally
on the ceiling
though having
always
in my eyes
the secret songs
of the poet's
dead
orchestra

ΝΥΚΤΕΡΙΝΗ ΜΑΡΙΑ

Τήν ἐπομένη ἀκριβῶς τοῦ θανάτου μου, ἤ μᾶλλον τῆς θανατώσεώς μου, πῆρα νά διαβάσω ὅλες τίς ἐφημερίδες, γιά νά μάθω ὅσο τό δυνατόν περισσοτέρας λεπτομερείας ὡς πρός τά τῆς ἐκτελέσεώς μου. Φαίνεται ὅτι ὡδηγήθην εἰς τό ἰκρίωμα ὑπό αὐστηρᾶς συνοδείας. Φοροῦσα, λέει, κιτρίνου χρώματος ἐπενδύτην, δικτυωτόν λαιμοδέτην καί περικεφαλαίαν. Τά μαλλιά μου ἤτανε ὅμοια μέ βούρτσα, ἴσως μπογιατζῆ, ἴσως πιτυοκάμπτη. Κατόπι πετάξανε τό πτῶμα μου μακριά, σ' ἕνα βαλτοτόπι, ὅπου ἤτανε ἄλλοτε λημέρι τοῦ γάλλου Καρτεσίου κι' ὅπου βρισκόταν ἐπίσης, χρόνια τώρα, βορά τῶν ὀρνέων καί μιᾶς ἱεροδούλου λεγομένης Εὐτέρπης, τό ἔνδοξο πτῶμα τοῦ ἀειμνήστου Καραμανλάκη. Κι' ἐνῶ πολλά ἐλέγοντο ἱεροκρυφίως, ὅτι κατά τήν ἐποχήν ἐκείνην εὑρισκόμουνα, κατ' ἄλλους μέν στό Μαρακαΐμπο τῆς Νοτίου Ἀμερικῆς, κατ' ἄλλους δέ στόν Πειραιᾶ, στό Πασσᾶ Λιμάνι, ἐγώ βρισκόμουνα ἁπλούστατα στό Ἑλμπασσάν (τῆς Ἀλβανίας). Καί τό μόνο πρᾶμα τῆς προκοπῆς, πού ἔτυχε νά διαβάσω ἐκεῖνες τίς ἡμέρες, ἤτανε μιά μακροσκελεστάτη ἐπιστολή τοῦ Ἰταλοῦ Γουλιάμου Τσίτζη, τοῦ ἐγκαρδίου καί μοναδικοῦ μου φίλου, τόν ὁποῖον ἄλλωστε δέν γνώρισα ποτέ καί γιά τόν ὁποῖον ἀμφιβάλλω ἀκόμα κι' ἄν ὑπάρχη. Μέ λίγες λέξεις, ὅλο τό περιεχόμενο τῆς ἐπιστολῆς του αὐτῆς ἤτανε τό ἑξῆς: «Εἶσαι», ἔλεγε, ὑπονοῶν βέβαια τήν Πολυξένη, «εἶσαι ἕνα παλιό γραμμόφωνο μέ μπρούντζινο χουνί κάτω ἀπό ἕνα μαῦρο πανί».

NOCTURNAL MARIA

On the very next day after my death, or rather my being put to death, I set to reading all the newspapers, that I might learn every possible detail concerning my execution. It appears I was led to the scaffold under strict escort. I was wearing, it says, a yellow-colored topcoat, a string necktie and an ancient helmet. My hair was like a brush, perhaps that of a decorator, perhaps that of a pine-bender. Afterwards, they cast my body far away, in a marsh that was once the haunt of the Frenchman Descartes and where, for years, fodder for the vultures and a whore called Euterpe, had lain the illustrious corpse of the unforgettable Karamanlakis. And though much was secretly said, that at the time I was in Maracaibo in South America according to some, and according to others in Passalimani in Piraeus, I was quite simply in Elbasan (in Albania). And the one thing of note that I happened to read during those days was a most lengthy letter from the Italian, Guillaume Tsitzes, my one close friend, whom actually I have never met and whose existence I even doubt. In short, the entire content of that letter of his was as follows: "You," he said, meaning Polyxeni of course, "are an old gramophone with a brass horn beneath a black cloth."

ΤΑ ΚΛΕΙΔΟΚΥΜΒΑΛΑ ΤΗΣ ΣΙΩΠΗΣ

Tout porte à croire qu'il existe un certain point de l'esprit d'où la vie et la mort, le réel et l'imaginaire, le passé et le futur, le communicable et l'incommunicable, le haut et le bas cessent d'être perçus contradictoirement. Or, c'est en vain qu'on chercherait à l'activité surréaliste un autre mobile que l'espoir de détermination de ce point.

ANDRÉ BRETON "Second Manifeste du Surréalisme"

Ο ΣΕΒΑΧ ΘΑΛΑΣΣΙΝΟΣ

tu autem eras interior intimo meo et superior summo meo
ΙΕΡΟΥ ΑΥΓΟΥΣΤΙΝΟΥ
«Ἐξομολογήσεις», βιβλ. τρίτο, VI. ΙΙ

εἶν' ἡ ψυχή μου συχνά
ἕνα σοκάκι στή Μύκονο
σάν ἀρχινάη νά βραδιάζη
καί πιάνουν οἱ γυναῖκες
καί τοποθετοῦν ἐρωτικά
χάμω στό δρόμο
σέ σχήματα γεωμετρικά
μονότονα
ὅλο μπλέ γυαλιά
– μπλέ ποτήρια
μπλέ καράφες
πόθους μπλέ
βιολιά
λουλούδια
χαλίκια
ὅλα
ἀπό μπλέ γυαλί –
μακριά ἀπ' τόν ἥλιο
πάνω στό χῶμα
στό δρόμο
ἀπ' ὅπου πέρασ' ὁ ἥλιος

From: *THE CLAVICEMBALOS OF SILENCE* (1939)

Tout porte à croire qu'il existe un certain point de l'esprit d'où la vie et la mort, le réel et l'imaginaire, le passé et le futur, le communicable et l'incommunicable, le haut et le bas cessent d'être perçus contradictoirement. Or, c'est en vain qu'on chercherait à l'activité surréaliste un autre mobile que l'espoir de détermination de ce point.

ANDRÉ BRETON "Second Manifeste du Surréalisme"

SINBAD THE SAILOR

tu autem eras interior intimo meo et superior summo meo
SAINT AUGUSTINE
Confessions, Book III, 6, 2

my soul is often
a lane in Mykonos
when night starts to fall
and the women take
and sensuously place
down in the street
in geometric shapes
monotonous
all of blue crystal
– blue glasses
blue carafes
blue desires
violins
flowers
pebbles
all
of blue crystal –
away from the sun
on the earth
in the street
where the sun once passed

καί δέν πρόκειται
– ἄλλωστε –
νά ξαναπεράσῃ πιά

τότες εἶν' ἀκριβῶς
ἡ ὥρα
ὅπου κι' ἐγώ
περνῶ ἀπαλά τό χέρι
στή βάση τοῦ κρανίου μου
καί τό βυθίζω ἀπότομα
– βαθιά –
μέσ' στό κεφάλι μου
καί τραβῶ ἔξω
τό μυαλό μου
καί στίβω ἤρεμα
τή φαιά μου
οὐσία
ἀνάμεσα
στά δάχτυλά μου

κι' ὅταν ὅλα
τά ὑγρά
χυθοῦν
– χωρίς φωνές –
καταγῆς
μνήσκει μονάχα
μέσα στήν ἀπαλάμη μου
– καί ζεῖ –
ἕνα μικρό λουλούδι
πού τό ζητοῦσα
ἀπό παιδί
καί πού μοῦ χαϊδεύει τό μέτωπο
μέ τά λευκά του

never
– though –
to pass again

this is precisely
the time
when I too
gently lift my hand
to the base of my skull
and suddenly plunge it
– deep –
into my head
and pull out
my mind
and calmly squeeze
my grey
matter
between
my fingers

and when all
the liquid
has spilled
– without any cries –
to the ground
all that remains
in my palm
– and lives –
is a tiny flower
that I have sought
since being a child
and that caresses my brow
with its white

χέρια
καί μοῦ μιλεῖ στοργικά
καί μοῦ
λέει
γιά τά ὄνειρα
πού σφυροῦν τή νύχτα
τόσο ἤρεμα
τόσο πονετικά
– σά δάχτυλα
σά δάκρυα –
μέσα στά ἐρείπια
τῆς
Παλμύρας
μέσα στά
νεκρά παλάτια
τῆς Βαβυλώνας
καί μοῦ λέει ἀκόμα
καί γιά τή ζωή
πού ζῶ
ἤσυχα
ἤρεμα
μέσα στό μεγάλο
ἔρημο σπίτι
– ὅλο ἀπό μπλέ γυαλί –
ἐκεῖ ὅπου ζοῦν
μόνο
τά πουλιά
ὁλομόναχος
ἀκίνητος
μέσα στά ἠλεκτροφόρα
σύρματα
τῆς κοιλιᾶς ΤΗΣ

hands
and speaks to me tenderly
and tells
me
of the dreams
that hum at night
so calmly
so compassionately
– like fingers
like tears –
in the ruins
of
Palmyra
in the
lifeless palaces
of Babylon

and it tells me too
of the life
I live
quietly
calmly
in the large
empty house
– all of blue crystal –
where only
birds
live
and I alone
unmoving
in the electric
cables
of HER belly

κι' ἐνῶ μαίνεται γύρω μου ἡ καταιγίδα
καί σκεπάζει
τό κατάστρωμα
τοῦ ἔρμου
καραβιοῦ μου
ἡ ἀγριεμένη
θάλασσα
μέ τά πόδια
γυμνά
σκαρφαλώνω
στό πιό ψηλό κατάρτι
καί κρατῶ σφιχτά
μέσα στά χέρια
ἕνα ποτήρι
ἀπό μπλέ γυαλί

– αὐτά τά χέρια
τό μέτωπό μου
πού δέν τό καῖν
τ' ἀστροπελέκια
κι' οἱ ἀετοί –
κι' εἶναι τό μπλέ τό γυάλινο
ποτήρι
αὐτό ἀκριβῶς
ὅπου ἔχω βάλει μέσα
τά δυό μου χέρια
τά ὑγρά
πού ἔπεσαν
ἀπό
τά δάχτυλά μου
τό μικρό
ἄσπρο

and while the storm rages about me
and the wild
sea
covers
the deck
of my deserted
ship
with feet
bare
I climb
the highest mast
and tightly hold
in my hands
a glass
of blue crystal

– these hands
my brow
unburned by
the lightning bolts
and eagles –
and the blue crystal
glass
is the very one
in which I have put
my two hands
the liquid
that fell
from
my fingers
the tiny
white

λουλούδι
κι' ἀκόμα ἕνα μακρύ
μακρύ
γυαλί
μπλέ
ἤ ρόζ
– δέ θυμᾶμαι –
ὅπου εἶναι
ἀπλούστατα
ΑΥΤΗ
....

κι' οἱ φωνές
ταράζουν
τή νύχτα
σά φωνές
σάν ἄγρια
μονωδία
μέ γυναίκειες κραυγές
τῇ συνοδείᾳ
– βέβαια –
πιάνου
βιολιοῦ
ἤ καί πλαγιαύλου
ἀκόμη

flower
and also a long
long
crystal
blue
or pink
– I don't recall –
that is
quite simply
HER
… … … … … … …..

and the voices
disturb
the night
like voices
like a wild
monody
with female cries
to the accompaniment
– naturally –
of piano
violin
or flute
even

ΕΠΕΙΣΟΔΙΟ

στά μέρη τῆς Πόλης φυτρώνει ἕνα πουλί πού οἱ ἐντόπιοι
τό λέν «μαγνόλια»

EPISODE

in Constantinople, in those parts, there sprouts a bird that the locals call "magnolia"

ΤΑ ΚΛΕΙΔΟΚΥΜΒΑΛΑ ΤΗΣ ΣΙΩΠΗΣ

... πολύ σιωπηλά εἶναι ὅλα, κι' ἡ σιωπή εἶναι
καλή μονάχα σάν κλείνη μέσα της χαρά.
Ἀλλοιῶς, τή φοβᾶμαι ...
ΛΗ

τά σπέρματα
τῶν λυκανθρώπων
κουράζουν
τά πηδάλια
τοῦ ὁρίζοντος
ρίχτουν
ἀναμμένες φλογέρες
μέσα
στά ματωμένα φουστάνια
πού κρέμονται
στά πυκνά κλαργιά
τῶν δέντρων
πνίγουν κοράκια
μέσ' στούς καθρέφτες
ζητοῦν
τή δικαιοσύνη
καί τόν οἶκτο
τῶν
παιδιῶν

ἐγώ
– ὅμως –
βάζω κόκκινα λουλούδια
μέσ' στά μαλλιά της
ὀρθώνομαι
ὁλόγυμνος
μέσα σέ

THE CLAVICEMBALOS OF SILENCE

> *… all is very silent, and silence is good*
> *only when it contains within it joy.*
> *Otherwise, I fear it …*
> LI

the sperm
of werewolves
wearies
the helms
of the horizon
casts
blazing flutes
amid
the bloodied skirts
hanging
from the thick branches
of the trees
smothers crows
in the mirrors
seeks
the justice
and pity
of
children

I
– however –
place red flowers
in her hair
rise
stark naked
in

κήπους
πορφυρούς
χάνομαι
μέσα σέ
σκοτεινές σπηλιές
πού κρύφτουν
βαθιά
ραφτομηχανές
καί ψάρια
κίτρινα
πού μιλοῦν
σά λουλούδια

κι' ἴσως
ἐγώ νά εἶμαι πιά
αὐτός ὁ λυκάνθρωπος
τῶν ἀστραπῶν
αὐτός πού λέν
– σά βραδιάζει –
ὁ «ἄνθρωπος παρένθεσις»
μέσ' στίς φυσοῦνες
τῆς πλεκτάνης
στά
σάβανα
τῆς πορείας
ἐν ὥρᾳ
νυκτός
ὅταν
πεθαίνη
ἕνα πουλί
σά θειαφοκέρι

κι' ἔτσι πέφτουν
– σταλαματιά σταλαγματιά –

purple
gardens
lose myself
in
dark caverns
that conceal
deep down
sewing machines
and fish
yellow ones
that talk
like flowers

and perhaps
I am now
that werewolf
of lightning flashes
the one called
– when darkness falls –
"parenthesis man"
in the bellows
of the plot
in the
shrouds
of the procession
at the hour
of night
when
like a sulfur wick
a bird
expires

and so fall
– drop by drop –

στούς κρόταφους
τῶν ἀπεγνωσμένων
κλειδοκυμβάλων
τά ζευγάρια
τῶν ἀπογοητευμένων
κι' ἕνα
βαρύ σύννεφο
ἀπό μακριά
ξανθά μαλλιά
– μέ μάτια φαιά –
πετάει ἀθόρυβα
μέσ' σέ
στενόμακρα ὑπόγεια
ὅπ' ἀνθοῦν μόνο
λιμάνια
καί
γυπαετοί

κι' εἶναι ἡ σιωπή
φωτιά
μιάν ἀνεμόσκαλα
πού τοποθετοῦν
προσεχτικά
στά χείλια
κι' ἕνα ἄσπρο
ἄλογο
πού εἶναι
ἕνα δέντρο
κοντά στή θάλασσα
κι' ἕνα κόκκινο
ἄλογο
σάν
σημαία

down the temples
of the despondent
clavicembalos
the disheartened
couples
and a
heavy cloud
of long
blonde hair
– with grey eyes –
floats noiselessly
in
narrow basements
where alone flourish
harbors
and
eagles

and the silence is
fire
a rope-ladder
carefully
placed
on the lips
and a white
horse
that is
a tree
by the sea
and a red
horse
like
a flag

καί τρέχω
πάνω στά νερά
– ἀκούραστα –
μέ τό λυρικό
ποδήλατο
μέ τήν περικεφαλαία
τῆς ἀγάπης

κι’ ὅταν φτάσω
στό τελευταῖο
σκαλί
τῆς σκοτεινῆς
αὐτῆς
σκάλας
κι’ ἀνοίξω
τήν πόρτα
τοῦ δωματίου
τότες μόνε ἀντιλαμβάνομαι
πώς τό δωμάτιο
ἦταν
– εἶναι –
ἕνας μεγάλος
κῆπος
γιομάτος μουσική
καί ζωγραφιές

– ἕνα δωμάτιο
γιομάτο σεντόνια
ριχμένα
μέσα στόν
κῆπο –

σεντόνια
π’ ἄλλα ἀνεμίζανε

and I race
– tirelessly –
over the waters
on my lyric
cycle
in my helmet
of love

and when I arrive
at the last
rung
of this
dark
ladder
and open
the door
of the room
only then do I realize
that the room
was
– is –
a huge
garden
full of music
and paintings

– a room
full of sheets
thrown
into the
garden –

sheets
some flapping

σά σημαῖες
κι' ὡσάν
ὑελοπίνακες
κι' ἄλλα ἤτανε
ριχμένα κάτω
σάν καθρέφτες
κι' ἄλλα
μιλοῦσαν
λέξεις ἄναρθρες
σάν καπνοδόχες
κι' ἄλλα στρωμένα
σέ κρεβάτια
σάν κομῆτες
ἄλλα ἔμοιαζαν
κανάτια
ἄλλα ἤτανε
σάν προβοσκίδες
κι' ἄλλα
ἔντυναν
μέ δροσιά
καί τραγικές κραυγές
γυναῖκες ὁλόγυμνες
κι' ὡραῖες

ἔτσι
πού πρέπει
– ἴσως νᾶν κι' ἀνάγκη ἀπόλυτη –
νά παραβάλω
τήν ὅλη
κατάσταση
μ' ἕνα γυαλί
πού ὅταν
βάζης
τό μάτι

like flags
and like
glass panes
others
thrown down
like mirrors
others
uttering
inarticulate words
like chimneys
others spread
over beds
like comets
others resembling
jugs
others
like proboscises
and others
garbing
in coolness
and tragic cries
women naked
and fair

so that
I must
– perhaps a consummate need –
compare
the whole
situation
to a glass
in which
when held
to the eye

βλέπεις
ἕνα βαθύ
πηγάδι
καί στό
βάθος
ἕνα
πουλί

you see
a deep
well
and in the
depths
a
bird

$$PO\Delta IA = SO_4H_2$$

ἄκουσε τά δάκρυα πῶς κυλοῦν
ὅμοια μέ δέντρ' ἀσάλευτα
βουβά
καί
ἔρημα
σάν πέφτη ἡ νύχτα

κι' ὅμως ὁ κῆπος
– λέω –
μέ τ' ἀμέτρητα παράθυρα
ἦταν ἀπέραντος
κι' οἱ πρασινάδες του
ἔφταναν κάτω κοντά στή θάλασσα
ἀκριβῶς ἐκεῖ π' ἀρχινᾶ
ἡ κίτρινη ἀμμουδιά
πάνω σ' αὐτή τήν κίτρινη
ἀμμουδιά
εἴπαμε
– μέ φαίνεται –
τά πιό ἔμορφά μας τραγούδια

κι' ὅμως ἐκεῖ
μᾶς πετροβόλησαν
μέ πέτρες
καί βότσαλα
χουφτιές

καί τά βότσαλα ἤτανε
τά λευκά
ἐρωτικά δόντια
τῶν γυναικῶνε
π' ἀγαπήσαμε

POMEGRANATES = SO_4H_2

listen to how the tears roll
like trees motionless
mute
and
desolate
when night falls

and yet the garden
– as I say –
with its countless windows
was vast
and its greenery
reached down to the sea
to where begin
the yellow sands
and on these yellow
sands
we sang
– so it seems to me –
our loveliest songs

yet there
we had stones
and pebbles
hurled at us
in handfuls

and the pebbles were
the white
amorous teeth
of women
we had loved

Η ΖΩΗ ΚΑΙ Ο ΘΑΝΑΤΟΣ ΤΩΝ ΠΟΙΗΤΩΝ

Σινώπη
εἶναι τό ὄνομα
– τό ἐπίσημο –
τῆς «Πόλεως-Σύννεφο»
τῆς καί «Πόλεως τῶν Πυρκαϊῶν» λεγομένης
πού
βρίσκεται κάπου κατά
τήν
Νότιον Ἀμερική

ἡ ὑδάτινη
καί μᾶλλον ἑλληνιστικοῦ πολιτισμοῦ
αὐτή πόλις
αἰωρεῖται στούς οὐρανούς
σάν σκυτάλη
καί τοποθετεῖται ἀσφαλῶς
ἀπό τούς εἰδικούς
ἄλλοτε μέν στή μέση ἀκριβῶς
μιᾶς εὐθείας γραμμῆς
χαραγμένης ἀνάμεσα στό Μαρακαΐμπο
καί στό Βαλπαραΐζο
τῆς Χιλῆς
ἄλλοτε δέ
ἀνάμεσα πάλε στό Μαρακαΐμπο καί
στό
Ἐλμπασσάν

ἐκεῖ
καθώς τά σπίτια εἶναι ὅλα καμωμένα ἀπό πυρκαϊές
οἱ κάτοικοι ζοῦν μέσα στίς φλόγες
καίγονται συνεχῶς
καί ξαναγεννιοῦνται συνεχῶς

THE LIFE AND DEATH OF POETS

Sinope
is the name
– the official one –
of the "Cloud-City"
also called "City of Fires"
which
lies somewhere over
in
South America

this aquatic
and probably Hellenistic
city
hangs in the skies
like a baton
and is placed with certainty
by the experts
sometimes exactly in the middle
of a straight line
drawn between Maracaibo
and Valparaíso
in Chile
and sometimes
between Maracaibo again
and
Elbasan

there
as the houses are all made of fires
the inhabitants live in the flames
are burned constantly
and are reborn constantly

ἀπό τήν τέφρα τους
ἀπαράλλαχτα ὅπως
τό πουλί
φοῖνιξ

ἐκεῖ ἀκριβῶς
ἐγεννήθη –ὡς γνωστόν –
καί ὁ μέγας ἕλλην ποιητής τῆς
ἀρχαιότητος
Ἀλέκτωρ

κατά τήν διάρκειαν ἀνασκαφῶν
ἀνευρέθη κάποτε ἀναμεσίς τῶν ἐρειπίων
κι' ἕνα παράξενο ποίημα
–ἐκείνης τῆς ἐποχῆς –
γραμμένο ἐπί χάρτου κοινοῦ
μέ σιδηροῦς
καί χαλκοῦς ἁρμούς ἐναλλάξ
καί μελάνην δακρύων

τό ποίημα δέ ἦταν τό ἑξῆς:

«ἐλᾶτε στοῦ Λατίου τά ἐλάτια
νά δῆτε τοῦ δύτου τήν δίνην»

λόγῳ τῆς παρουσίας τῆς λέξεως
«δύτης»
τό ποίημα ἀπεδόθη
– ἀρχικῶς –
στόν μέγαν

Ἰσίδωρον Ducasse*
ὅπου ἔτυχε νά κατάγεται ἀπό

* comte de Lautréamont

from their ashes
identical like
the phoenix
bird

there in this very place
– as everyone knows –
was born the great Greek poet of
antiquity
Alector

found among the ruins
during the excavations
was a strange poem
– from that time –
written on ordinary paper
with alternate
iron and bronze joints
and ink from tears

the said poem was as follows:

"look on the laurels of Latius
to see the swimmer's swirl"

because of the presence of the word
"swimmer"
the poem was attributed
– initially –
to the great

Isidore Ducasse*
who happened to originate from

---

*   comte de Lautréamont

κεῖνα
τά μέρη

κατόπιν –ὅμως –ὠρίμου σκέψεως
ἀπεδόθη ὁριστικά
– καί ἀμετακλήτως
πλέον –
σέ κάποια γυναῖκα λεγομένη
Ὡραία Κυρία
γνωστοτέραν μᾶλλον ὑπό
τό ξενικόν αὐτῆς
ὄνομα
Bella Donna

those
parts

after – however – due consideration
it was attributed finally
– and now
irrevocably –
to a woman called
Fair Lady
probably better known by
her foreign
name
Belladonna

ΕΝΑ ΤΑΞΙΔΙ ΣΤΟ ΕΛΜΠΑΣΣΑΝ

I

Σήμερα θά πῶ ταξιδιωτικές μου ἐντυπώσεις ἀπό τήν Ἀλβανίαν. Καί, πρίν ἀπ' ὅλα, πρέπει νά δηλώσω ὅτι δέν ὑπάρχει τίποτες εὐκολώτερο, τίποτες ἁπλούστερο, ἀπό μιά μετάβαση σ' αὐτήνα τή χώρα. Ὅμως, εἶναι ἀπαραίτητο νά προσμένη κανείς, γι' αὐτό τό σκοπό, τή γιορτή τ' Ἀι-Γιαννιοῦ, τό καλοκαίρι. Μόνο τότες, σά βραδιάξη, ὁ νοσταλγός τῶν μακρινῶν τόπων μπορεῖ, πηδώντας τίς φωτιές, νά βρεθῆ σ' ὅποια πόλη ἔχει ποτέ του ἐπιθυμήσει.

Ἐγώ, κάποτες, μιά μέρα ὀδυνηρῆς μοναξιᾶς, μιά μέρα ὅπου εἶχα ζήσει μακριά ἀπό τά πουλιά, πήδηξα, σά βράδιασε, τίς φωτιές πού εἶχαν ἀνάψει σέ μιάν ὁποιαδήποτε λαϊκή γειτονιά τῶν Ἀθηνῶν, μέ τό βαθύ πόθο τῆς Ἀλβανίας μέσ' στήν καρδιά μου. Πήδηξα μιά, πήδηξα δυό. Τίποτες. Τήν τρίτη φορά βρέθηκα ἀπότομα στό Ἐλμπασσάν.

II

Τό Ἐλμπασσάν εἶναι μία πόλις μεγάλη, ὅπου μπορῶ νάν τήν περιγράψω λεπτομερέστατα λέγοντας γιά ἕνα τραγούδι – σέ ἄγνωστη, βέβαια, γλῶσσα – πάνω σέ τρεῖς νότες πού ἐπανέρχονται ἀτέλειωτα, μονότονα, πάντα οἱ ἴδιες, ἀπό τό πρωῒ ἴσαμε τό βράδυ, στή φλογέρα πού παίζει ὁ τυφλός ἐπαίτης στή γωνιά τοῦ δρόμου.

Τά σοκάκια – στό Ἐλμπασσάν – εἶναι σ' ἀφάνταστο βαθμό στενά, κι' ἀπό κάθε μεριά ὑψώνονται τοῖχοι γυμνοί, θεώρατοι, πού φτάνουν κοντά, λές, στόν οὐρανό. Οὔτε βλέπεις πουθενά κανένα πορτί, οὔτε βέβαια κάνα κλαδί δέντρου νά ξεπερνᾶ.

III

Λογυρνοῦσα μέσα σ' αὐτή τήν πολιτεία μέ μεγάλη περιέργεια. Γαλήνη βασίλευε μέσ' στήν καρδιά μου καί τραγουδοῦσα μάλιστα, ἀνάμεσ' ἀπ' τά δόντια, κι' ἕνα τραγούδι ἀπό τά παιδικά μου χρόνια.

A JOURNEY TO ELBASAN

I

Today, I am going to relate my travel impressions of Albania. And, first of all, I have to say that nothing is easier, nothing is simpler than a journey to that land. Yet, to this end, it is essential to await the summer and the feast of St John. Only then, as night falls, the dreamer of distant lands may, by leaping over the fires, find himself in any city he has ever wished.

Once, as night fell, after a day of aching loneliness, a day when I had lived far from the birds, I leapt over the fires that had been lit in some lowly district of Athens with a deep craving for Albania in my heart. I leapt once, leapt twice. Nothing. The third time I suddenly found myself in Elbasan.

II

Elbasan is a large city, which I can describe in the utmost detail by talking of a song – naturally in an unknown tongue – upon three notes repeated endlessly, monotonously, ever the same, from morning till night, on the flute played by the blind mendicant at the corner of the street.

The lanes – in Elbasan – are to an unimaginable degree narrow, and on each side loom enormous, bare walls that seem to reach up to the sky. Nowhere is any wicket to be seen, nor even the protruding branch of a tree.

III

I wandered through the township with great curiosity. Peace prevailed in my heart and, under my breath, I even sang a song from my childhood.

Οἱ ἄνθρωποι πού συναντοῦσα στό διάβα μου ἤτανε κάτι ψηλοί φουστανελλοφόροι, μέ φουστανέλλες μακρυές ἴσαμε καταγῆς. Τό βῆμα τους ἤτανε ἀργό, «μεγαλόπρεπο –ἔλεγα –καθώς εἶναι, πάντα, στήν Ἀνατολή». Ἄλλοι φοροῦσαν φέσια ἄσπρα στό κεφάλι, κι' ἄλλοι, πάλι, μεγάλα τραγικά γυναικεῖα καπέλλα μέ φτερά. Ὅμως, ξάφνου, μι' ἀνέκφραστη ἀγωνία πλάκωσε τήν καρδιά μου. Οἱ ἄνθρωποι αὐτοί δέν εἶχαν μάτια! Τούς εἶχα προσέξει: ἤδη μ' ἀνησυχοῦσε τό βλέμμα τους! Ὁ φόβος μέ σταμάτησε, μέ κάρφωσε, γιά κάμποσο, γι' ἀρκετά, ἐκεῖ, μά ἐντελῶς ἀκούνητο, δίχως μιλιά. Κι' ὅταν μπόρεσα κάπως νά κουνηθῶ, νά τρέξω, νά καταλάβω τέλος πάντων, εἶδα μέ φρίκη, σάν πῆρα τό κατόπι τους, πώς μόλις ἔστριβαν τή γωνιά, χανόντουσαν σάν ὄνειρο... Χανόντουσαν, γιά νά ξαναφανερωθοῦν, πάλε, στήν ἄλλη γωνιά, ἀπ' ὅπου εἶχαν ξεκινήσει, νά συνεχίσουν ἀτάραχοι τό ἀπαίσιο σεργιάνι τους.

Καμιάν ἀμφιβολία δέ χωροῦσε πιά. Μιάν ἀνήκουστη ἀπάτη παιζόταν εἰς βάρος μου. Κατάλαβα πώς εἶχα πέσει ἀνίδεο θῦμα μιᾶς αἰσχρῆς καί τρομερᾶς πλεκτάνης. Ἀμέσως ἀνελογίσθην τό μέγεθος τοῦ ὅλου σφάλματός μου, κάθησα χάμω καί ἔκλαψα πικρά.

The people I met on my way were tall and wore fustanellas, long fustanellas down to the ground. Their step was slow, "majestic – I reflected – as it always is in the East." Some wore white fezzes on their heads, while others again wore large tragic women's hats with feathers.

Yet, suddenly, an inexpressible anxiety afflicted my heart. These people had no eyes! I had noticed them: already their gaze had been troubling me! The fear made me halt, rooted me to the spot, for some time, for quite a while, there, absolutely motionless, speechless. And when I was able to move somewhat, to run, at any rate to understand, I saw to my horror when I followed after them, that, on turning the corner, they vanished like a dream .... Vanished, to appear again at the same corner from where they had begun, continuing their frightful stroll unperturbed.

There was no longer any room for doubt. An incredible hoax was being staged at my expense. I realized that I had fallen victim to a foul and terrible plot. I straightaway saw the magnitude of my error, sank to the ground and wept bitterly.

Η ΠΛΕΚΤΑΝΗ ΤΩΝ ΝΑΥΑΓΙΩΝ

Δέν γνωρίζω τί γένεται τή νύχτα, ἤ καί τή μέρα ἀκόμη, στ᾽ ἄγρια, τά ψηλά βουνά. Ξέρω, ὅμως, νά πῶ γιά τά μυστηριώδη καί παράξενα στοιχειά πού κατοικοῦνε μόνα τους στίς κορφές τῶν ἔρημων λόφων. Ξέρω νά πῶ πολλά γιά τίς συνήθειές τους, καί πώς δέν ἀπομακρύνονται ποτές ἀπό τά σημεῖα –πάντα τά πιό ὑψηλά –ὅπου ἐδιάλεξαν γιά μόνιμη διαμονή τους. Πώς περνώντας ὁ διαβάτης, ἀπό μακριά ἤ ἀπό κοντά, μεσημέρι γιά βράδυ, τά διακρίνει, τά βλέπει, ἄλλοτε ν᾽ ἀνεμίζουνε σάν πολεμικά μπαϊράκια, ἄλλοτε νά παίρνουν σχήματα ἀλλόκοτα, κατά προτίμησιν τεσσάρων ξύλων μέ μιά σκεπή ἀπό ξερά κλαριά πεύκου, ἴδια μέ τά τσαρντάκια πού στήνουν οἱ ἀλβανοί ποιμένες σάν ἦχο φλογέρας. Ἄλλοτε πάλι ταξιδεύουν σέ μακρινά κι᾽ ἀνεξερεύνητα πελάγη, ἐπιβαίνοντα πεπαλαιωμένων πετρελαιοφόρων, πάντοτε δέ, ὑπό ἑλληνοκαθολικήν σημαίαν, εἰς μνήμην βέβαια τοῦ θεοῦ Πανός. Κι᾽ ἔτσι, ἁπλή, φυσική, λογική, κι᾽ ἴσως ἀκόμη καί ψυχαναλυτική συνέπεια εἶναι ν᾽ ἀφήνουν, και τή νύχτα, ἀναμμένα τά φῶτα στά ἐργοστάσια, καθώς κι᾽ αὐτές τίς θεώρατες στίβες σκουπιδιῶν καί τενεκέδων μέσ᾽ στά χωράφια. Ὅλα γιά τό μεγάλο θεό Πάνα. Ὅμως, τά ἠλεκτρικά φῶτα εἶναι τελείως ἄχρηστα καί μόνο ποῦ καί ποῦ, κι᾽ αὐτό σε πολύ ἀραιά διαστήματα, χρησιμεύουν νά φωτίζουν ἀκρογιάλια πού δέρνει ὁ ἄνεμος, ξύλινες ἐγκαταλελειμμένες μπαράγκες, φύκια κι᾽ ἀπολιθωμένα κόκκαλα προκατακλυσμιαίων τεράτων, ὡς καί μαρμάρινες προτομές αὐτοκρατόρων καί ποιητῶν.

THE SHIPWRECKS' PLOT

I am not aware of what happens at night, or even in daytime, in the rugged, high mountains. I do know, however, about the mysterious and strange spirits that live alone atop desolate hills. I know much about their habits, and how they never abandon the places – always the highest ones – that they have chosen for their permanent abode. How, when a passer-by approaches, close by or far off, at noon or night, he spies them, sees them, sometimes flapping like battle standards, sometimes assuming weird shapes, preferably four poles with a dry pine-branch roof, identical to the shacks built by Albanian shepherds like a flute's sound. At other times they journey to distant and unexplored seas, embarking on old oil tankers, always though, under a Greek-catholic flag, in memory, no doubt, of the god Pan. And thus, a simple, natural, logical, perhaps also psychoanalytical, consequence is that they leave the lights lit, even at night, in the factories, together with those enormous piles of rubbish and tins in the fields. All for the great god Pan. Yet the electric lights are completely useless and only occasionally, and this at very rare intervals, are they used to light shores swept by the wind, abandoned wooden huts, seaweed and petrified bones of antediluvian monsters, even marble busts of emperors and poets.

ΤΟ ΣΚΥΡΟΚΟΝΙΑΜΑ ΤΩΝ ΗΡΩΪΚΩΝ ΠΑΡΘΕΝΩΝ

λησμονοῦνται
οἱ σεμνές παρθένες
πού ἔπεσαν
– ἄχ τόσο πρόωρα –
μαχόμενες
ἡρωϊκά
πάνω στά ὁδοφράγματα

στόν τόπο ὅμως
ὅπου κύλησε τό
νεκρό κεφάλι τους
καί σούρθηκαν
τά μακριά μαλλιά τους
ἐκεῖ
ἀρέσει στόν ποιητή
ν' ἀπομονώνεται
σέ μιάν ὑπερήφανη
– καί γαλάζια –
μοναξιά

ἐκεῖ
σ' αὐτό τό ἔρμο
ἀκροθαλάσσι
εἶναι π' ἀνάφτουν τή
νύχτα τά
φανάρια
πού παραπλανοῦν
τούς ναυτικούς
ἐκεῖ γίνεται ἡ
σκέψις
μιά φλογισμένη ρόδα
πού κυλάει
στόν ὁρίζοντα

THE CONCRETE OF HEROIC MAIDENS

soon forgotten are
the modest maidens
who fell
– oh so untimely –
fighting
heroically
at the street barricades

yet on the spot
where their dead heads
rolled
and their long hair
trailed
there
the poet likes
to withdraw
in a haughty
– and azure –
solitude

there
on that desolate
shore
is where at night
they light the
lamps
that mislead
sailors

there
thought becomes
a flaming wheel
rolling
on the horizon

ἐκεῖ εἶναι τά νησιά
πού γένονται σάβανα
ὅταν τρελλαίνη ὁ ἄνεμος
τά
φύλλα
τῶν φοινικοδένδρων

ἐκεῖ ἐντοπίζεται
ἡ ὅλη κίνησις τοῦ λιμανιοῦ
μέ σωρούς ἀπό
νεκρές φώκιες
καί τούς
κρουνούς
τοῦ πετρελαίου

ἐκεῖ φυτρώνουν καί
τά δέντρα
πού παράγουν
τούς παράξενους κι' ὡραίους καρπούς
πού προσφέρουν στόν
ποιητή
γιά τίς
μελλούμενές του
πικρίες

there lie the islands
that become shrouds
when the wind enrages
the
leaves
of the palms

there is located
all the bustle of the port
with piles of
dead seals
and the
oil
hydrants

there too grow
the trees
that produce
the strange and lovely fruit
presented to the
poet
for his
future
sorrows

Η ΨΥΧΑΝΑΛΥΣΙΣ ΤΩΝ ΦΑΝΤΑΣΜΑΤΩΝ

... ἀγάπην δέ μή ἔχω, γέγονα χαλκός ἠχῶν
καί κύμβαλον ἀλαλάζον.
ΑΠ. ΠΑΥΛΟΣ

Σά μπαίνη τό καράβι τῆς ἀγάπης, τή νύχτα, μέσ' στό λιμάνι, τό ὑποδέχονται οἱ μυστηριώδεις μουσικές τῆς ἐρημιᾶς. Γύρω, τά νερά γιομίζουν λουλούδια ὅλων τῶν εἰδῶν καί ὅλων τῶν χρωμάτων, καί μιάν ἄσπρη σειρά ἀπό γυμνές γυναῖκες μᾶς περιμένει στήν προκυμαία. Εἶναι ἔτοιμες, ὅλες τους, στό πρῶτο μας νεῦμα, νά φορέσουν ἀμέσως τήν κόκκινη στολή τῶν βουτηχτάδων. Ὄχι ὅμως γιά νά κατεβοῦν στά βάθη τῆς θάλασσας, ἀλλά μόνο καί μόνο γιά νἄρθουν νά μᾶς περιμένουν, ἴσως κι' ὧρες ὁλόκληρες, ἀκούραστα, στοργικά, στήν εἴσοδο τοῦ ὑπογείου σιδηροδρόμου. Ἐμεῖς, φυσικά, φτάνουμε ἀναπάντεχα, κουνώντας τά μεγάλα φτερά μας καί φωνάζοντας λόγια ἀσυνάρτητα κι' ὡραῖα. Τότες γίνεται ἀπότομα πιό αἰσθητή ἡ ἡσυχία τοῦ ἐξοχικοῦ τοπίου, κι' ἔτσι μέσ' στά σκοτάδια, ἀπ' τά χωράφια, ξεπετιοῦνται ἄνθρωποι μαυροντυμένοι, πού εἶναι οἱ κομῆτες, καί πιάνα ὀρθά, μέ τά λευκά τους πλῆκτρα, πού εἶναι τά ἄστρα. Οἱ σημαῖες κυματίζουν στόν ἄνεμο, σέ κανονικά διαστήματα ἠχοῦν τά μυδραλλιοβόλα, καί τά παιδιά τραγουδοῦν. Στ' αὐτιά μας ἀκοῦμε τά προφητικά ὀνόματα τῶν γυναικῶν πού θ' ἀγαπούσαμε. Ἐπίσης καί τό ὄνομα μιᾶς πόλεως: Σινώπη. Ἐγώ ὅμως δέν φοβοῦμαι τό θάνατο, γιατί ἀγαπῶ τή ζωή.

THE PSYCHOANALYSIS OF PHANTOMS

> *... and have not love, I am become*
> *as sounding brass or a tinkling cymbal.*
> SAINT PAUL

When, at night, the ship of love enters the port, it is greeted by the mysterious melodies of the desert. Round about, the waters fill with flowers of all kinds and all colors, and a white line of naked women awaits us on the quay. They are ready, all of them, at the first sign from us, to immediately don the red suit worn by divers. Though not to descend to the sea's depths, but quite simply to come and wait for us, perhaps for hours on end, tirelessly and lovingly, at the entrance to the underground railway. We, naturally, arrive unexpectedly, flapping our large wings and shouting words incoherent and fine. Then the calm of the countryside becomes suddenly more perceptible, and so amid the darkness, from out of the fields spring black-clad men, that are comets, and upright pianos, with their white keys, that are stars. The flags flap in the wind, at regular intervals the machine-guns rattle and the children sing. In our ears we hear the prophetic names of women we would have loved. As well as the name of a city: Sinope. Yet I do not fear death, because I love life.

ΥΔΡΑ

κατηγγέλθη
ὡς ἐξαιρετικά ἐπικίνδυνος
γιά τήν δημόσια
ἀσφάλεια
– γιά τήν εἰρήνη
τῶν φιλησύχων πολιτῶν –
τήν ὥρα πού
σοβαροί
– ἤ μᾶλλον σοβαροφανεῖς –ἱερεῖς
μᾶλλον ἡλικιωμένοι
καί λίαν ἄξιοι ἤ ἀνάξιοι σεβασμοῦ
ἐπεκαλοῦντο
τήν μνήμην
τῶν μεγάλων ναυμάχων
τῆς Σαλαμῖνος
καθώς
καί τήν μνήμην τῶν
Μιαούλη, Κανάρη, Τομπάζη, Λαζάρου Κουντουριώτη
καί Ἰσιδώρου Ducasse*

χαράματα τόν
ἔπιασαν
πισθάγκωνα τόν ἔδεσαν
καί τόν ἐπῆγαν σηκωτό
σά λείψανο
σάν μιά παρθένα λεπτή
λευκή
λεγομένη Μαρία
πού ἔπλεκε
μιᾶς σπάνιας ἐμορφιᾶς

* comte de Lautréamont

HYDRA

he was denounced
as an exceptional menace
to public
safety
– to the peace
of law-abiding citizens –
at the very time that
serious
– or rather seemingly serious – priests
rather aged
and most worthy or unworthy of respect
invoked
the memory
of great naval commanders
of Salamis
together
with the memory of
Miaoulis, Kanaris, Tombazis, Lazaros Koundouriotis
and Isidore Ducasse*

they seized him
at dawn
bound his hands behind him
and frogmarched him
like a relic
like a virgin slender
and white
by the name of Maria
who was weaving
singularly beautiful

---

* comte de Lautréamont

νταντέλλα
– νταντέλλα σάν τή ζωγραφική μου –
στή σκιά τοῦ
δάσους
τοῦ βουνοῦ
καί τοῦ πράσινου
κήπου

τόν πέταξαν
–μοῦ εἶπαν οἱ γυναῖκες –
μέσα σέ μιά σέρρα
μέ κόκκινα λουλούδια
μέ κόκκινα βελούδινα
παραπετάσματα
στά παράθυρα
λατάνιες
καί ἔπιπλα παλαιά
ὅμως καθαρά
μέ τή λάμπα
τό γυαλί τῆς λάμπας
καθότι ἤτανε
– λέν πάλε οἱ γυναῖκες –
σάββατο βράδυ
καί ξημέρωνε
Κυριακή

σάββατο βράδυ
Κυριακή πρωΐ

ἀπό τήν πόρτα
φαίνονταν ἡ θάλασσα
–ἕνα κομμάτι θάλασσας
γαλάζιο –
ἡ σκάλα ἀνέβαινε ψηλά

lace
– lace like my painting –
in the shade of
the forest
of the mountain
and of the verdant
garden

they cast him
– the women told me –
into a conservatory
with red flowers
with red velvet
curtains
at the windows
bourbon palms
and old furniture
though clean
with the lamp
the glass of the lamp
since it was
– said the women again –
saturday night
before daybreak
on Sunday

saturday night
Sunday morning

through the door
appeared the sea
– a stretch of azure
sea –
the stairs led high

κι' ὠνόμαζα θλιμμένα
τήν καρδιά μου
κατά διαστήματα κανονικά –ἤ μᾶλλον ἀκανόνιστα –
Ἕκτωρ
ἀλογᾶ Ἕκτωρ

ἐνῶ Ἑκάβη
–σ' αὐτήνα τήν περίπτωση –
ἤτανε ἡ μεγάλη
ἡ φοβερή σκιά
τοῦ
ἐγκεφάλου μου

and sorrowfully I named
my heart
at regular intervals – or rather irregular ones –
Hector
horse-owning Hector

while Hecuba
– in that case –
was the great
the terrible shadow
of
my brain

ΜΟΛΙΣ ΣΗΜΑΝΟΥΝ ΤΑ ΜΕΣΑΝΥΧΤΑ,
Ο JEF ΤΟ ΜΕΓΑ ΑΥΤΟΜΑΤΟΝ...

est-ce quelque dédale où ta raison perdue
ne se retrouve pas?
FR. DE MALHERBE

Μόλις σημάνουν τά μεσάνυχτα, ὁ Jef, τό μέγα αὐτόματον, λέει ὑπερήφανα κι᾽ ἀργά τίς λέξεις τίς αἰώνιες καί τίς ἀπατηλές, τίς τόσο μάταιες, ἀλλά καί τίς τόσο λυσιτελεῖς, γιά τ᾽ ἀτλαζένια μάτια π᾽ ἀγαπούσαμε, θυμάστε; Θυμάστε, ἤ μήπως προσπαθεῖτε, μᾶλλον, νά δαμάσετε σέ φωνές σειρήνας τά δίχτυα τῶν μαλλιῶνε, αὐτά π᾽ αὐλάκωναν –ὀδυνηρά –τά πλεχτά καί σβηστά φανάρια τῆς νεροσυρμῆς;... τῆς φωνοσυρμῆς;... τῆς φαντασίας;... τῶν μεγάλων πλατιῶν κρεβατιῶν τοῦ ἔρωτα. Τίποτα ἀπ᾽ ὅλα αὐτά; Τίποτε. Τότε μᾶς πρέπουν τά ὕψη. Πρέπει ν᾽ ἀτενίζουμε τά ὕψη. Σάν τόν μηδενιστή, ὅπου τινάζεται στόν ἀγέρα, ζωντανό λουλούδι. Καί καθώς, φεῦ, πρέπει πάντα νά ξαναγυρίσουμε κάποτε ἀπό κεῖ ψηλά, ἄς ξαναγυρίσουμε. Ἀλλά, τότε πάλι, μέ λουλούδια, σάν λουλούδια, μέ παλάτια, μ᾽ ἐαρινές μουσικές, μέ λόγια ἀγάπης, μέ μάτια ἀγάπης. Παραμερίστε, ἔτσι νά χαρῆτε, τά μεγάλα ματόκλαδα κι᾽ ἀνοῖξτε τά μεγάλα βλέφαρα τοῦ σύννεφου. Ἰδέστε: πάνω σέ χαλιά δροσιᾶς, ἀραδιασμένα κανονικά, σειρές, σειρές, τά μεταλλικά σουραύλια. Νά, αὐτό εἶναι πού λέγαμε: «ἡ χαρά». Νά, αὐτή εἶναι ἡ λεγόμενη «λεπτή θωπεία ἀγαπημένης γυναικός». Αὐτό εἶναι πού λέν «ῥῆτρον ζωῆς», «μπροστέλλα τοῦ ἥλιου», «ἥλιος σιγῆς». Προσέχτε καλά τοῦτα τά λόγια. Ἔχουν τόσες φανερές ὅσο καί κρυφές σημασίες. Εἶναι λέξεις γιομάτες μεταφυσικῶν ἐννοιῶν, εἶναι τά βάραθρα τῆς πικρίας καί τά βουνά τῆς χαρᾶς. Εἶναι τά λόγια πού λέει ἡ ζωή, τά λόγια πού λέει τό κύμβαλον τό ἀλαλάζον τῆς ἀγάπης, ὁ χαλκός ὁ ἠχῶν τῆς ἀγάπης, ἐγώ, ὁ Jef, τό μέγα αὐτόματον τοῦ μεσονυχτίου.

THE MOMENT MIDNIGHT STRIKES,
JEF THE GREAT AUTOMATON...

est-ce quelque dédale où ta raison perdue
ne se retrouve pas?
FR. DE MALHERBE

The moment midnight strikes, Jef, the great automaton, proudly and slowly utters words eternal and deceptive, words so vain yet so profitable, concerning the satin eyes we loved, do you recall? Do you recall, or are you trying, rather, to tame in a siren's cries the nets of hair, those that – painfully – furrowed the laced and extinguished lamps of the watercourses?... of the voice's courses?... of the imagination?... of the large wide beds of passion? None of these things? None. Then we are deserving of the heights. We must turn our gaze to the heights. Like the nihilist, who blows himself up, a living flower. And since, alas, we have always to return eventually from up there, let's return. Yet, once again, with flowers, like flowers, with palaces, with vernal melodies, with words of love, with looks of love. Move aside the large eyelashes to feel joy and open the cloud's huge eyelids. Regard: on carpets of dew, arrayed properly, in rows, in rows, the metal flutes. There, that's what we called: "joy." There, that's the so-called "soft caress of a beloved woman." That's what they call "life's proviso," "the sun's pinafore," "silence's sun." Mark well these words. They have as many obvious as hidden meanings. They are words full of metaphysical concepts, they are the chasms of sorrow and the peaks of joy. They are the words uttered by life, the words uttered by love's sounding brass, by love's tinkling cymbal, by me, Jef, midnight's great automaton.

ΑΚΡΙΒΩΣ ΟΠΩΣ

ta mémoire pareille aux fables incertaines…
CH. BAUDELAIRE

Ο ΧΟΡΟΣ:
τί ζητοῦσες
–μόνος –
πάνω σ᾽ ἐκεῖνο
τό στενόμακρο μπαλκόνι
μέ τή μαύρη μακρυά νταντέλλα
τή νύχτα;

τί ζητοῦσες
ὅταν πετοῦσες
κάτω στό δρόμο
τόσα λουλούδια
καί τήν τόση χαρά μιᾶς νυχτιᾶς;

τί ζητοῦσες
ὅταν γυρνοῦσες μόνος
– φορώντας
τά φορέματα τ᾽ οὐρανοῦ –
τή νύχτα
μέσα στά καλειδοσκόπια
καί τή μέρα
μέσα στούς κινητῆρες
τῶν μηχανῶν;

εἶσαι ὁ ἥλιος
τό ψάρι
ἡ βάρκα-κατάρτι
τό δέντρο
ἤ ὁ Νεκτεναβός;

JUST AS

ta mémoire pareille aux fables incertaines...
CH. BAUDELAIRE

CHORUS:
what were you seeking
– all alone –
on that
narrow balcony
with the long black lacework
at night?

what were you seeking
when you threw
on the street below
so many flowers
and such a night's joy?

what were you seeking
when you returned alone
– wearing
the sky's attire –
at night
inside kaleidoscopes
and during the day
inside machines'
engines?

are you the sun
fish
boat-mast
tree
or Nectanabos?

Ο ΠΟΙΗΤΗΣ:
ὄχι

εἶμαι ἐκεῖνος πού εἶδε
τόν ἀρχιτέκτονα
καί τή μητέρα
τόν ποιητή καί τή μητέρα*
ζητοῦσα δέ
τή χαρά
τό σπόρο τῆς
νύχτας
τό βιολί τοῦ ὕπνου
τή
στάχτη

Ο ΧΟΡΟΣ:
κι' ὅμως

πές μας
τί βρῆκες;

Ο ΠΟΙΗΤΗΣ:
μέσα στό δάσος
μέ τά χαμηλά πεῦκα

βρῆκα

τήν ξύλινη
φιγούρα
τοῦ καραβιοῦ
πού κυματίζανε
τά ξανθά μαλλιά της

* πρβλ. καί Γεωργίου de Κήρυκο "Autoritratto con la madre".

POET:
no

I am the one who saw
the architect
and the mother
the poet and the mother*
and I was seeking
joy
the seed of
night
the violin of sleep
the
ash

CHORUS
even so

tell us
what did you find?

POET:
in the forest
of low pines

I found

the wooden
image
of the ship
where her fair hair
flapped

* cf. Giorgio de Chirico "Autoritratto con la madre."

στόν
ἄνεμο

εἶχε σειρές
περιδέραια
ἀπό λαμπρά ἄστρα
γύρω
στό λαιμό
της
....
τίς νύχτες
ὅταν αὐλακώνουν βαθιά
τό πρόσωπό μου
ποτάμι
τά δάκρυα
ὅπου κυλοῦν
ἀπό τά μάτια μου

τώρα
σάν ξυπνῶ
τήν κυττάζω
καί τήνε βλέπω πλάγι μου
νά φέγγη
ἡ κοιλιά
ΤΗΣ
ὡσάν
φανάρι

in the
wind

she had strings
upon strings
of bright stars
round
her
neck
… … … … … …
at night
when my face
is deeply furrowed
by tears
a river
flowing
from my eyes

now
when I awake
I gaze at her
and see her beside me
HER
belly
shining
like a
lamp

ΜΠΟΛΙΒΑΡ

ἕνα ἑλληνικό ποίημα

ΦΑΣΜΑ ΘΗΣΕΩΣ ΕΝ ΟΠΛΟΙΣ ΚΑΘΟΡΑΝ, ΠΡΟ
ΑΥΤΩΝ ΕΠΙ ΤΟΥΣ ΒΑΡΒΑΡΟΥΣ ΦΕΡΟΜΕΝΟΝ
Le cuer d' un home vaut tout l' or d' un païs

Γιά τούς μεγάλους, γιά τούς ἐλεύθερους, γιά τούς γενναίους, τούς
δυνατούς,
Ἁρμόζουν τά λόγια τά μεγάλα, τά ἐλεύθερα, τά γενναῖα, τά δυνατά,
Γι' αὐτούς ἡ ἀπόλυτη ὑποταγή κάθε στοιχείου, ἡ σιγή, γι' αὐτούς τά
δάκρυα, γι' αὐτούς οἱ φάροι, κι' οἱ κλάδοι ἐλιᾶς, καί τά φανάρια
Ὅπου χοροπηδοῦνε μέ τό λίκνισμα τῶν καραβιῶν καί γράφουνε στούς
σκοτεινούς ὁρίζοντες τῶν λιμανιῶν,
Γι' αὐτούς εἶναι τ' ἄδεια βαρέλια πού σωριαστήκανε στό πιό στενό, πάλι
τοῦ λιμανιοῦ, σοκάκι,
Γι' αὐτούς οἱ κουλοῦρες τ' ἄσπρα σκοινιά, κι' οἱ ἁλυσίδες, οἱ ἄγκυρες, τ'
ἄλλα μανόμετρα,
Μέσα στήν ἐκνευριστικιάν ὀσμή τοῦ πετρελαίου,
Γιά ν' ἁρματώσουνε καράβι, ν' ἀνοιχτοῦν, νά φύγουνε,
Ὅμοιοι μέ τράμ πού ξεκινάει, ἄδειο κι' ὁλόφωτο μέσ' στή νυχτερινή
γαλήνη τῶν μπαχτσέδων,
Μ' ἕνα σκοπό τοῦ ταξειδιοῦ: πρός τ' ἄστρα.

Γι' αὐτούς θά πῶ τά λόγια τά ὡραῖα, πού μοῦ τά ὑπαγόρευσε ἡ Ἔμπνευσις,
Καθώς ἐφώλιασε μέσα στά βάθια τοῦ μυαλοῦ μου ὅλο συγκίνηση
Γιά τίς μορφές, τίς αὐστηρές καί τίς ὑπέροχες, τοῦ Ὀδυσσέα Ἀνδρούτσου
καί τοῦ Σίμωνος Μπολιβάρ.

Ὅμως γιά τώρα θά ψάλω μοναχά τόν Σίμωνα, ἀφήνοντας τόν ἄλλο γιά
κατάλληλο καιρό,
Ἀφήνοντάς τον γιά νάν τ' ἀφιερώσω, σάν ἔρθ' ἡ ὥρα, ἴσως τό πιό ὡραῖο
τραγούδι πού ἔψαλα ποτέ,

BOLIVÁR (1944)

a greek poem

ΦΑΣΜΑ ΘΗΣΕΩΣ ΕΝ ΟΠΛΟΙΣ ΚΑΘΟΡΑΝ ΠΡΟ
ΑΥΤΩΝ ΕΠΙ ΤΟΥΣ ΒΑΡΒΑΡΟΥΣ ΦΕΡΟΜΕΝΟΝ
Le cuer d' un home vaut tout l' or d' un païs

For the great, the free, the brave, the strong,
The fitting words are great and free and brave and strong,
For them, the total subjection of every element, silence, for them
    tears, for them beacons, and olive branches, and the lanterns
That bob up and down with the swaying of the ships and scrawl on
    the harbors' dark horizons,
For them are the empty barrels piled up in the narrowest lane, again
    in the harbor,
For them the coils of white rope, the chains, the anchors, the other
    manometers,
Amidst the irritating smell of petroleum,
That they might fit out a ship, put to sea and depart,
Like a tram setting off, empty and ablaze with light, in the nocturnal
    serenity of the gardens,
With one purpose behind the voyage: ad astra.

For them I'll speak fine words, dictated to me by Inspiration's Muse,
As she nestled deep in my mind full of emotion
For the figures, austere and magnificent, of Odysseus Androutsos
    and Simon Bolivar.

But for now I'll sing only of Simon, leaving the other for an appro-
    priate time,
Leaving him that I might dedicate, when the time comes, perhaps the
    finest song that I've ever sung,

Ἴσως τ' ὡραιότερο τραγούδι πού ποτές ἐψάλανε σ' ὅλο τόν κόσμο.

Κι' αὐτά ὄχι γιά τά ὅτι κι' οἱ δυό τους ὑπῆρξαν γιά τίς πατρίδες, καί τά
ἔθνη, καί τά σύνολα, κι' ἄλλα παρόμοια, πού δέν ἐμπνέουν,
Παρά γιατί σταθήκανε μέσ' στούς αἰῶνες, κι' οἱ δυό τους, μονάχοι
πάντα, κι' ἐλεύθεροι, μεγάλοι, γενναῖοι καί δυνατοί.

Καί τώρα ν' ἀπελπίζουμε πού ἴσαμε σήμερα δέν μέ κατάλαβε, δέν
θέλησε, δέ μπόρεσε νά καταλάβη τί λέω, κανείς;
Βέβαια τήν ἴδια τύχη νἄχουνε κι' αὐτά πού λέω τώρα γιά τόν Μπολιβάρ,
πού θά πῶ αὔριο γιά τόν Ἀνδροῦτσο;
Δέν εἶναι κι' εὔκολο, ἄλλωστε, νά γίνουν τόσο γλήγορα ἀντιληπτές
μορφές τῆς σημασίας τ' Ἀνδρούτσου καί τοῦ Μπολιβάρ,
Παρόμοια σύμβολα.
Ἀλλ' ἄς περνοῦμε γρήγορα: πρός Θεοῦ, ὄχι συγκινήσεις, κι' ὑπερβολές,
κι' ἀπελπισίες.
Ἀδιάφορο, ἡ φωνή μου εἴτανε προωρισμένη μόνο γιά τούς αἰῶνες.
(Στό μέλλον, τό κοντινό, τό μακρυνό, σέ χρόνια, λίγα, πολλά, ἴσως ἀπό
μεθαύριο, κι' ἀντιμεθαύριο,
Ἴσαμε τήν ὥρα πού θέ ν' ἀρχινίση ἡ Γῆς νά κυλάη ἄδεια, κι' ἄχρηστη, καί
νεκρή, στό στερέωμα,
Νέοι θά ξυπνᾶνε, μέ μαθηματικήν ἀκρίβεια, τίς ἄγριες νύχτες, πάνω
στήν κλίνη τους,
Νά βρέχουνε μέ δάκρυα τό προσκέφαλό τους, ἀναλογιζόμενοι ποιός
εἴμουν, σκεφτόμενοι
Πώς ὑπῆρξα κάποτες, τί λόγια εἶπα, τί ὕμνους ἔψαλα.
Καί τά θεόρατα κύματα, ὅπου ξεσποῦνε κάθε βράδυ στά ἑφτά τῆς
Ὕδρας ἀκρογιάλια,
Κι' οἱ ἄγριοι βράχοι, καί τό ψηλό βουνό πού κατεβάζει τά δρολάπια,
Ἀέναα, ἀκούραστα, θέ νά βροντοφωνοῦνε τ' ὄνομά μου.)

Ἄς ἐπανέλθουμε ὅμως στόν Σίμωνα Μπολιβάρ.

Μπολιβάρ! Ὄνομα ἀπό μέταλλο καί ξύλο, εἴσουνα ἕνα λουλούδι μέσ'
στούς μπαχτσέδες τῆς Νότιας Ἀμερικῆς.

Perhaps the finest song that's ever been sung in the whole world.

And this not for what they both were for their countries, their nations,
their people, and other such like that fail to inspire,

But because they remained throughout the ages, both of them, alone
always, and free, great, brave and strong.

And shall I now despair that to this very day no one has understood,
has wanted, has been able to understand what I say?

Shall the fate then be the same for what I say now of Bolivar, for what
I'll say tomorrow of Androutsos?

Besides, it's no easy thing for figures of the importance of Androutsos
and Bolivar to be so quickly understood,

Symbols of a like.

But let's move on quickly: for Heaven's sake, no emotion, exaggera-
tion or despair.

Of no concern, my voice was destined for the ages alone.

(In the future, the near, the distant, in years to come, a few, many,
perhaps from the day after tomorrow or the day after that,

Until the time that, empty and useless and dead, the Earth begins to
drift in the firmament,

The young, with mathematical precision, will awake in their beds on
wild nights,

Moistening their pillows with tears, wondering at who I was, reflecting

That once I existed, what words I said, what songs I sang.

And the gigantic waves that every evening break on Hydra's seven
shores,

And the savage rocks, and the high mountain that brings down the
blizzards,

Will eternally and untiringly thunder my name.)

But let's get back to Simon Bolivar.

Bolivar! A name of metal and wood, you were a flower in the gardens
of South America.

Εἶχες ὅλη τήν εὐγένεια τῶν λουλουδιῶν μέσ' στήν καρδιά σου, μέσ' στά
μαλλιά σου, μέσα στό βλέμμα σου.
Ἡ χέρα σου εἴτανε μεγάλη σάν τήν καρδιά σου, καί σκορποῦσε τό καλό
καί τό κακό.

Ροβόλαγες τά βουνά κι' ἐτρέμαν τ' ἄστρα, κατέβαινες στούς κάμπους, μέ
τά χρυσά, τίς ἐπωμίδες, ὅλα τά διακριτικά τοῦ βαθμοῦ σου,
Μέ τό ντουφέκι στόν ὦμο ἀναρτημένο, μέ τά στήθια ξέσκεπα, μέ τίς
λαβωματιές γιομάτο τό κορμί σου,
Κι' ἐκαθόσουν ὁλόγυμνος σέ πέτρα χαμηλή, στ' ἀκροθαλάσσι,
Κι' ἔρχονταν καί σ' ἔβαφαν μέ τίς συνήθειες τῶν πολεμιστῶν Ἰνδιάνων,
Μ' ἀσβέστη, μισόνε ἄσπρο, μισό γαλάζιο, γιά νά φαντάζῃς σά
ρημοκκλήσι σέ περιγιάλι τῆς Ἀττικῆς,
Σάν ἐκκλησιά στίς γειτονιές τῶν Ταταούλων, ὡσάν ἀνάχτορο σέ πόλη
τῆς Μακεδονίας ἐρημική.

Μπολιβάρ! Εἴσουνα πραγματικότητα, καί εἶσαι, καί τώρα, δέν εἶσαι
ὄνειρο.
Ὅταν οἱ ἄγριοι κυνηγοί καρφώνουνε τούς ἄγριους ἀετούς, καί τ' ἄλλα
ἄγρια πουλιά καί ζῶα,
Πάν' ἀπ' τίς ξύλινες τίς πόρτες στ' ἄγρια δάση,
Ξαναζῇς, καί φωνάζεις, καί δέρνεσαι,
Κι' εἶσαι ὁ ἴδιος ἐσύ τό σφυρί, τό καρφί κι' ὁ ἀητός.

Ἄν στά νησιά τῶν κοραλλιῶν φυσοῦνε ἄνεμοι, κι' ἀναποδογυρίζουνε τά
ἔρημα καΐκια,
Κι' οἱ παπαγάλοι ὀργιάζουνε μέ τίς φωνές σάν πέφτει ἡ μέρα, κι' οἱ κῆποι
εἰρηνεύουνε πνιγμένοι σ' ὑγρασία,
Καί στά ψηλά δεντρά κουρνιάζουν τά κοράκια,
Σκεφτῆτε, κοντά στό κῦμα, τοῦ καφφενείου τά σιδερένια τά τραπέζια,
Μέσ' στή μαυρίλα πῶς τά τρώει τ' ἀγιάζι, καί μακρυά τό φῶς π' ἀνάβει,
σβύνει, ξανανάβει, καί γυρνάει πέρα δῶθε,
Καί ξημερώνει –τί φριχτή ἀγωνία –ὕστερα ἀπό μιά νύχτα δίχως ὕπνο,
Καί τό νερό δέν λέει τίποτε ἀπό τά μυστικά του. Ἔτσ' ἡ ζωή.

You had all the gentleness of flowers in your heart, in your hair, in
your gaze.
Your hand was huge like your heart, and scattered both good and evil.
You swept through the mountains and the stars trembled, you came
down to the plains, with your gold finery, your epaulets, all the
insignia of your rank,
With a rifle hanging on your shoulder, with chest bared, with your
body covered in wounds,
And stark naked you sat on a low rock, at the sea's edge,
And they came and painted you in the ways of Indian braves,
With wash, half white, half blue, so you'd appear like a lonely chapel
on one of Attica's shores,
Like a church in the districts of Tatavla, like a palace in a deserted
Macedonian town.

Bolivar! You were reality, and you are, even now, you are no dream.
When the wild hunters nail the wild eagles, and the other wild birds
and animals,
Over their wooden doors in the wild forests,
You live again, and shout, and grieve,
And you are yourself the hammer, nail and eagle.

If on the isles of coral, winds blow and the empty fishing boats
overturn,
And the parrots are a riot of voices when the day ends and the gardens
grow quiet drowned in humidity,
And in the tall trees the crows perch,
Consider, beside the waves, the iron tables of the cafeneion,
How the damp eats at them in the gloom, and far off the light that
flashes on, off, on again, turning back and forth.
And day breaks – what frightful anguish – after a night without sleep,
And the water reveals nothing of its secrets. Such is life.

Κι' ἔρχετ' ὁ ἥλιος, καί τῆς προκυμαίας τά σπίτια, μέ τίς νησιώτικες
καμάρες,
Βαμμένα ρόζ, καί πράσινα, μ' ἄσπρα περβάζια (ἡ Νάξο, ἡ Χίος),
Πῶς ζοῦν! Πῶς λάμπουνε σά διάφανες νεράϊδες! Αὐτός ὁ Μπολιβάρ!

Μπολιβάρ! Κράζω τ' ὄνομά σου ξαπλωμένος στήν κορφή τοῦ βουνοῦ
Ἔρε,
Τήν πιό ψηλή κορφή τῆς νήσου Ὕδρας.
Ἀπό δῶ ἡ θέα ἐκτείνεται μαγευτική μέχρι τῶν νήσων τοῦ Σαρωνικοῦ,
τή Θήβα,
Μέχρι κεῖ κάτω, πέρα ἀπ' τή Μονεβασιά, τό τρανό Μισίρι,
Ἀλλά καί μέχρι τοῦ Παναμᾶ, τῆς Γκουατεμάλα, τῆς Νικαράγκουα,
τοῦ Ὀντουράς, τῆς Ἀϊτῆς, τοῦ Σάν Ντομίγκο, τῆς Βολιβίας,
τῆς Κολομβίας, τοῦ Περοῦ, τῆς Βενεζουέλας, τῆς Χιλῆς, τῆς
Ἀργεντινῆς, τῆς Βραζιλίας, Οὐρουγουάη, Παραγουάη, τοῦ
Ἰσημερινοῦ,
Ἀκόμη καί τοῦ Μεξικοῦ.
Μ' ἕνα σκληρό λιθάρι χαράζω τ' ὄνομά σου πάνω στήν πέτρα, νἄρχουνται
ἀργότερα οἱ ἄνθρωποι νά προσκυνοῦν.
Τινάζονται σπίθες καθώς χαράζω –ἔτσι εἴτανε, λέν, ὁ Μπολιβάρ –καί
παρακολουθῶ
Τό χέρι μου καθώς γράφει, λαμπρό μέσα στόν ἥλιο.

Εἶδες γιά πρώτη φορά τό φῶς στό Καρακάς. Τό φῶς τό δικό σου,
Μπολιβάρ, γιατί ὡς νἄρθης ἡ Νότια Ἀμερική ὁλόκληρη εἴτανε
βυθισμένη στά πικρά σκοτάδια.
Τ' ὄνομά σου τώρα εἶναι δαυλός ἀναμμένος, πού φωτίζει τήν Ἀμερική,
καί τή Βόρεια καί τή Νότια, καί τήν οἰκουμένη!
Οἱ ποταμοί Ἀμαζόνιος καί Ὀρινόκος πηγάζουν ἀπό τά μάτια σου.
Τά ψηλά βουνά ἔχουν τίς ρίζες στό στέρνο σου,
Ἡ ὀροσειρά τῶν Ἄνδεων εἶναι ἡ ραχοκοκκαλιά σου.
Στήν κορφή τῆς κεφαλῆς σου, παλληκαρᾶ, τρέχουν τ' ἀνήμερα ἄτια καί
τ' ἄγρια βόδια,
Ὁ πλοῦτος τῆς Ἀργεντινῆς.
Πάνω στήν κοιλιά σου ἐκτείνονται οἱ ἀπέραντες φυτεῖες τοῦ καφφέ.

And the sun comes, and the houses on the wharf, with their island-
style arches,
Painted pink, and green, with white sills (Naxos, Chios),
How they live! How they shine like translucent fairies! Such is
Bolivar!

Bolivar! I cry out your name, reclining on the peak of Mount Ere,
The highest peak on the isle of Hydra.
From here the view, enchanting, extends as far as the Saronic isles,
Thebes,
Beyond Monemvasia, far below, to august Misr,
And as far as Panama, Guatemala, Nicaragua, Honduras, Haiti, San
Domingo, Bolivia, Colombia, Peru, Venezuela, Chile, Argentina,
Brazil, Uruguay, Paraguay, Ecuador,
As far even as Mexico.
With hard stone I carve your name in rock, that afterwards men may
come in pilgrimage.
As I carve sparks fly – such, they say, was Bolivar – and I watch my
hand as it writes, gleaming in the sun.

You saw the light for the first time in Caracas. Your light,
Bolivar, for before you came the whole of South America was plunged
in bitter darkness.
Now your name is a blazing torch, lighting America, North and
South, and all the world!
The Amazon and Orinoco rivers spring from your eyes.
The high mountains are rooted in your breast,
The Andes range is your backbone.
On the crown of your head, brave palikar, run unbroken stallions and
wild cattle,
The wealth of Argentina.
On your belly sprawl vast coffee plantations.

Σάν μιλᾶς, φοβεροί σεισμοί ρημάζουνε τό πᾶν,
Ἀπό τίς ἐπιβλητικές ἐρημιές τῆς Παταγονίας μέχρι τά πολύχρωμα
    νησιά,
Ἡφαίστεια ξεπετιοῦνται στό Περοῦ καί ξερνᾶνε στά οὐράνια τήν ὀργή
    τους,
Σειοῦνται τά χώματα παντοῦ καί τρίζουν τά εἰκονίσματα στήν Καστοριά,
Τή σιωπηλή πόλη κοντά στή λίμνη.
Μπολιβάρ, εἶσαι ὡραῖος σάν Ἕλληνας.

Σέ πρωτοσυνάντησα, σάν εἴμουνα παιδί, σ' ἕνα ἀνηφορικό καλντιρίμι
    τοῦ Φαναριοῦ,
Μιά καντήλα στό Μουχλιό φώτιζε τό εὐγενικό πρόσωπό σου.
Μήπως νἆσαι, ἄραγες, μιά ἀπό τίς μύριες μορφές πού πῆρε, κι' ἄφησε,
    διαδοχικά, ὁ Κωσταντῖνος Παλαιολόγος;

Μπογιάκα, Ἁγιακοῦτσο. Ἔννοιες ὑπέρλαμπρες κι' αἰώνιες. Εἴμουν ἐκεῖ.
Εἴχαμε ἀπό πολλοῦ περάσει, ἤδη, τήν παλιά μεθόριο: πίσω, μακρυά, στό
    Λεσκοβίκι, εἶχαν ἀνάψει φωτιές.
Κι' ὁ στρατός ἀνέβαινε μέσα στή νύχτα πρός τή μάχη, π' ἀκούγονταν
    κιόλα οἱ γνώριμοί της ἦχοι.
Πλάϊ κατέρχουνταν, σκοτεινή Συνοδεία, ἀτέλειωτα λεωφορεῖα μέ τούς
    πληγωμένους.

Μήν ταραχθῆ κανείς. Κάτω ἐκεῖ, νά, ἡ λίμνη.
Ἀπό δῶ θά περάσουν, πέρ' ἀπ' τίς καλαμιές.
Ὑπομονευτῆκαν οἱ δρόμοι: ἔργο καί δόξα τοῦ Χορμοβίτη, τοῦ
    ξακουστοῦ, τοῦ ἄφταστου στά τέτοια. Στίς θέσεις σας ὅλοι. Ἡ
    σφυρίχτρα ἠχεῖ!
Ἐλᾶτε, ἐλᾶτε, ξεζέψτε. Ἄς στηθοῦν τά κανόνια, καθαρίστε μέ τά
    μάκτρα τά κοῖλα, τά φυτίλια ἀναμμένα στά χέρια,
Τά τόπια δεξιά. Βράς!
Βράς, ἀλβανιστί φωτιά: Μπολιβάρ!

When you speak, terrible earthquakes spread devastation,
From Patagonia's formidable deserts as far as the colorful islands,
Volcanoes erupt in Peru and vomit their wrath in the heavens,
Everywhere the earth trembles and the icons creak in Kastoria,
The silent town beside the lake.
Bolivar, you have the beauty of a Greek.

I first encountered you, as a child, in one of Phanar's steep cobbled
   streets,
A lighted lamp in Mouchlio illumined your noble face.
Are you, I wonder, one of the myriad forms assumed, and succes-
   sively discarded by Constantine Palaeologus?

Boyaca, Ayacucho. Ideas both illustrious and eternal. I was there.
We'd already left the old frontiers far behind:
Back in the distance, fires were burning in Leskovik.
And in the night, the army moved up towards the battle, its familiar
   sounds could already be heard.
Opposite, a grim Convoy of endless trucks returned with the
   wounded.

Let no one be alarmed. Down there, see, the lake.
This is the way they'll come, beyond the rushes.
The roads have been mined: the work and repute of that Hormovo
   man, renowned, unrivalled in such matters. Everyone to their
   stations. The whistle's sounding!
Come on, come on. Get the cannons uncoupled and set up, clean the
   barrels with the swabs, fuses lit and held ready,
Cannon-balls to the right. Vrass!
Vrass, Albanian for fire: Bolivar!

Κάθε κουμπαρᾶς, π' ἐξεσφενδονιζόταν κι' ἄναφτε,
Εἴταν κι' ἕνα τριαντάφυλλο γιά τή δόξα τοῦ μεγάλου στρατηγοῦ,
Σκληρός, ἀτάραχος ὡς στέκονταν μέσα στόν κορνιαχτό καί τήν ἀντάρα,
Μέ τό βλέμμ' ἀτενίζοντας πρός τ' ἀψηλά, τό μέτωπο στά νέφη,
Κι' εἴταν ἡ θέα του φριχτή: πηγή τοῦ δέους, τοῦ δίκιου δρόμος,
λυτρώσεως πύλη.

Ὅμως, πόσοι καί πόσοι δέ σ' ἐπιβουλευτῆκαν, Μπολιβάρ,
Πόσα «ντολάπια» καί δέ σοῦ 'στησαν νά πέσης, νά χαθῆς,
Ἕνας πρό πάντων, ἕνας παλιάνθρωπος, ἕνα σκουλήκι, ἕνας
Φιλιππουπολίτης.
Ἀλλά σύ τίποτα, ἀτράνταχτος σάν πύργος στέκουσαν, ὄρθιος, στοῦ
Ἀκογκάγκουα μπρός τόν τρόμο,
Μιά φοβερή ξυλάρα ἐκράταγες, καί τήν ἐκράδαινες πάνω ἀπ' τήν
κεφαλή σου.
Οἱ φαλακροί κόνδωρες σκιάζουνταν, πού δέν τούς τρόμαξε τῆς μάχης τό
κακό καί τό ντουμάνι, καί σέ κοπάδια ἀγριεμένα πέταγαν,
Κι' οἱ προβατογκαμῆλες γκρεμιοτσακίζουντάνε στίς πλαγιές, σέρνοντας,
καθώς πέφταν, σύννεφο τό χῶμα καί λιθάρια.
Κι' οἱ ἐχθροί σου μέσα στά μαῦρα Τάρταρα ἐχάνοντο, λουφάζαν.
(Σάν θἄρθη μάρμαρο, τό πιό καλό, ἀπό τ' Ἀλάβανδα, μ' ἁγίασμα τῶν
Βλαχερνῶν θά βρέξω τήν κορφή μου,
Θά βάλω ὅλη τήν τέχνη μου αὐτή τή στάση σου νά πελεκήσω, νά στήσω
ἑνοῦ νέου Κούρου τ' ἄγαλμα στῆς Σικίνου τά βουνά,
Μή λησμονώντας, βέβαια, στό βάθρο νά χαράξω τό περίφημο ἐκεῖνο
«Χαῖρε παροδίτα».)

Κι' ἐδῶ πρέπει ἰδιαιτέρως νά ἐξαρθῆ ὅτι ὁ Μπολιβάρ δέν ἐφοβήθηκε, δέ
«σκιάχτηκε» πού λέν, ποτέ,
Οὔτε στῶν μαχῶν τήν ὥρα τήν πιό φονικιά, οὔτε στῆς προδοσίας, τῆς
ἀναπόφευκτης, τίς πικρές μαυρίλες.
Λένε πώς γνώριζε ἀπό πρίν, μέ μιάν ἀκρίβεια ἀφάνταστη, τή μέρα, τήν
ὥρα, τό δευτερόλεφτο ἀκόμη: τή στιγμή,
Τῆς Μάχης τῆς μεγάλης πού εἴτανε γι' αὐτόνα μόνο,

Every pineapple that was hurled and exploded,
Was a rose to the glory of the great general,
As he stood, stern and unshaken, amid the dust and tumult,
Gazing on high, his forehead in the clouds,
And the sight of him caused dread: fount of awe, path of justice, gate
of salvation.

Yet, how many conspired against you, Bolivar,
How many traps did they not set for you to fall into and vanish,
One man, above all, a rogue, a snake, a native of Philippoupolis.
But what was that to you, like a tower you stood firm, upright, before
Acongagua's terror,
Holding a mighty cudgel and wielding it above your head.
The bald-headed condors, unafraid of the carnage and smoke of
battle, took fright and flew up in terrified flocks,
And the llamas hurled themselves down the mountain slopes, drag-
ging, as they fell, a cloud of earth and rocks.
And into the dark of Tartarus your enemies disappeared, lay low.
(When the marble arrives, the best from Alabanda, I'll sprinkle my
brow with Blachernae's holy water,
I'll use all my craft to hew your stance, to erect the statue of a new
Kouros in Sikynos' mountains,
Not forgetting, of course, to engrave on its base that famous "Hail,
passer-by.")

And here it should above all be stressed that Bolivar was never afraid,
was never, as they say, "struck with fear,"
Not even at the most murderous hour of battle, nor in the bitter
gloom of unavoidable treachery.
They say he knew beforehand, with unimaginable precision, the day,
the hour, even the second: the moment,
Of the Great Battle that was for him alone,

Κι' ὅπου θέ νἄτανε αὐτός ὁ ἴδιος στρατός κι' ἐχθρός, ἡττημένος καί
νικητής μαζί, ἥρωας τροπαιοῦχος κι' ἐξιλαστήριο θῦμα.

(Καί ὡς τοῦ Κύριλλου Λουκάρεως τό πνεῦμα τό ὑπέροχο μέσα του
στέκονταν,
Πῶς τίς ξεγέλαγε, γαλήνιος, τῶν Ἰησουϊτῶνε καί τοῦ ἐλεεινοῦ
Φιλιππουπολίτη τίς ἀπαίσιες πλεχτάνες!)
Κι' ἄν χάθηκε, ἄν ποτές χάνετ' ἕνας Μπόλιβάρ! πού σάν τόν Ἀπολλώνιο
στά οὐράνια ἀνελήφθη,
Λαμπρός σάν ἥλιος ἔδυσε, μέσα σέ δόξα ἀφάνταστη, πίσω ἀπό βουνά
εὐγενικά τῆς Ἀττικῆς καί τοῦ Μορέως.

ἐπίκλησις

Μπολιβάρ! Εἶσαι τοῦ Ρήγα Φερραίου παιδί,
Τοῦ Ἀντωνίου Οἰκονόμου –πού τόσο ἄδικα τόν σφάξαν –καί τοῦ
Πασβαντζόγλου ἀδελφός,
Τ' ὄνειρο τοῦ μεγάλου Μαξιμιλιανοῦ ντέ Ρομπεσπιέρ ξαναζεῖ στό
μετωπό σου.
Εἶσαι ὁ ἐλευθερωτής τῆς Νότιας Ἀμερικῆς.
Δέν ξέρω ποιά συγγένεια σέ συνέδεε, ἄν εἴτανε ἀπόγονός σου ὁ ἄλλος
μεγάλος Ἀμερικανός, ἀπό τό Μοντεβίντεο αὐτός,
Ἕνα μονάχα εἶναι γνωστό, πώς εἶμαι ὁ γυιός σου.

In which he himself would be army and enemy, both vanquished and
victor, triumphant hero and sacrificial victim.
(And the lofty spirit of such as Cyril Loukaris reared within him,
How he calmly eluded the despicable plots of the Jesuits and that
wretched man from Philippoupolis!)

And if he was lost, if ever lost is such a one as Bolivar! who like
Apollonius vanished into the heavens,
Resplendent like the sun he disappeared, in unimaginable glory,
behind the gentle mountains of Attica and the Morea.

invocation

Bolivar! You are a son of Rigas Ferraios,
Of Antonios Economou – so unjustly slain – and brother to
Pasvantzoglou,
The dream of the great Maximilien de Robespierre lives again on
your brow,
You are the liberator of South America.
I don't know how you were related, if one of your descendants was
that other great American, the one from Montevideo,
One thing alone is sure, that I am your son.

ΧΟΡΟΣ

στροφή

(*entrée des guitares*)

Ἄν ἡ νύχτα, ἀργή νά περάσῃ,
Παρηγόρια μᾶς στέλνῃ τίς παλιές τίς σελῆνες,
Ἄν στοῦ κάμπου τά πλάτη φαντασμάτων σκοτάδια
Λυσικόμους παρθένες μ' ἀλυσίδες φορτώνουν,
Ἦρθ' ἡ ὥρα τῆς νίκης, ἦρθε ὥρα θριάμβου.
Εἰς τά σκέλεθρα τ' ἄδεια στρατηγῶν πολεμάρχων
Τρικαντά θά φορέσουν πού ποτίστηκαν μ' αἷμα,
Καί τό κόκκινο χρῶμα ποὔχαν πρίν τή θυσία
Θά σκεπάσῃ μ' ἀχτίδες τῆς σημαίας τό θάμπος.

ἀντιστροφή

(*the love of liberty brought us here*)

τ' ἄροτρα στῶν φοινικιῶν τίς ρίζες
κι' ὁ ἥλιος
πού λαμπρός ἀνατέλλει
σέ τρόπαι' ἀνάμεσα
καί πουλιά
καί κοντάρια
θ' ἀναγγείλῃ ὡς ἐκεῖ πού κυλάει τό δάκρυ
καί τό παίρνει ὁ ἀέρας στῆς
θαλάσσης
τά βάθη
τόν φριχτότατον ὅρκο
τό φρικτότερο σκότος
τό φριχτό παραμύθι:
Libertad

CHORUS

strophe

(entrée des guitares)

If the night, slow in passing,
Sends moons of old to console us,
If in the wide plain phantom shades
Burden flowing-haired maidens with chains,
The hour of victory, of triumph has come.
On hollow skeletons of belligerent generals
Cocked hats soaked in blood will be placed,
And the red that was theirs before the sacrifice
Will cover with rays the flag's luster.

antistrophe

(the love of liberty brought us here)

the ploughs at the palms' roots
and the sun
that rises resplendent
amid trophies
and birds
and spears
will announce as far as a tear rolls
carried by the breeze to
the sea's
depths
the most terrible oath
the more terrible darkness
the terrible tale:
Libertad

ἐπῳδός

(χορός ἐλευθεροτεκτόνων)

Φύγετε μακρυά μας ἀρές, μή ζυγώσετε πιά, corazón,
Ἀπ' τά λίκνα στ' ἀστέρια, ἀπ' τίς μῆτρες στά μάτια, corazón,
Ὅπου ἀπόγκρημνοι βράχοι, καί ἡφαίστεια καί φώκιες, corazón,
Ὅπου πρόσωπο σκοῦρο, καί χείλια πλατειά, κι ὀλόλευκα corazón,
    δόντια, corazón,
Ἄς στηθῇ ὁ φαλλός, καί γιορτή ἄς ἀρχίση, μέ θυσίες ἀνθρώπων,
    μέ χορούς, corazón,
Μέσ' σέ σάρκας ξεφάντωμα, στῶν προγόνων τή δόξα, corazón,
Γιά νά σπείρουν τό σπόρο τῆς καινούργιας γενιᾶς, corazón,

epode

(freemasons' dance)

Away with you curses, come near us no more, corazón,
From the cradle to the stars, from the womb to the eyes, corazón,
Where precipitous rocks, where volcanoes and seals, corazón,
Where swarthy faces, thick lips and gleaming white teeth, corazón,
Let the phallus be raised, the revels begin, with human sacrifice,
    dance, corazón,
In a carnival of flesh, to our ancestors' glory, corazón,
That the seed of the new generation be sown, corazón.

ΣΥΜΠΕΡΑΣΜΑ:

Μετά τήν ἐπικράτησιν τῆς νοτιοαμερικανικῆς ἐπαναστάσεως στήθηκε στ' Ἀνάπλι καί τή Μονεμβασιά, ἐπί ἐρημικοῦ λόφου δεσπόζοντος τῆς πόλεως, χάλκινος ἀνδριάς τοῦ Μπολιβάρ. Ὅμως, καθώς τίς νύχτες ὁ σφοδρός ἄνεμος πού φυσοῦσε ἀνατάραζε μέ βία τήν ρεντιγκότα τοῦ ἥρωος, ὁ προκαλούμενος θόρυβος εἴτανε τόσο μεγάλος, ἐκκωφαντικός, πού στέκονταν ἀδύνατο νά κλείση κανείς μάτι, δέν μποροῦσε νά γενῆ πλέον λόγος γιά ὕπνο. Ἔτσι οἱ κάτοικοι ἐζήτησαν καί, διά καταλλήλων ἐνεργειῶν, ἐπέτυχαν τήν κατεδάφιση τοῦ μνημείου.

CONCLUSION:

Following the success of the South-American revolution, a bronze statue of Bolivar was erected in Nauplion and Monemvasia, on a deserted hill overlooking the town. However, the fierce wind that blew at night caused the hero's frock-coat to flap furiously, creating a noise so great, so deafening, that it was impossible for anyone to get a wink of sleep, any thought of sleep was now out of the question. So the inhabitants demanded and, through the appropriate steps, were able to have the monument torn down.

ΥΜΝΟΣ ΑΠΟΧΑΙΡΕΤΙΣΤΗΡΙΟΣ ΣΤΟΝ ΜΠΟΛΙΒΑΡ

(Ἐδῶ ἀκούγονται μακρυνές μουσικές πού παίζουν, μ' ἄφθαστη μελαγχολία, νοσταλγικά λαϊκά τραγούδια καί χορούς τῆς Νοτίου Ἀμερικῆς, κατά προτίμησιν σέ ρυθμό sardane).

στρατηγέ
τί ζητοῦσες στή Λάρισα
σύ
ἕνας
Ὑδραῖος;

SONG OF FAREWELL TO BOLIVAR

(Here the strains of distant music are heard; the playing, with incomparable melancholy, of nostalgic folk songs and dances from South America, preferably in sardana time).

general
what were you doing in Larissa
you
from
Hydra?

Η ΕΠΙΣΤΡΟΦΗ ΤΩΝ ΠΟΥΛΙΩΝ

Forth from the war emerging, a book I have made,
The words of my book nothing, the drift of it
    everything,
A book separate, not link'd with the rest nor felt
    by the intellect,
But you ye untold latencies will thrill to every page.
                    WALT WHITMAN

ΟΙ ΦΩΝΕΣ

εἰς Ἀνδρέαν Breton

μέσ' ἀπ' τίς γρίλλιες τίς κλειστές
στήν κίτρινη
τή φλόγα
τοῦ μεσημεριοῦ
– ὅταν τ' ἀγάλματα σιωποῦν
κι' οἱ μῦθοι στέργουν –
οἱ φωνές
δονοῦν
πρῶτα
ἀχνά
ἀργά
κι' ὕστερα
βροντερά
καί γρήγορα
μέσ' στό σοκάκι

κι' ἀποκαλύπτουν ξάφνου τά αἰώνια μυστικά

ἄλλοτε
– φυσικά –
εἶν' τρομερές καί φοβερές
σάν τάφοι

From: *THE RETURN OF THE BIRDS* (1946)

Forth from the war emerging, a book I have made,
The words of my book nothing, the drift of it
     everything,
A book separate, not link'd with the rest nor felt
     by the intellect,
But you ye untold latencies will thrill to every page.
                              WALT WHITMAN

THE VOICES

                              to André Breton

through the closed shutters
in the yellow
flame
of midday
– when the statues fall silent
and the myths concur –
the voices
vibrate
first
faintly
slowly
and then
thunderously
and quickly
in the lane

and suddenly reveal the eternal secrets

sometimes
– naturally –
these are terrible and frightful
like graves

κι' ἄλλοτε
πάλε
στοργικές
σάν τάφοι πάλι
κι' ὡσάν θωπεία
μακρυῶν
λεπτῶν
δακτύλων

καί λέν
τό κάθε τί
μέ τ' ὄνομά του

λέν τό νερό
τῆς βρύσης
στόμα
τά μαῦρα
τά ψηλά
τά δέντρα
λήθη
τή νύχτα μέσ'
στίς ρεματιές
Ὀμφάλη

λέν τά κλαμμένα μάτια
«φίλη»
τά δροσερά ἅλικα χείλια
φύλλα
τά ἐρωτικά τά δόντια
ἐφιάλτη

τοῦ ἔρωτα τά πορφυρά κρεββάτια
ἀβύσσους
τοῦ λιμανιοῦ τά μαῦρα

and sometimes
again
tender
again like graves
and like the caresses
of long
delicate
fingers

and they call
each thing
by its name

they call water
from the tap
mouth
the black
tall
trees
oblivion
the night in
the ravines
Omphali

they call tearful eyes
"girlfriend"
cool crimson lips
leaves
amorous teeth
nightmare

the purple beds of passion
abysses
the harbor's black

τά νερά
λυχνάρι
καί λέν τίς
σκουριασμένες ἄγκυρες
τ' ὀνείρου
θρῆνο

βάζουν πολύχρωμα φτερά
στό θλιβερό
τ' Ὀρφέα βλέμμα
στ' Ὀρφέα
τά χέρια
βάζουνε βεντάλιες
ξεσκίζουνε
τά φλογισμένα του
φουστάνια
κοσμοῦν
τήν κεφαλή του
μέ νταντέλλες
πολύ λεπτές

(στ' Ὀρφέα
τήν κορφή
μπήγουν
σημαῖες)

πετοῦν μέσ'
στῶν χρησμῶν τό χάος
αἷμα
καί ξαναλέν τίς
φοινικιές
δαυλιά

στέκουνε μέ λυγμούς

waters
lamp
and they call
dream's
rusty anchors
lament

they lay colorful plumes
on Orpheus'
sorrowful gaze
on Orpheus'
hands
they lay fans
they rip
his blazing
frocks
adorn
his head
with laces
most delicate ones

(in the crown
of Orpheus' head
they stick
flags)

amid the chaos' oracles
they hurl
blood
and again call the
palm trees
torches

sobbing they halt

στή λέξη σφύρα
ὀνόμασαν σιγή
τή λέξη θύρα
τό θάνατο εἶπαν
μουσική μέσ' στά
μηνίγγια
καί λένε δάσος
μέσ' στή νύχτα
τήν καρδιά
μου

at the word mallet
the word portal
they named silence
death they called
music in the
temples
and forest in the night
is what they call
my
heart

ΧΟΡΟΣ ΑΙΣΘΗΜΑΤΙΚΟΣ ΚΙ' ΕΥΓΕΝΙΚΟΣ

C'est le bal de l'abîme où l'amour est sans fin;
Et la danse vous noie en sa houleuse alcôve.

ALFRED JARRY: "Les Minutes de Sable Mémorial"

Ὁ μέγας ποιητής Κάλφογλους δέν εἴταν μόνον ὁ ἄφταστος διδάσκαλος τοῦ λόγου καί τοῦ ὀνείρου, ὅπου γνωρίζουμε. Ὑπῆρξε, κι' αὐτό εἶναι μιά ἀπό τίς πολλές σκοτεινές καί μυστικές πλευρές τῆς ζωῆς τῶν ποιητῶν, ὑπῆρξε κι' ἕνας μεγάλος, ἕνας πολύ μεγάλος μουσικός. Πάντα, βέβαια, μέσα στόν δικό του φανταστικό ρυθμό, τῶν λουλουδιῶν. Αὐτός εἶναι, μάλιστα, πού, πρίν ἀπό κάθε ἄλλον, ἐμεταχειρίστηκε τό πιάνο σάν πνευστό ὄργανο. Γιά νά ἐκτελέση ἕνα ὁποιοδήποτε κομμάτι, καί τό δυσκολώτερο ἀκόμη, μ' αὐτό τόν τρόπο, μετεμφιέζετο πρῶτον σέ μαρμάρινο ἄγαλμα, τό ὁποῖον ἔστηναν, κατά προτίμηση, μέσα σ' ἔρημους, ἐγκαταλελειμμένους κήπους. Κατόπιν, μόλις ἄρχιζαν ν' ἁπλώνωνται τά κόκκινα χρώματα τῆς δύσεως στόν οὐρανό, ἔσκαβαν, μέ τρόπο, στή ράχη τ' ἀγάλματος, ἕναν μικρό κρυψῶνα, ὅπου μποροῦσε νά μπῆ καί νά χωρέση ἕνα παιδί, γιά νά μιλῆ ὡσάν νά μιλοῦσε, δῆθεν, τό ἄγαλμα. Τότε ὁ ποιητής, νεκρός πλέον, ἅρπαζε στά δυνατά του χέρια ἕνα μεγάλο σφυρί, μιά «βαρειά», καί τό κατάφερνε ἀλύπητα, μέ βιάση κι' ἀγκομαχητά, πάνου στό πιάνο πού ἐτινάζονταν σέ κομμάτια. Ἀμέσως ἠχοῦσαν βαθειά, μ' ἀναστεναγμούς, τά σιδερένια πλευρά τῶν καραβιῶν. Τά πουλιά φώναζαν, τρομαγμένα. Λαμαρίνες σφύριζαν στόν ἀγέρα, καθώς τίς ἐπαράσερνε ὁ σφοδρός τοῦτος ἄνεμος πάνω ἀπό τίς στέγες τῶν ἀποθηκῶν. Κάθε τί ἐσαρώνετο σ' αὐτήνα τή φοβερή ὀργή Κυρίου: ἀπό τά πιό ὑπερήφανα παλάτια μέ τίς καμάρες ἴσαμε τήν πιό ταπεινή προσευχή τοῦ σκαφτιᾶ. Καί μόνο νταντέλλες ἀραχνοΰφαντες ἔπεφταν αὐτόματα, ἀπό μισή σέ μισή ὥρα, καί μισοσκέπαζαν τή θερμή γύμνια τῶν ὡραίων γυναικῶν. Ἐρασταί αὐτοκτονοῦσαν συνεχῶς, ἀπό τό πρωΐ. Πίδακες ἀνάβλυζαν ἐκεῖ πού πρίν δέν εἶσαν παρά γραμμένες οἱ δυό μόνε λέξεις: «ψιλῶ ὀνόματι», ἤ ἀκόμη «ἐν ὀνόματι», ἤ, πάλε, «φυγεῖν ἀδύνατον». Μιά νύχτα, στά μέρη τῆς Βοιωτίας, ἔσβυσαν ὅλα τά φανάρια, καί τά συνεπῆρε κι' αὐτά ἡ θάλασσα. Κι' ὅταν ὁ ποιητής,

NOBLE AND SENTIMENTAL DANCE

C'est le bal de l'abîme où l'amour est sans fin;
Et la danse vous noie en sa houleuse alcôve.
ALFRED JARRY: "Les Minutes de Sable Mémorial"

Kalfoglous, the great poet, was not only the incomparable master of discourse and dream that we know. He was also, and this is one of the many dark and secret sides of poets' lives, a great, a very great, musician. Always, of course, in his own imaginary rhythm, that of flowers. He it was, in fact, who, before anyone else, employed the piano as a wind instrument. In order to perform whatever piece, even the most difficult, in this way, he first assumed the guise of a marble statue, which they erected, preferably, in desolate, deserted gardens. Then, as soon as dawn's red hues began to spread in the sky, with discretion, they carved out a small hidey-hole in the statue's back, into which a child could enter and fit, to speak as though it were the statue supposedly speaking. Then the poet, now dead, took in his powerful hands a large hammer, a "sledge," and, puffing through haste, mercilessly brought it down again and again on the piano, which shattered in pieces. Straightaway the ship's iron sides deeply resounded with sighs. The birds cried out in fear. Metal sheets whistled in the air, raked by this fierce wind over the rooftops of the warehouses. Everything was swept in this terrible wrath of the Lord: from the proudest palaces with their arches to the digger's humblest prayer. And alone gossamer lacework automatically fell, from one half-hour to the next, half-covering the warm nakedness of beautiful women. Lovers committed suicide constantly, from the morning. Fountains gushed where before were written but two simple words: "bare name," or even "in name," or, again, "escape impossible." One night, in Boeotian lands, all the beacons went out, and these too were swept off by the sea.

πάνω στό κορύφωμα τῆς λυρικῆς μανίας, ἐναπόθετε χάμω, ἤρεμα, τήν τρομερή βαρειά, ἁπαλή εἰρήνη ἁπλώνονταν στόν κόσμο καί πράσινα λαμπρά ὄστρακα κοσμοῦσαν τίς μακρυές χρυσές πλεξοῦδες της. Τό πιάνο εἶχεν ἐκτελέσει τόν προορισμό του καί μετεβάλλετο, κι' αὐτό αὐτομάτως, σέ μιά σειρά χάλκινα σαμντάνια, καί πάλι σέ μιά σειρά λευκές καί ρόδινες, ἐναλλάξ, δωρικές κολῶνες, καί μιά σειρά μεγάλα θλιμμένα γυναικεῖα μάτια, πολύ ὡραῖα, διαφόρου χρώματος ἀνά ζεῦγος. Περιττό νά προσθέσω, ἴσως, ὡς ἀπαραίτητο συμπλήρωμα, καί γιά τό σεβασμό, ἀλλά καί τήν ἀποκατάσταση, τῆς ἀληθείας, πώς ὁ μέγας ποιητής Κάλφογλους δέν ἐχρησίμευσε πραγματικά ἐδῶ παρά σάν ἕνα πρόσχημα, ἕνα ἁπλό πρόσχημα. Καθότι κι' ὁ ποιητής, καί τό ἄγαλμα, καί τό μικρό παιδί, κι' ἡ ἀγχόνη πού εἶπα, δέν εἴσαν παρά ἐγώ, μόνον ἐγώ, ὁ ἴδιος, ἴσως σέ παλαιούς, ἴσως ἀκόμη καί σέ πρόσφατους, σέ πολύ πρόσφατους μάλιστα καιρούς.

And when at the height of his lyrical frenzy, the poet calmly put down the fearful sledgehammer, gentle peace spread throughout the world and glistening green shells adorned her long golden braids. The piano had served its purpose and was transformed, this too automatically, into a series of copper candelabra and again into a series of alternately white and pink Doric columns, and a series of large sad female eyes, most lovely ones, each pair a different color. No need for me to add, perhaps, as a necessary supplement, and out of respect, but also for the sake of truth, that Kalfoglous the great poet was actually used here only as a pretext, a simple pretext. For the poet, and the statue, and the small child, and the gallows I mentioned, were but me, only me, me myself, perhaps in older, perhaps even in recent, in fact in very recent times.

Η ΕΠΙΣΤΡΟΦΗ ΤΗΣ ΕΥΡΥΔΙΚΗΣ

μέσ' στό χαμένο
τό μικρό
λιμάνι
π' ἄγγιξαν
σάν τίς στερνές
σταγόνες
τοῦ
ἥλιου
τῶν ψαριῶν
τά δάκρυα
ὑψώνεται ἡ ζωή
κάθετη κι' ἤρεμη
σέ μαρμαρένιες
γοῦρνες
καί λωτούς
πικρούς
μέ τούς νοσταλγικούς
ρυθμούς
τῶν βαρυαύλων
καί τῆς
νύχτας

καί νά
ὅπου μᾶς πρόφταξε ἡ ὥρα
καί ζωντάνεψαν
τά ὄνειρα
πού εἰπώθηκαν
στούς παιδικούς ἀχάτες
κι' οἱ φοινικιές ἐτρελλαθήκανε
καί καίγονται
κι' ὀρθώσανε
πρός τ' ἄστρα

THE RETURN OF EURYDICE

in the lost
little
harbor
touched
like the last
drops
of
sun
by the fish's
tears
life rears itself
erect and calm
in marble
basins
and bitter
lotuses
with the nostalgic
strains
of bassoons
and of the
night

and there it was
that time caught up with us
and the dreams
told
in the children's agates
came to life
and the palm trees became crazed
and burn
and raised
their white

τ' ἄσπρα
χέρια τους
καί στά σκοτάδια
τίς κραυγές
τῶν πόθων

καί τώρα
τά μηνύματα
ἁρπάξανε
τά φλάμπουρα
π' ἀνέμιζαν
στοῦ ἄγριου
δάσους
τούς ἀπόρθητους
κρυψῶνες
κι' οἱ στοργικές
φωνές
πάλι
ἀκούστηκαν
νἄρχωνται
ἀπό
τά τρίσβαθα
τά φωτεινά
τῶν
ὁριζόντων

καί οἱ λυγμοί
ὅπου
σά βάσκανες ματιές
χρωμάτιζαν
τοῦ πυρετοῦ τά ντέφια
στῆς λατρείας
τά κλωνάρια

arms
to the stars
and in the darkness
their cries
of longing

and now
the messages
seized
the
pennants
that flapped
in the wild
wood's
impregnable
hideouts
and the tender
voices
again
were heard
coming
from
the shining
depths
of the
horizon

and the sobs
that
like cursing looks
tinged
the fever's tambourines
in the ritual's
branches

ἀργά ἀργά
σιγοῦν
μιά πού
πιό γρήγορα
θά ξεχαστῆ
τοῦ χωρισμοῦ
τό κλάμμα

ἀφοῦ προβέλνει
τό θηρίο
τ' ἀνεμόδαρτο
ἴδιο ξυλάρμενο
μέσα στῆς ζήλειας
τό δρολάπι
–κι' ὄχι ὁ
συνηθισμένος
ὁ Μινώταυρος
ὁ γνώριμος
ἀλλά
ἕνας ταῦρος
μέ ἀνθρώπινο
κεφάλι –

καί πίσω
τά πλατειά
φτερά
ἀνεμίζουνε
– ὡσάν τ' ἀγρίμι
π' οὔρλιαξε
σέ βάθρα
ἀγαλμάτων –
καί τά λυχνάρια
δείχνουνε
τό δρόμο

gradually
fall silent
since
more quickly
separation's
tears
will be forgotten

since the beast
weather-beaten
like a ship under bare poles
advances
into jealousy's
snare
– and not the
usual
familiar
Minotaur
but a bull
with human
head –

and behind
the wide
wings
flap
– like the wildling
that howled
on a statue's
base –
and the lamps
show
the way

πού ἔρχουνται
καί οἱ δαυλοί
ὁρίζουν
τῆς πομπῆς
τό δρόμο

κι᾽ ἔρχονται
οἱ ἀνέραστες
παρθένες
πού ἀσέλγησαν
σ᾽ ἀντιφωνάρια
λυτρωμοῦ
καί
πόρπες
σαβανῶτρες
κι᾽ ἔρχονται
καί μοῦ
δείχνουν
μέ τά
ματωμένα χέρια τους
τό δέντρο
τῆς ζωῆς
καί τοῦ
θανάτου

ὅμως δέν μέ γελοῦν
γιατί τά
χείλια
μου
τά ξέσκισ᾽ ἄσπλαχνα
ἡ
ἐκδίκησις
κι᾽ ὁ
πελεκάνος

they come
and the torches
mark
the
procession's
path

and so come
the loveless
virgins
who acted indecently
on deliverance's
antiphonaries
and the clasps
of the shrouders
they come
and with
their
bloodied hands
show me
the tree
of life
and of
death

yet they deceive me not
because
my
lips
were mercilessly torn
by
revenge
and the
sacrificial

τῆς θυσίας
καί γιατί
μέσ᾽ στά
μάτια μου
βαθειά
ριζώσανε
τά
μανιασμένα
ἀστροπελέκια
τοῦ
πελάγους

κι᾽ ἄν ὁ
ἀνίερος κύκλος
δέν κατάφερε
νά ζήση
μέσ᾽ στό
εἶναι μου
τά σαρκοβόρα
τρεχαντήρια
οἱ
ὑπερήφανες
ἀγριοφωνάρες
μου
ξυπνήσανε
τίς
ἐρημιές
τίς
φοβερές
πού
ζώνει
ἡ
νύχτα

axe
and because
deeply
within
my eyes
the
raging
thunderbolts
of the
sea
had taken root

and if the
impious circle
was unable
to live
in
my being
the carnivorous
sailboats
the
proud
wild cries
awoke
in me
the
most
terrible
wildernesses
that
the
night
encircles

κι' ἄν ἡ πομπή
κυλάη
τό δρόμο
τῆς
μέσ' στῶν δαυλῶν
τά φῶτα
καί τά σεῖστρα
καί μπρός
πάντα
πηγαίνει
ὁ ταῦρος
ὁ
ἀνθρωπόμορφος
καί
τελευταῖες
οἱ παρθένες
μέ τά μῦρα

ὅμως
τό
ξέρω:
εἶμαι
ὁ μόνος
πού ἐδάκρυσε
ὅταν
περάσανε
αὐτά
τά
λυρικά
σφαχτάρια
καί ξέρω
ὅτι
τό δέντρο
ὅπου

and if the procession
rolls
on its
way
amid the torches'
lights
and the sistra
and in front
always
goes
the
man-like
bull
and behind
the virgins
with the myrrh

yet
I
know:
I am
the only one
who cried
when
these
lyrical
beasts of sacrifice
passed
by
and I know
that
the tree
that

ἐφάνταξε
εἶναι
τό δέντρο
τῆς ζωῆς
μονάχα

εἶναι
τό δέντρο
πού
στίς
δροσερές
παλάμες του
κρατᾶ
τό αἰώνιο
μυστικό
τῆς
λήθης

κι' εἶναι
τό
δέντρο
πού
καρτερικά
πάντοτε
πρόσμενα
νά γινῶ ἕνα
μέ τίς
πυκνές
τίς
φυλλωσιές
του

εἶναι
τό δέντρο

appeared
is
the tree
of life
alone

it is
the tree
that
in its
cool
hands
holds
the eternal
secret
of
oblivion

and it is
the
tree
with
whose
thick
leafage
patiently
always
I expected
to
become
one

it is
the precious

τό μονάκριβο
πού
τά λουλούδια
του
ἐλέγαν
πάντα
τό
τραγούδι
τῆς
χαρᾶς
μου

κι᾿ εἶν᾿ ἡ Εὐρυδίκη

ἡ Εὐρυδίκη πού ἔρχεται
καί φεύγει
καί ΞΑΝΑΡΧΕΤΑΙ
γιά
νά
σταθῆ
ὁριστικά
μέσ᾿ στή
φρικτή
πληγή
τῶν
ἀγριεμένων
σωθικῶν
μου

(κι᾿ ἴσως
καί
γιά
νά δικαιωθῆ
ὁ παληός

tree
the flowers
of
which
always
sang
the
song
of
my
joy

and it is Eurydice

Eurydice who comes
and goes
and COMES AGAIN
so as
to
remain
forever
in the
horrible
wound
of
my
enraged
innards

(and perhaps
so as
also
to vindicate
the old

χρησμός
πού
κάποτ' ὥρισε
πώς εἶμαι
ὁ Ὀρφέας
ὁ ψηλός
λεπτός
κι' ἀθάνατος
βγαλμένος ἀπό
τά πλατειά
τά στήθια
τοῦ
Ἑρμῆ
τοῦ
Τρισμεγίστου)

καί τώρα
πού
τό ὄνειρο
ἐθριάμβεψε
μέσ'
στό μικρό
λιμάνι
ὅπου ἄραξε
ἡ πυρκαϊά τῶν φοινικιῶν
στίς
μαρμαρένιες
γοῦρνες
πάλι ἡ χαρά τοῦ ἥλιου
ὁλοῦθε
ἁπλώνεται
κι' ἠχοῦν
μόναχα
οἱ

oracle
that
once decreed
that I am
Orpheus
tall
slender
and immortal
plucked from
the
broad
breast
of
Hermes
Trismegistus)

and now
that
the dream
has triumphed
in
the little
harbor
where
the palm trees' fire
moored
in the marble
basins
again the sun's joy
spreads
all around
and only
the
bassoons

βαρύαυλοι
σάν
ἔρθη
ἡ
νύχτα

sound
when
the
night
comes

ΔΥΑΔΙΚΟΣ ΑΥΤΟΜΑΤΙΣΜΟΣ

Τό νοῦ σας! Φυλαχτῆτε! Προσέχτε! Ἤδη οἱ ἄνεμοι πού φυσοῦν ἐφέρανε ἴσαμε τ᾽ αὐτιά μας τά μυστηριώδη μηνύματα. Τό κάθε τί ἐγκυμονεῖ γύρω μας καί μιάν ἀπειλή. Μαχαλᾶς δέν ἔμεινε πού νά μήν τόνε πλάκωσε ὁ φόβος. Κάθε ἀντικείμενο κρύφτει μέσα του καί μιά ψυχή. Νά φύγουμε, ἐλᾶτε. Ἡ ὥρα χτυπᾶ. Ἡ σκουριασμένη ἀνεμοδούρα μᾶς κράζει ἔξαλλη μέσα στή νύχτα. Τά μαγγανοπήγαδα σταματοῦν καί τά τυφλά ἀλόγατα γινῆκαν ἕνα μέ τά φυτά τά λεγόμενα «μπιγκόνιες». Νά φύγουμε. Ἐμπρός. Νά φύγουμε κάπου μακρυά. Στά Γάλβανα! Στά Γάλβανα! Ἐκεῖ, πού εἶναι ἡ σωτηρία, τῆς λήθης τ᾽ ἀπάνεμο λιμάνι. Ἡ γαλήνη. Ἐκεῖ!... Θύματα ἐξιλαστήρια τῆς ἀγάπης, τῆς νύχτας ἀσκητικοί στρατοκόποι, τῆς αὐγῆς ὑπερήφανοι περπατητές, ἀνάφτε τό θαλασσινό φανάρι. Ποιός ἔχει τακάτι, τίνος τό λέει στ᾽ ἀλήθεια ἡ καρδιά, ἅς ἐρθῆ. Μή χρονοτριβοῦμε ἄδικα σέ μάταιες ἀνασκοπήσεις τοῦ παρελθόντος. Οἱ καιροί εἶν᾽ ἀβέβαιοι. Καμμιάν ἀσφάλεια δέν ἔχουν οἱ δρόμοι, καί σέ πολλά σημεῖα ἡ πλημμύρα κατέκλυσε τό πᾶν. Στά σκοτεινά χαντάκια στοιβάχτηκαν, σέ στάσεις εἰρωνικές, οἱ καρυάτιδες, οἱ ποθοκρατόρισσες τῶν ἐρωτικῶν μας χρόνων. Τό περίφημό τους χαμόγελο ἐπέταξε μακρυά κι᾽ ἀνθεῖ τώρα σέ κάτι χαμένα ἐρημονήσια. Τ᾽ ἀστροπελέκι μᾶς δείχνει τό δρόμο. Ἐμπρός! Στά Γάλβανα τῆς Λυκαονίας, ἐκεῖ θ᾽ ἀναπαυθοῦμε. Ἀφοῦ στεφθοῦν τά εὐγενικά μέτωπά μας μέ ἄνθη ροδιᾶς, ἀφοῦ προσφέρουμε τίς νενομισμένες σπονδές στά πουλιά. Ἐκεῖ, πού μέσα στά ξύλινα μεγαλόπρεπα τεμένη τῆς παλαιᾶς πρωτεούσης θά σφάξουμε τό νέο μοσχάρι, καί θ᾽ ἀναβλύσει μέσ᾽ ἀπ᾽ τό χυμένο αἷμα φλογοβόλα κολώνα. Ἐκεῖ πού ζώστηκαν τά ἰθυφαλλικά μπαϊράκια κόρες ὡραιότερες κι᾽ ἀπ᾽ τά πιό ἀπροσδόκητα συμπεράσματα τῆς δυναμίτιδος. Ἐκεῖ πού ζεῖ ὁ Ἕλλην Παντελᾶς ἐν μέσῳ τῶν ἀγρίων Σουδανῶν, ὅπου τά λουλούδια τά πιό φωτεινά εἶναι σοφά ἀπομεινάρια νεκρῶν καλλονῶν. Ἐκεῖ πού εἶναι ἀνώφελα κι᾽ ἄσκοπα τά δάκρυα τοῦ καρχαρία, οἱ αἰνιγματώδεις δεήσεις τοῦ Ζαχαρία, οἱ ψυχροί ἐναγκαλισμοί τοῦ πιγκουΐνου. Ἐκεῖ πού τά δάκρυα τά πύρινα τῶν τελευταίων αὐτοκρατόρων καί οἱ ἐρωτικοί σπασμοί εἶναι ἕν καί τό αὐτό πρόσωπο. Ὅπου ἡ προσφορά τοῦ λοστρόμου στ᾽ ἀχνάρια τῆς ὑποτεινούσης τῶν ἀνωμάλων ἕλξεων θά συνοδεύεται μέ ὑπόκρουσιν ἅρπας καί ἀγγέλων. Κι᾽ ὅπου ἡ μεγαλόπρεπη παρουσία μας θά σημαίνει τήν διά παντός ἐπικράτησιν τῆς ἐλευθερίας, καί τοῦ πόθου τῆς ἐλευθερίας, σ᾽ ὁλόκληρο τόν κόσμο.

BINARY AUTOMATISM

Be mindful! Take care! Watch out! Already the winds that are blowing have brought mysterious messages to our ears. Everything around us is fraught with peril. Not a neighborhood remains that is not racked by fear. Every object conceals a soul within it. Come, let us leave. The time is ticking. The rusted weathercock is crowing to us frenziedly in the night. The wheel wells have ceased and the blind horses have become one with the plants known as "begonias." Let us leave. Come on. Let us leave for somewhere far. For Galvana! For Galvana! There, where lies our salvation, oblivion's sheltered harbor. Tranquility. There!... Scapegoats of love, night's ascetic wayfarers, dawn's proud walkers, light the sea beacon. Come whoever has the mettle, whoever's heart is truly in it. Let us not delay with futile reviews of the past. The times are uncertain. The streets are unsafe, and in many places the deluge has left nothing uncovered. Stacked in dark ditches, in ironic postures, are the caryatids, the keepers of desire in our amorous years. Their renowned smile has taken wing for afar and now blossoms on remote barren islands. The lightning bolt shows us the way. Come on! To Galvana in Lykaonia, there we will find rest. After our noble brows have been crowned with pomegranate blossom, after we have offered due libations to the birds. There, where in the majestic wooden shrines of the old capital we will slaughter the new calf, and from its spilt blood will sprout a flaming column. There, where maidens fairer than dynamite's most unexpected outcomes buckled on the phallic standards. There where Pantelas the Greek lives amidst the savage Sudanese, where the brightest flowers are sage remains of dead beauties. There where the shark's tears, Zacharias' puzzling prayers and the penguin's cold embraces are futile and pointless. There, where the burning tears of the last emperors and passion's convulsions are one and the same person. Where the boatswain's contribution to the traces of the hypotenuse of irregular attractions will be to the accompaniment of harp and angels. And where our majestic presence will signify the prevalence once and for all of freedom, and of the longing for freedom, throughout the world.

ΠΟΙΗΜΑ ΠΟΥ ΤΟΥ ΛΕΙΠΕΙ Η ΧΑΡΑ
ΑΦΙΕΡΩΜΕΝΟ ΣΕ ΓΥΝΑΙΚΑ ΥΠΕΡΟΧΗ
ΔΩΡΗΤΡΙΑ ΠΟΘΟΥ ΚΑΙ ΓΑΛΗΝΗΣ

ἀφοῦ τό θέλεις
γυναῖκα ἁρμονική κι' ὡραία
ἔτσι καθώς ἕνα βράδυ τοῦ Μαΐου ἐτοποθέτησες ἁπλά κι' εὐγενικά μιάν
    ἄσπρη ζωντανή γαρδένια
ἀνάμεσα στά νεκρά λουλούδια
μέσα στό παλιό –ἰταλικό μοῦ φαίνεται –βάζο μέ παραστάσεις γαλάζιες
    τεράτων καί χιμαιρῶν
ἔλα
πέσε στά χέρια μου
καί χάρισέ μου
–ἀφοῦ τό θέλεις –
τή θλίψη τοῦ πρασίνου βλέμματός σου
τή βαθειά πίκρα τῶν κόκκινων χειλιῶν σου
τή νύχτα τῶν μυστηρίων πού εἶναι πλεγμένη μέσα στά μακρυά μαλλιά
    σου
τή σποδό τοῦ ὑπέροχου σώματός σου

POEM DEVOID OF JOY
DEDICATED TO A WONDERFUL WOMAN
DONATOR OF LONGING AND SERENITY

since you so wish
woman graceful and fair
just as one evening in May simply and gently you placed a
     living white gardenia
between the dead flowers
in the old vase – an Italian one I think – with its scenes
     of blue monsters and chimeras
come
fall into my arms
and give me
– since you so wish –
the sorrow in your green gaze
the deep rancor in your red lips
the night of mysteries plaited in your long hair
the ashes of your wonderful body

ΘΕΑΝΩ

οἱ μεγάλοι Μύστες
μέ τά θερμά
ὡραῖα κορμιά
κάτω
ἀπό τά λινά φορέματα
μέ τίς ἁρμονικές
πτυχώσεις
μοῦ παρουσιάστηκαν
στή τζαμαρία τοῦ παρισινοῦ καφφενείου
καί μέ νοήματα
ζητῆσαν
νά βγῶ καί νάν τούς ἀνταμώσω ἔξω

στό δρόμο τό λιθόστρωτο γυάλιζε κάτω ἀπ' τή νυχτερινή νεροποντή
κι' ἀντανακλοῦσε φῶτα
φωτεινά σχήματα
καί προβολεῖς αὐτοκινήτων

λησμόνησα νά πῶ πώς ἡ σκηνή αὐτή ἔλαβε χώρα στήν Κωνσταντινούπολη
κάπου στήν Ξηροκρήνη –κοντά στά Παλαιά Τείχη –
καί μάλιστα ἐκεῖνο τό βράδυ ὁ γειτονικός κινηματογράφος ἔτυχε νά
    παίζη
τήν περίφημη ταινία
Pax tibi Marce Evangelista meus

THEANO

the great Mystics
with their warm
fine bodies
beneath
linen garments
with symmetrical
folds
appeared to me
in the Paris café window
and beckoned to me
through gestures
to go outside to meet them

on the street the pavement glistened from the nocturnal
        downpour
and reflected lights
bright shapes
and car headlights

I forgot to mention that this scene took place in Constantinople
somewhere in Xirokrini – near the Old Walls –
and actually that evening the local cinema happened to be
        showing
that famous film
Pax tibi Marce Evangelista meus

ΚΗΠΟΙ ΜΕΣ' ΣΤΟ ΛΙΟΠΥΡΙ

τό λευκό σῶμα αὐτῆς τῆς γυναικός
φωτίζονταν
ἐκ τῶν ἔσωθεν
μ' ἕνα φῶς τόσο λαμπρό
ὥστε
ἐδέησε
νά πάρω τή λάμπα
καί νά τήν
ἀκουμπήσω
χάμω στό πάτωμα
πού
νά μπορέσουνε
οἱ σκιές
τῶν δύο τόσο εὐγενικῶν μας σωμάτων
νά προβληθοῦν
στόν
τοῖχο
μέ μίαν ἱερατικότητα βιβλική

ἡ λάμπα ἔκαιε συνεχῶς
–ἡ πηγή τοῦ πετρελαίου εἴτανε ἀνεξάντλητη –
ὅλη τή νύχτα
τήν ἀκόλουθη μέρα
κι' ὅλη τήν ἐπομένη νύχτα
χάμω στό πάτωμα
πάνω στά πλούσια
στοιβαγμένα
χαλιά
τά ὡραιότερα φροῦτα

GARDENS IN THE SCORCHING SUN

this woman's white body
was lit
from within
by a light so bright
that
she implored
me to take the lamp
and to
place it
on the floor
so
the shadows
of our two most noble bodies
might be projected
on
the wall
with biblical sanctimoniousness

the lamp burned constantly
– the supply of oil was inexhaustible –
all night long
the next day
and all the following night
on the floor
on the rich
piles
of rugs
the finest fruits

τά λαμπρότερα λουλούδια
–ὅπου ἐπικρατοῦσαν
οἱ πικροδάφνες
ἄσπρες καί ρόδινες –

ἡ ἀτμόσφαιρα –συμβολική –ἀπό ἕνα κίτρινο: ἕνα κίτρινο χρυσό

the loveliest flowers
– prevalent among which
were the white and pink
oleanders –

the atmosphere – a symbolic one – was of yellow: a yellow
    gold

ΠΙΚΑΣΣΟ

εἰς Παῦλον Πικασσό

ὁ ταυρομάχος τώρα πλέον ζεῖ στήν Ἐλασσόνα
εἰς τή λιθόστρωτη πλατεῖα κάτω ἀπ' τά πλατάνια
κι' ὁ καφφετζῆς ἀέναα πηγαινοέρχεται κι' ἀνανεώνει
τόν καφφέ στό φλυτζάνι καί τόν καπνό στόν ἀργελέ τοῦ ταυρομάχου
ὡς ὅτου νά περάσουνε νοσταλγικά
τῆς μέρας οἱ ὧρες
καί συναχτοῦν πουλιῶν μυριάδες
μέσ' στίς πυκνές τίς φυλλωσιές τῶν πλατανιῶνε
ὅπου σημαίνει πώς ὁ ἥλιος δύει

τότε οἱ συνωμότες ἕνας ἕνας γλυστρᾶνε στό σοκάκι
σιωπηλά ὡς πέφτει ἡ νύχτα καί βοηθᾶ τους
ἀπαρατήρητοι νά συναχτοῦν κι' αὐτοί σάν
τά πουλιά
ἐκεῖ πού θέλουν
καί δάκρυα βαρειά κυλοῦν ἀπό τά δόλια τους τά μάτια

καί ἡ μητέρα ὅπου ζητεῖ ν' ἀναχαιτίση τούς φασίστες
μέσα στό σκοτεινό δωμάτιο κεῖ πού σιγομιλοῦν οἱ συνωμότες
καί κρέμονται ἀπ' τό ταβάνι πιπεριές γιά νά στεγνώνουν
μέ τά ροζιάρικα τά χέρια πού τά κοσμοῦν ροδάρια
βγάζει τῆς λάμπας τό γυαλί καί τήν ἀνάφτει
καί τά ροζιάρικα πάλι τά χέρια πού τά λερῶσαν τά πετρέλαια
ἥσυχα ἥσυχα τά σφουγγίζει στήν ποδιά της

καί καθώς εἴπαμε ὅτι ποθεῖ ν' ἀναχαιτίση τούς φονιάδες
παίρν' ἡ γριά τή λάμπα ἀπ' τό τραπέζι
κι' ἀνοίγει τό παράθυρο μέ βιάση
κι' ὄξω τεντώνει
– μέσ' στή νύχτα –
τή χερούκλα πού κρατᾶ τή λάμπα

PICASSO

to Pablo Picasso

the toreador now lives in Elassona
in the cobbled square beneath the plane trees
and the café-owner ever comes and goes and replenishes
the coffee in the cup and the tobacco in the toreador's narghile
until nostalgically
the day's hours pass
and myriads of birds gather
in the plane trees' thick leafage
which means that the sun is setting

then one by one the conspirators slip into the back street
silently as night falls and helps them
inconspicuous to gather too
like the birds
where they want
and large tears roll from their wretched eyes

and the mother who wants to contain the fascists
in the somber room where the conspirators whisper
and peppers hang from the wall to dry
with her callused hands adorned by rosaries
removes the lamp's glass and lights it
and quietly wipes these same callused hands
smeared with the oil on her apron

and wanting as we said to contain the murderers
the old woman takes the lamp from the table
and hastily opens the window
stretching out
– into the night –
the large hand holding the lamp

γριά μάνα! τῆς φωνάζουν
ποῦ τήν πᾶς τή λάμπα;
ὅμως μέσ' στά χωράφια τῆς Ἀβίλας δές σαλέψαν
ὕποπτες σκιές μ' αὐτόματα στήν ἀμασκάλη
κι' ὡς ἀπό μακρυά ἐφάνταζε σάν ἄστρο
τό φῶς πού εἶχε βγαλθῆ στό παραθύρι
ἄρχισαν λίγο λίγο ν' ἀντηχοῦν κιθάρες

κι' οἱ γύφτισσες ἐπιάσαν νά χορεύουν
μέ τίς ὡραῖες λαγόνες καί τά πολύχρωμα ἀνεμιζούμενα πλατειά
φουστάνια
ἐνῶ ἀπ' τά θερμά βαμμένα στόματά τους ἴδια κραυγές πόνου
ἐξέφευγαν τοῦ τραγουδιοῦ τά λόγια:
«θά σοῦ πῶ τή μοναξιά μου μέ τό Soleares»

κι' οἱ majos λυσσάγαν πάνω στίς κιθάρες
καί τά φασιστικά καθάρματα πολυβολούσανε τά πλήθη
κι' αὐτές μέ τά μεταξωτά γοβάκια τους
– μέ τά ψηλά τακούνια –
χάμω –πάνω στό καρντερίμι –τσαλαπατοῦσαν τήν καρδιά μου

τότες ἐγίνηκε «πού νά σοῦ φύγη τό καφάσι»
σάν ἕνας ταῦρος κοκκινότριχος πετάχτηκε στή μέση
φλόγες καθώς τοῦ βγαίνανε ἀπ' τά ρουθούνια
κι' οἱ μπαντερίλλιες τοῦ βελόνιαζαν ὀδυνηρά τό σβέρκο καί τήν πλάτη

κι' ἄρχισε δῶ καί κεῖ νά κουτουλάη
νά ξεκοιλιάζη
νά λιανίζη σάρκες μέ τά κερατά του
ψηλά στόν ἀέρα νά τινάζη
ὅσους χτυποῦσε
καί νά σωριάζωνται βουνό κουφάρια ἕνα γύρο
ἀλόγων ἄνθρωπων
μέσ' σέ ποτάμια αἷμα

old woman! they call to her
where are you taking the lamp?
but look moving in the fields of Avila were
suspicious shadows with automatics underarm
and from afar the light held out of the window
looked like a star
gradually guitars began to resound

and gypsy women took up the dance
with their lovely loins and colorful billowing wide skirts
while like cries of pain from their warm reddened mouths
the song's lyrics escaped
"I'll tell you of my solitude with Soleares"

and the majos went wild on the guitars
and the fascist rabble shot at the crowds
and those women with their satin slippers
– with their high heels –
on the ground – on the cobbles – trampled on my heart

it was then that something to "blow your mind" happened
when a red-haired bull appeared on the scene
the flames faring from its nostrils
and banderillas painfully piercing its neck and back

and here and there it began to butt
to gore
to carve flesh with its horns
to toss high in the air
whoever it struck
so all around piled the carcasses
of horses of men
in rivers of blood

(τό σβέρκο καί τή ράχη του όδυνηρά ΚΟΣΜΟΥΣΑΝ μπαντερίλλιες)

κι' οί κόρες μέ τούς ώραίους μαστούς άνάσκελα έξαπλωθῆκαν χάμω
καί μέσ' στά ώραῖα μάτια τους δύανε
κι' άνατέλλαν
ἥλιοι

(banderillas painfully ADORNED its neck and back)

and the maidens with their beautiful breasts lay down on their
    backs
and in their radiant eyes suns
set and
rose

OPNEON 1748

(ἑρμηνεία τῶν ζωγράφων)

καλός ἤ κακός ἵμερος ὡδήγησε
τήν ἀμφιλύκην τῶν
νεαρῶν πελταστῶν
στ' ἀπάτητα ὄρη τῆς νύχτας
μέσα στ' ἄγρια ρουμάνια τῆς Ὀρθοδοξίας
στίς πυκνές συστάδες τῶν κυπαρισσιῶν τοῦ πανικοῦ
στήν ἠθική προβολή
σκληρῆς Μοίρας σέ κιονοστοιχία ὄρθρου καί ληθάργου;

ποιός νἄταν ὁ πρωτοστάτης
τῆς ἀνταρσίας;
τῆς φήμης;
τοῦ ἔρωτος;
ὁ ρήτωρ;
ὑπῆρξαν πιστοί στά κελεύσματα
–ποιῶν ἄλλων: τῶν κελευστῶν –
πατροκτόνοι καί παιδερασταί καλοί
μέ μόνη τήν
παρασημαντική νεκροφιλίας
ὡς δικαίωση
στίς ἀλλεπάλληλες –ἀπιστεύτου δριμύτητος –ἐπιθέσεις
τῶν δοξογράφων;

ἄραγες –ἀκούοντας, ὦ παῖδες, –τῶν φιλοπόνων ζωγράφων ἡ μεταφυσική
    πολιτεία
μέσα στούς ἀναρτημένους πίνακες νά βρίσκεται κρυμμένη;

κι' ἐνῶ πέφτουν κατακέφαλα
τά πολεμικά σκεπάρνια
καί βουΐζουν οἱ ρεματιές

VULTURE 1748

(painters' interpretation)

was it a good or bad libido that led
the morning twilight of the
young targeteers
to the untrodden peaks of night
in Orthodoxy's wild thickets
in the dense clusters of panic's cypresses
in the moral projection
of a harsh Fate in the colonnade of reveille and lethargy?

who was the instigator
of the mutiny?
of the rumor?
of the passion?
the orator?
were they loyal to the command
– of who else: of the commanders –
fine patricides and pederasts
with only the
parasemantics of necrophilia
as justification
in the successive – incredibly harsh – attacks
of the doxographers?

perhaps – listen, o lads, – the industrious painters'
        metaphysical realm
is to be found hidden in the hanging paintings?

and while the war hatchets
rain down upon heads
and the ravines hum

ἀπό τόν ὄλεθρο τῆς μάχης
καί τά τροπάρια
πολεμιστῶν ἁγίων
ἀκούγεται φωνή:

«Μίρκο Κράλη, τί ζητᾶς;
ἐδῶ δέν εἶναι παῖξε γέλασε:
ἐδῶ εἶναι Μπαλκάνια»

with the destruction of battle
and the hymns
of warrior saints
a voice is heard:

"Mirko Kralje, what is it you want?
this is no playground:
this is the Balkans"

ΕΛΕΟΝΩΡΑ II

ἡ νύχτα λύσσαξε στό παραθύρι
αὐτά εἶναι –πού λέν –τοῦ Διοκλητιανοῦ τά παλάτια;
ἀκολουθῶ τά ἴχνη τοῦ βλέμματός σου πάνω στή θάλασσα
οἱ μυστικές χαρές τοῦ σώματός σου εἶναι ξαπλωμένες πάνω στά βράχια
    στό περιγιάλι
ὁ ἥλιος ἔζωσε μέσα στά μάτια τά πιό ψηλά του κυπαρίσσια
ἅς προσχωρήσουμε στίς μουσικές τῶν τροπικῶν
τ' ἄϋλα λόγια πόθου καί πίστεως γρηγοροῦν
Ἀμαληκῖται γρηγοροῦν
τ' ἄλογα πού καλπάζουν
τ' ἀμάξι ἄφισε τώρα τό δρόμο καί προχωρεῖ στήν καρδιά τοῦ δάσους
ταχύτης καί ἀδράνεια
κόρη τῆς Ἀλασίας ὡραιοτική
ὑπερφίαλοι κι' ἀλαζόνες καί βέβηλοι ἐρασταί
– ὅμως ἐρασταί –
ἐδῶ ἐγκατεστάθηκαν ὑδραυλικά πριόνια ἀνάμεσα στό χῶμα τό κόκκινο
    καί τό πράσινο τῶν πεύκων
ἐκεῖ τό τέμενος τῆς Σοφίας
πιό πέρα τό γεφύρι τό κάστρο ἡ σπηλιά
πού ζοῦμε
τά σώματά μας θά χαθοῦν θά σβύσουν
ἀπό μᾶς θά μείνη μέχρι τῆς συντελείας τῶν αἰώνων
αὐτό τό «σέ ἀγαπῶ» πού σοῦ ψιθύρισα στίς ὧρες μας τίς πιό κρυφές

ELEONORA II

the night raged at the window
are these – as they say – Diocletian's palaces?
I follow the traces of your gaze over the sea
your body's secret joys recline upon the rocks on the shore
the sun enclosed in the eyes its tallest cypresses
let us turn to the tropics' melodies
the intangible words of longing and faith are vigilant
Amalekites are vigilant
the horses that are galloping
the car has now left the road and proceeds into the heart of the
      forest
speed and inertia
Alasia's fairest maiden
arrogant and conceited and profane lovers
– yet lovers –
here hydraulic saws were set between the soil's red and the
      pines' green
there the shrine of Wisdom
and further the bridge the castle the cave
where we live
our bodies will vanish will fade
what will remain of us till the end of time
is that "I love you" whispered to you in our most secret
      moments

Ο ΜΑΘΗΤΕΥΟΜΕΝΟΣ ΤΗΣ ΟΔΥΝΗΣ

ξεκίνησε αὐγή
–χαράματα –
νά κλέψη
τ᾽ ἄστρα
ξεκίνησε
νύχτα
καί σκότωσε
ὅλα τά
ὄνειρα
αὐτό τό ἄγαλμα

– καί μπλέχονταν
ὡς βάδιζε
τά γυμνά πόδια του
στούς βάτους
καί μάτωναν στ᾽ ἀγκάθια –

καί τά εὐγενικά εὐλογημένα χέρια του
ἴδια πουλιά τῆς Ἄνοιξης χαϊδεῦαν
τά γεράνια π᾽ ὀνομάτιζε μιά νύχτα ἀγάπης
καί τοῦ παρθενικοῦ ὀνειροκρίτη της
τίς βαθειές πόρπες

καί τῶν βυζιῶν της $\left\{ \begin{array}{l} \text{τις κραυγές} \\ \text{τίς κόκκινες} \\ \text{και τους κρυφούς} \\ \text{και τους κρυφούς θυσάνους} \end{array} \right.$

GRIEF'S APPRENTICE

this statue
set out at dawn
– at break of day –
to steal
the stars
it set out
at night
and killed
all the
dreams

– and as it walked
its bare feet
became tangled
in the bushes
and bled on the thorns –

and its gentle gifted hands
like to birds in spring caressed
the geraniums that it named a night of love
and the deep clasps
of her virginal dream-interpreter

and her breasts'   {   red
                   cries
                   and hidden
                   tassels

ΕΛΕΥΣΙΣ

... N'en déplaise à quelque impatients fossoyeurs, je prétends en savoir plus long qu'eux sur ce qui porrait signifier au surréalisme son heure dernière: ce serait la naissance d'un mouvement plus émancipateur. Un tel mouvement, de par la force dynamique même que nous continuons à placer audessus de tout, mes meilleurs amis et moi nous tiendrions à honneur, du reste, de nous y rallier aussitôt. Il faut croire que le nouveau mouvement n'a pas été, n'est pas encore...

ANDRÉ BRETON: Lecture at Yale.

ΤΟ ΓΕΡΑΚΙ

Ἕνα γέλιο γυναικεῖο ἀκούγεται μακρυά. Μιά κυρία γελάει κάπου, μακρυά μας, κι' ὁ ἄνεμος φέρνει τόν ἦχο τοῦ γέλιου της μέχρις ἐδῶ. Μέχρις ἐδῶ, σ' αὐτό τό ἔρμο περιγιάλι, κάτω ἀπ' τό μολυβή οὐρανό, κοντά στ' ἀφρισμένα κύματα, ὅπου, στή στάση «τρεῖς φιλόσοφοι στ' ἀκροθαλάσσι», ζοῦμε μέσα σέ μιά καταθλιπτική μοναξιά. Στά γυμνά πόδια μας φυτρώνουν, λίγο-λίγο, φτερά. Ἴσως ἐμεῖς νἄμαστε αὐτός ὁ θεός Ἑρμῆς, τόν καιρό τῆς νειότης του. Αὐτή ἡ φοβερή μοναξιά μας! Αὐτή ἡ τραγική μοναξιά σας! Γιατί, δέν χωρεῖ καμμιάν ἀμφιβολία, εἴμαστε μόνοι, μόνοι, πάντα μόνοι, αἰώνια, βασανιστικά, μόνοι. Ὅλοι. Ὅλοι. Ἐμεῖς, ἐσεῖς, ὅλοι. Ὅμως ἐγώ εἶμαι ὁ μόνος, πάλι, πού δέν τή δέχεται τήν αἰσχρή τούτη καταδίκη, καί διαμαρτύρουμαι, καί χτυπιέμαι, καί τό φωνάζω. Μόνον ἐγώ. Καί μιά λεπτομέρεια: ἡ κυρία δέν γελοῦσε. Ἔκλαιγε. Μᾶς εἶχε γελάσει ὁ ἄνεμος. Ὁ ἄνεμος παρεμόρφωσε τόν ἦχο. Στό μολυβή οὐρανό πετοῦν πουλιά. Μιά βάρκα παλεύει πάνω στ' ἀφρισμένα κύματα. Εἶναι μακρυά, ἀλλ' ὁλοέν πλησιάζει.

From: *ELEUSIS* (1948)

... N'en déplaise à quelque impatients fossoyeurs, je prétends en savoir plus long qu'eux sur ce qui porrait signifier au surréalisme son heure dernière: ce serait la naissance d'un mouvement plus émancipateur. Un tel mouvement, de par la force dynamique même que nous continuons à placer audessus de tout, mes meilleurs amis et moi nous tiendrions à honneur, du reste, de nous y rallier aussitôt. Il faut croire que le nouveau mouvement n'a pas été, n'est pas encore...

ANDRÉ BRETON: Lecture at Yale.

THE HAWK

Female laughter is heard afar. Somewhere, far from us, a woman is laughing, and the wind brings the sound of her laughter here. Here, to this lonely shore, beneath a leaden sky, beside the waves' foam, where, with a stance of "three philosophers on the seashore," we live in a depressing solitude. Wings slowly sprout on our naked feet. Perhaps we are the god Hermes, in his youth. That terrible solitude of ours! That tragic solitude of ours! For there is not the slightest doubt, we are alone, alone, ever alone, eternally, tortuously alone. Everyone. Everyone. All of us, all of you, everyone. Though, again, I am the only one not to accept this disgraceful sentence, and I protest, and rail and cry out. I alone. And one detail: the woman was not laughing. She was crying. We were deceived by the wind. The wind distorted the sound. Birds fly in the leaden sky. A boat struggles atop the waves' foam. It is far off, but is ever getting nearer.

ΤΑ ΧΡΥΣΑ ΟΡΟΠΕΔΙΑ

στό Γκαμπόν
στίς ὄχθες τοῦ Ὀγκουέ
φιάξανε μιά μουτσούνα
κι' ὅποιος τή φορᾶ
παριστάνει
τό φεγγάρι καί τόν ἥλιο
τήν ὥρα τοῦ χοροῦ

γιά μάτια τῆς ἐβάλανε μιά περιστέρα
γιά ματόκλαδα ἐβάλαν τό παράπονο τῆς περιστέρας
γιά στόμα τῆς ἐβάλαν τ' ὄνομα τοῦ Μπολιβάρ
μιά τρύπα μ' ἀναμμένα κάρβουνα
καί δάκρυα
κι' ἱερά λείψανα μαρτύρων
εἶναι τό γένι της
κι' ὁ ποταμός Ὀγκουέ εἶναι τό χτένι της κι' ἡ ἀγάπη της

τώρα ἡ βάρκα μας πλέει ἁπαλά στόν ποταμό
ἀπό τίς ὄχθες μᾶς γνέφουν καί μᾶς χαιρετοῦν τά δέντρα
κι' ἐγώ κρατῶ πάνω στό στῆθος μου τή
μάσκα
λέω τίς προσευχές τῆς Βιθυνίας
βυθίζω ἁπαλά τό χέρι μου στό νερό τό χλιαρό

στίς ἐκβολές τοῦ ποταμοῦ
τά σκυλόψαρα μᾶς βλέπουνε λοξά
καί τραβοῦν πέρα
– δέν ἁρμόζουνε θωπεῖες στά σκυλόψαρα –
χελιδονόψαρα
πετοῦν τριγύρω μας
στό πρόσταγμά μας

THE GOLDEN PLATEAUX

in Gabon
on the shores of the Ogooué
they fashioned a mask
and whoever wears it
represents
the moon and sun
during the dance

for its eyes they used a dove
for its eyelids the dove's complaint
for its mouth the name of Bolivár
a hole with lighted coals
and tears
and the sacred relics of martyrs
are its beard
and the River Ogooué its comb and its love

now our boat floats gently on the river
from the shores the trees nod and greet us
and I hold to my breast the
mask
recite the prayers of Bithynia
gently dip my hand into the tepid water

at the river's estuary
dogfish look at us askance
and make way
– caresses do not befit dogfish –
flying fish
leap all around us
at our command

τά φοινικόδεντρα
κατά τό σχῆμα τους
εἶν' ἄλλοτε ἡ βεντάλια
ἄλλοτε τό παρασόλι τοῦ Παρασκευᾶ
τήν ὥρα τοῦ χοροῦ

τό πουλί μου
εἶναι
τό
πουλί
μου
καί πάντα μου
Εὐθαλία Ἀθανασία Θάμαρ Καλλιόπη
σᾶς ἀγαπῶ

the palm trees
in keeping with their shapes
are sometimes fans
sometimes Paraskevas' parasol
during the dance

my bird
is
my
bird
and always
Euthalia Athanassia Tamar Calliope
I will
love you

Η ΝΕΑ ΛΑΟΥΡΑ

οἱ τεράστιοι θησαυροί
– γιά τούς ὁποίους τόσα θρυλλοῦνται –
τῆς πτωχῆς
περιαλγοῦς
κόρης
εἶναι
τά μόνα
χείλη της
τά μόνα
ἡδύγευστα χείλη της

πόσο μοῦ λείπουν καί πόσο τά νοσταλγῶ
– καί τά δοξάζω –
σά βρίσκομαι μακρυά
νά περιπλανιέμαι
σέ τοῦτα τ' ἄχαρα
τ' ἀπίστευτα ταξείδια
πού κάθε τόσο
ἐπιχειρῶ

κι' ὅμως πόσο
τά χαίρομαι
– καί τά δοξάζω –
σά βρίσκομαι
κοντά
της

εἶναι ἡ ζωή

βγαίνει καί παίρνει γύρα
σοκάκια
καί μαχαλάδες

THE NEW LAURA

the vast treasures
– about which so much is rumored –
of the poor
distressed
girl
are
her singular
lips
her singular
luscious lips

how I miss them and how I yearn for them
– and praise them –
when I am far away
wandering
on these thankless
incredible journeys
that every so often
I undertake

and yet how
I rejoice in them
– and praise them –
when I find myself
beside
her

she is life

she emerges and takes to
the back streets
and neighborhoods

καί μέ λυγμούς
μέ φωνάζει
καί μέ ζητᾶ

ἔλα
μήν κάνεις ἔτσι
εἴμαστε Ἕλληνες
σύ εἶσαι
– τί θαῦμα! –
μιά κόρη
Ἑλληνίς

ὅταν κοιμοῦμαι
τά λουλούδια τῆς ἀμασχάλης σου
ἔρχονται
καί μοῦ θωπεύουν
ὅλο τό κορμί
καί σάν ζωγραφίζω
τότε
ἔρχονται
τά μάτια σου
τά ὡραῖα
στήν ἄκρια τοῦ χρωστῆρα μου
καί
σεργιανίζουν
πάνω
σ' ὅλη τήν ἐπιφάνεια
τοῦ
μουσαμᾶ

γιά νά ξέρης:
σ' ἔχω κάνει ἀθάνατη

and sobbing
she calls to me
and seeks me

come
don't go on like that
we are Greeks
you are
– what a miracle! –
a girl
a Greek girl

when I sleep
the flowers from your armpit
come
and caress
all my body
and when I paint
then
your eyes
your beautiful eyes
come
to the edge of my palette
and
wander
over
the entire surface
of the
canvass

so you might know:
I have made you immortal

ΥΜΝΟΣ ΔΟΞΑΣΤΙΚΟΣ
ΓΙΑ ΤΙΣ ΓΥΝΑΙΚΕΣ Π' ΑΓΑΠΟΥΜΕ

Dans les peuples vraiment libres, les femmes sont libres et adorées.
SAINT-JUST

T.

εἶν' οἱ γυναῖκες π' ἀγαποῦμε σάν τά ρόδια
ἔρχονται καί μᾶς βρίσκουνε
τίς νύχτες
ὅταν βρέχη
μέ τούς μαστούς τους καταργοῦν τή μοναξιά μας
μέσ' στά μαλλιά μας εἰσχωροῦν βαθειά
καί τά κοσμοῦνε
σά δάκρυα
σάν ἀκρογιάλια φωτεινά
σά ρόδια

εἶν' οἱ γυναῖκες π' ἀγαποῦμε κύκνοι
τά πάρκα τους
ζοῦν μόνο μέσα στήν καρδιά μας
εἶν' τά φτερά τους
τά φτερά ἀγγέλων
τ' ἀγάλματά τους εἶναι τό κορμί μας
οἱ ὡραῖες δεντροστοιχίες εἶν' αὐτές οἱ ἴδιες
ὀρθές στήν ἄκρια τῶν ἐλαφρῶν ποδιῶν
τους
μᾶς πλησιάζουν
κι' εἶναι σάν μᾶς φιλοῦν
στά μάτια
κύκνοι

εἶν' οἱ γυναῖκες π' ἀγαποῦμε λίμνες
στούς καλαμιῶνες τους

HYMN OF PRAISE FOR THE WOMEN WE LOVE

Dans les peuples vraiment libres, les femmes sont libres et adorées.
SAINT-JUST

T.

the women we love are like pomegranates
they come and find us
at night
when it rains
with their breasts they end our loneliness
deeply they penetrate into our hair
and adorn it
like tears
like luminous shores
like pomegranates

the women we love are swans
their parks
live only in our hearts
their wings are
angels' wings
their statues are our bodies
the lovely lines of trees are their very selves
erect on the tips of their light
feet
they approach us
and it is as if we are kissed
on our eyes
by swans

the women we love are lakes
on their reeds

τά φλογερά τά χείλια μας σφυρίζουν
τά ὡραῖα πουλιά μας κολυμποῦνε στά νερά τους
κι' ὕστερα
σάν πετοῦν
τά καθρεφτίζουν
–ὑπερήφανα ὡς εἶν' –
οἱ λίμνες
κι' εἶναι στίς ὄχθες τους οἱ λεῦκες λύρες
πού ἡ μουσική τους πνίγει μέσα μας
τίς πίκρες
κι' ὡς πλημμυροῦν τό εἶναι μας
χαρά
γαλήνη
εἶν' οἱ γυναῖκες π' ἀγαποῦμε
λίμνες

εἶν' οἱ γυναῖκες π' ἀγαποῦμε σάν σημαῖες
στοῦ πόθου τούς ἀνέμους κυματίζουν
τά μακρυά μαλλιά τους
λάμπουνε
τίς νύχτες
μέσ' στίς θερμές παλάμες τους κρατοῦνε
τή ζωή μας
εἶν' οἱ ἁπαλές κοιλιές τους
ὁ οὐράνιος θόλος
εἶναι οἱ πόρτες μας
τά παραθύρια μας
οἱ στόλοι
τ' ἄστρα μας συνεχῶς ζοῦνε κοντά τους
τά χρώματά τους εἶναι
τά λόγια τῆς ἀγάπης
τά χείλη τους
εἶναι ὁ
ἥλιος τό φεγγάρι

their ardent lips whistle to us
our beautiful birds bathe in their waters
and then
when they fly up
they are mirrored
– proud as they are –
by the lakes
and on their shores the poplars are lyres
whose music drowns
all bitterness within us
and as they inundate our being
with joy
with peace
the women we love are
lakes

the women we love are like flags
flying in desire's breezes
their long hair
shines
at night
in their warm palms they hold
our life
their soft bellies are
the celestial vault
they are our doors
our windows
fleets
our stars live forever beside them
their colors are
love's words
their lips
are the
sun the moon

καί τό πανί τους εἶν' τό μόνο σάβανο πού μᾶς ἁρμόζει:
εἶν' οἱ γυναῖκες π' ἀγαποῦμε σά σημαῖες

εἶν' οἱ γυναῖκες π' ἀγαποῦμε δάση
τό κάθε δέντρο τους εἶν' κι' ἕνα μήνυμα τοῦ πάθους
σάν μέσ' σ' αὐτά τά δάση
μᾶς πλανέψουνε
τά βήματά μας
καί χαθοῦμε
τότες εἶν'
ἀκριβῶς
πού βρίσκουμε τόν ἑαυτόνε μας
καί ζοῦμε
κι' ὅσο ἀπό μακρυά ἀκοῦμε νἄρχωνται οἱ μπόρες
ἤ καί μᾶς φέρνει
ὁ ἄνεμος
τίς μουσικές καί τούς θορύβους
τῆς γιορτῆς
ἤ τίς φλογέρες τοῦ κινδύνου
τίποτε –φυσικά –δέ μπορεῖ πιά νά μᾶς φοβίση
ὡς οἱ πυκνές οἱ φυλλωσιές
ἀσφαλῶς μᾶς προστατεύουν
μιά πού οἱ γυναῖκες π' ἀγαποῦμε εἶναι σά δάση

εἶν' οἱ γυναῖκες π' ἀγαποῦμε σάν λιμάνια
(μόνος σκοπός
προορισμός
τῶν ὡραίων καραβιῶν μας)
τά μάτια τους
εἶν' οἱ κυματοθραῦστες
οἱ ὦμοι τους εἶν' ὁ σηματοφόρος
τῆς χαρᾶς
οἱ μηροί τους
σειρά ἀμφορεῖς στίς προκυμαῖες
τά πόδια τους

and their linen the only shroud befitting us
the women we love are like flags

the women we love are forests
their every tree is a message of passion
when in these forests
our steps
mislead us
and we become lost
it is then
precisely
that we find ourselves
and live
and while from afar we hear the rains coming
or the wind
brings us
the melodies and noises
of the festivity
or the fifes of danger
nothing – of course – can frighten us any longer
as the dense foliage
naturally protects us
since the women we love are like forests

the women we love are like harbors
(the one goal
the destination
of our fine ships)
their eyes
are breakwaters
their shoulders are the semaphore
of joy
their thighs
a line of amphorae on the wharves
their legs

οἱ στοργικοί
μας
φάροι
–οἱ νοσταλγοί τίς ὀνομάζουν Κατερίνα –
εἶναι τά κύματά τους
οἱ ὑπέροχες θωπεῖες
οἱ Σειρῆνες τους δέν μᾶς γελοῦν
μόνε
μᾶς
δείχνουνε τό δρόμο
– φιλικές –
πρός τά λιμάνια: τίς γυναῖκες π᾽ ἀγαποῦμε

ἔχουν οἱ γυναῖκες π᾽ ἀγαποῦμε θεία τήν οὐσία
κι᾽ ὅταν σφιχτά στήν ἀγκαλιά μας
τίς κρατοῦμε
μέ τούς θεούς κι᾽ ἐμεῖς γινόμαστ᾽ ὅμοιοι
στηνόμαστε ὀρθοί σάν ἄγριοι πύργοι
τίποτε δέν εἶν᾽ πιά δυνατό νά μᾶς κλονίση
μέ τά λευκά τους χέρια
αὐτές
γύρω μας γαντζώνουν
κι᾽ ἔρχονται ὅλοι οἱ λαοί
τά ἔθνη
καί μᾶς προσκυνοῦνε
φωνάζουν
ἀθάνατο
στούς αἰῶνες
τ᾽ ὄνομά μας
γιατί οἱ γυναίκες π᾽ ἀγαποῦμε
τήν μεταδίνουν
καί σ᾽ ἐμᾶς
αὐτή
τή θεία τους
οὐσία

our
loving
beacons
– the more nostalgic call them Katerina –
their waves are
wonderful caresses
their Sirens do not deceive us
but
– friendly as they are –
show us
the way
to the harbors: the women we love

the women we love are divine in essence
and when in our embrace
we hold them tight
we too become like to gods
we stand erect like frightful towers
nothing can now shake us
with their white arms
they
clasp us all around
and all peoples and nations
come
and worship us
they cry out
our name
immortal
forever
for the women we love
impart
to us too
that
divine essence
of theirs

ΠΟΙΗΣΗ 1948

τούτη ἡ ἐποχή
τοῦ ἐμφυλίου σπαραγμοῦ
δέν εἶναι ἐποχή
γιά ποίηση
κι' ἄλλα παρόμοια:
σάν πάει κάτι
νά
γραφῆ
εἶναι
ὡς ἄν
νά γράφονταν
ἀπό τήν ἄλλη μεριά
ἀγγελτηρίων
θανάτου

γι' αὐτό καί
τά ποιήματά μου
εἶν' τόσο πικραμένα
(καί ποτέ –ἄλλωστε –δέν εἶσαν;)
κι' εἶναι
– πρό πάντων –
καί
τόσο
λίγα

POETRY 1948

this age
of civil strife
is no age
for poetry
and such like:
when something starts
to
be written
it is
as though
it were being written
on the back
of death
notices

which is why
my poems
are so bitter
(and when – indeed – were they not?)
and are
– above all –
also
so
few

Ο ΑΤΛΑΝΤΙΚΟΣ

Ἱλαρῶς διαπλέομεν ὠκεανόν...
Ψαλμός εὐαγγελιστῶν

Τί εἴμαστε; ποῦ πᾶμε;
PAUL GAUGUIN

τό καράβι ἠχεῖ
τό τραῖνο σφυρίζει
ἀπό τούς πυργίσκους τό σύνθημα δίνουν
τό νοῦ σας
τό ταξείδι ἀρχίζει
ἐλᾶτε
φεύγουμε
σέ ξένη γῆ

στόν καφφενέ τῆς λιθόστρωτης ἀρβανίτικης πλατείας
χαμένοι μέσ᾿ στό πλῆθος
τῆς ἥρεμης
ἀτάραχης συνηθισμένης πελατείας
ἐκεῖ πού βασιλεύει ἦθος
σεμνότης σιγή
δέν μένουμε πιά
τό ταξείδι μᾶς κράζει
ἐλᾶτε : φεύγουμε σέ ξένη γῆ

πᾶνε πιά οἱ ρεμβασμοί στοῦ Πειραιᾶ τά σοκάκια
δέν μᾶς βρίσκει ἡ νύχτα στίς γνωστές γειτονιές
σάν ἀνάφτουν τίς λάμπες
ὡς φωνάζουν παιδάκια
στό μουράγιο δέν μᾶς θέλγουν σά χτές
οἱ οἰκεῖες γωνιές
τῶν ὡραίων μεγάρων οἱ νεκρές οἱ προσόψεις
δέν ζητοῦν προβολή τοῦ εὐγενικοῦ μας κορμιοῦ

THE ATLANTIC (1954)

Merrily we ply the ocean waves…
Evangelical Hymn

What are we? Where are we going?
PAUL GAUGUIN

the boat sounds its siren
the train blows its whistle
from up in the towers the signal is given
careful
the journey's beginning
come on then
we're leaving
for another land

in the café of the cobbled Arvanite square
lost in the crowd
of quiet
calm regular customers where
what prevails is ethos
modesty silence
we're no longer sitting
the journey's at hand
come on: we're leaving for another land

gone now the daydreaming in Piraeus' streets
night finds us no more in the usual districts
when the streetlamps are lit
to the shouting of kiddies
we are not like yesterday drawn
by the pier's familiar haunts
the grand mansions' dead façades
seek not the sight of our noble bodies

– προσβολή εἶν' τῆς χτές τά προσόψια
ἡ πάλη –
ἐγκαταλείπουμε τά ἴδια καί τά ἴδια
ξεκινοῦμε γιά τά νέα ταξείδια
ξεκινοῦμε γιά ξένη μιά γῆ

ὁ ρυθμός δέν εἶν' πιά ὁ σκοπός μας
ἀπ' τήν πόρτα ἔχει φύγει ὁ σκοπός μας
στήν ἐκκλησία σβύνουν οἱ πολυελαῖοι τά μανουάλια
πού φωτίζαν τίς εἰκόνες
– χάνεται μέσα στό σκοτάδι ὁ γυναικωνίτης πού συχνάζαν
    οἱ κοκκῶνες –
καί μπρός στό τέμπλο ἡ καντήλα ἀρχίζει τό νυχτέρι
ἐμᾶς ὅμως μᾶς κράζουνε τά ξένα μέρη
κι' ὡς νά φωτίση καί πάλι
αὐγή
ἐμεῖς ξεκινᾶμε
γιά ξένη γῆ

ἡ καπελλοῦ συνταιριάζει φτερά ζωντανά πουλιά
δροσερά λουλούδια γιά τά καπέλλα
ὁ γραμματοκομιστής βαρέθηκε τό πάγαιν'- ἔλα
ὁ γαλατάς ἑτοιμάζει τά γιαούρτια
γιά τό βράδυ
κι' ἡ ὡραία παρθένος πλάι στό παραθύρι ἀκόμη ράβει
καί νά σέ λίγο θ' ἀποθέση τή βελόνα
καί στά σγουρά της τά μαλλιά τοποθετεῖ τοῦ μαρτυρίου κορώνα
ὡς πρόκειται μονορρούφι νά κατεβάση
τό φαρμάκι πού ἔχει ἑτοιμάσει ἀπ' τό πρωΐ
ἡ βρύση τρέχει ἡ στάμνα γιομίζει
τό μύλο ὁ μυλωνάς γυρίζει
βασιλεύει τό φεγγάρι ἡ Πούλια θά βγῆ
ἐμεῖς ξεκινᾶμε
γιά ξένη γῆ

– struggle is a slight on the face-towels
of yesterday –
abandoning the same old ways
now we're off on new journeys
off to another land

rhythm is our goal no more
our goal has gone out of the door
in church the chandeliers the candle stands lighting the icons grow
dim
– the darkness hides the women's pews which genteel ladies sit in –
and by the screen's votive lamp the nightly vigil starts
but we are called by foreign parts
when day breaks
at dawn's command
we're off
to another land

the milliner matches living birds' plumes
finds for the hats fresh blooms
the postman has tired of the toing and froing
the milkman is preparing the yoghurts
for the evening
and the fair maid beside the window is still sewing
regard in a while she'll put down the needle
and on her wavy hair place torment's crown
when at one go she'll down
the bitter potion she prepared that morning
the tap is running the pitcher fills
the wheel is turned by the miller in his mill
the moon's almost set the Pleiades appear and
we're off
to another land

στό πηδάλιο βάλαμε
τόν πιό νηφάλιο
στήν τσιμινιέρα
μιά μπαγιαντέρα
κι' οἱ πολυθρόνες μας εἶν' ροκοκό :
ἔ! θά περάσουμε Ἀτλαντικό !
σίφουνες μπόρες θά μᾶς βαρέσουν
καί – μᾶς ἀρέσουν δέ μᾶς ἀρέσουν –
τί τρικυμίες καί τί κακό !
θά ὁρμᾶνε τά κύματα νά μᾶς καταποντίσουν
οἱ κεραυνοί θά καμτσικίζουνε τόν οὐρανό
ἁρμυρά νερά πού θά μᾶς ραντίσουν
σάν κάτω νά βρισκόμαστε ἀπό κρουνό !
ὅμως νά ξέρετε: δέν θά χαθοῦμε
κανείς
κανένας δέ θά πνιγῆ
ὡς μᾶς προσμένει
μιά ξένη
γῆ

ἥλιος μπουνάτσα οὐρανός γαλάζιος οὔτε ἕνα νέφος
τά νερά ἥσυχα πράσινα σκοῦρα
– ὡσάν σέ πίνακα τοῦ Ἀλταμούρα –
στήν κουπαστή σκυμμένοι θ' ἀπολαμβάνουμε τήν ἄφατη εἰρήνη
καί μακρυά θά βλέπουμε τίς φαλαινοθηρίδες
νά κυνηγοῦνε τό πλουτοφόρο τους κυνήγι
καί οὔτε σύγκρυα οὔτε ρίγη
παρ' ὅλη τή δριμύτητα τῆς ἀτμοσφαίρας
καί – ὡς ὅλα ἀλλάζουν – νά ἡ ὁμίχλη
τό καράβι διεισδύει μέσ' στήν ὁμίχλη
ἀδύνατο νά δοῦμε ἐμπροστά μας
μπερντέδες ἡ θολούρα σκάλες σκάλες
κι' ἀρχίζουνε νά πέφτουνε

at the helm we placed
the soberest
on the funnel there
a bayadere
and our armchairs are rococo:
we'll cross the Atlantic! what ho!
we'll be hit by waterspouts and squalls
and – whether we like it or no –
what tempests what evils will befall!
waves will surge to make us founder
lightning bolts will lash the heavens
we'll be drenched by saltwater
as if we were under a faucet!
but rest assured: we won't be lost
no one will drown
not one hand
for awaiting us
is another
land

sun calm sea blue sky, not one cloud
tranquil dark green water
– like in a painting by Altamoura –
we'll enjoy ineffable peace bent over the rails
and far in the distance we'll see the whalers
hunting their profitable prey
and not one shiver or shudder of fear
despite the harsh atmosphere
and – when it all changes – see the fog
the boat penetrates into the fog
impossible for us to see ahead
layer after layer the murk a curtain
and the drops

οἱ στάλες
οἱ πρῶτες τῆς βροχῆς
κι' ἄνεμος ἄγριος ξάφνης σηκώνεται
μᾶς παίρνει ξάρτια
παίρνει τίς βάρκες παίρνει κατάρτια
τά πάντα ἀπ' τό καράβι μᾶς ξερριζώνει
μέ μουγγρητά μᾶς περιζώνει
καί τό ξυλάρμενο σκαμπανεβάζει
– τί μακρυά πού εἶστε τῆς πάτριας γῆς εἰκόνες ! –
κάτω μας ἀνοίγονται τῆς ἄβυσσου οἱ λειμῶνες
κάποτε στόν ὁρίζοντα ἡ θολούρα
– ἄν εἶναι δυνατό ! –
πυκνώνει
νυχτώνει
ξημερώνει
τούς μπερντέδες τῆς ὁμίχλης διαδέχονται οἱ κουρτίνες τῆς βροχῆς
ὁ ἥλιος – ὁ λαμπρός – κρυμμένος
καί μόνο ὁ ἄνεμος ὁ ἀφορεσμένος
ἀναμαλλιάζει τίς θολές τίς φοινικιές στά μάκρυνα νησιά
ἀργεῖ τό πλοῖο μας
πολύ ἀργεῖ
πότε θά φτάσουμε
στήν ξένη
γῆ;

ὁ Ἀτλαντικός σᾶς ξαναλέω μᾶς περιζώνει
εἶναι θεώρατος εἴμαστε μόνοι
εἴμαστε ἤπιοι εἶν' φοβερός
σάν καρυδότσουφλα μᾶς κλωθογυρίζει
καί μέσ' στ' αὐτί μας μᾶς ψιθυρίζει
μηνύματα ἄγρια (μᾶς ἀπειλεῖ)
πρός Θεοῦ μή χάνουμε τό ἠθικό μας !
παιδιά ἐλπίζετε στό ριζικό μας !
ὁποῦ καί νᾶναι

the first drops of rain
begin to fill the air
and suddenly a raging wind gets up
seizing our rigging
seizing lifeboats and masts
stripping our boat to the very last
it surrounds us and howls
and the vessel pitches under bare poles
– how distant you are images of our homeland! –
beneath us the abyss' pastures expand
then the murkiness on the horizon
– who would believe it! –
grows even thicker
deep night
then daylight
sheets of rain succeed the blankets of fog
the sun – the bright sun – is concealed
and only the accursed wind
tousles the dim palms on islands far off
so slow our boat
so very slow
when will we reach
the other
land?

the Atlantic as I told you is all around us
it's enormous and we're all alone
we're meek it's ferocious
it tosses us like a cockleshell
and in our ears whispers
angry messages (threatening us)
for heaven's sake let's not lose our morale!
trust in our destiny lads!
how long will it be

δέ θά φανῆ ;
– ἐκεῖ πού πᾶμε –
ἡ ξένη γῆ ;

ΚΟΥΒΕΝΤΑ:

ἄνθρωπε σύ πού βολοδέρνεις
μόνος – ὁλόμονος – τί γυροφέρνεις
μέσ' στόν ἀπέραντο ὠκεανό ;
πῶς δέ φοβᾶσαι μή ναυαγήσης ;
ἤ – τό λιγότερο –
πολύ ν' ἀργήσης
ὥσπου ν' ἀράξης
στήν ξένη γῆ ;

ΑΠΟΚΡΙΣΙΣ:

μοῦ λέτε ἄν χαθῶ ἄν ναυαγήσω
ἤ καί ν' ἀργήσω τέλος ν' ἀράξω
μποροῦσα ἄλλως ποτέ νά πράξω ;
ἔτσι
μέ ρίξανε
          στόν
               ὠκεανό

τό ταξείδι ἐξελίσσεται σύμφωνα μέ τήν προδιαγεγραμμένη πορεία
          ὑπάρχει πίστη ; τήν ἀπορία
σ' αὐτή τήν ἀέναη ἐναλλαγή
τῆς τρικυμίας καί τῆς γαλήνης
τοῦ φουρτουνιάσματος καί τῆς εἰρήνης
τί νά τήν κάνουμε ; τί ὠφελεῖ ;
κάπου θά πᾶμε κάπου θά πᾶμε
κι' ὅμως γιά λίγο
– πολύ λυπᾶμαι –

before we stand
– in the place we're going –
the other land?

REMARK:

man you who are afflicted
alone – all alone – what do you seek
in the vast ocean?
aren't you afraid lest you flounder
or – at the very least –
with much delay
drop anchor
in the other land?

REPLY:

what if I flounder or am lost you say
or even drop anchor with delay
what else could I have done?
this is how
I was cast
      into
             the ocean

the journey proceeds according to the preordained course
is there faith? the question
in this perpetual alternation
of tempest and calm seas
of storm and peace
serves what purpose? what possible use?
somewhere we'll go somewhere we'll go
though for only a while
– I'm sorry to let you know –

συλλογιστῆτε
τί θά γινοῦμε
ἄν δέν ὑπάρχη
ἡ ξένη γῆ

τώρα βρισκόμαστε στόν ὠκεανό

consider
what will become of us
if there is no
other land

now we're all on the ocean

ΕΝ ΑΝΘΗΡΩ ΕΛΛΗΝΙ ΛΟΓΩ

Dichten ist zeugen
NOVALIS

Η ΜΝΗΜΗ

... les croque-morts porterait des gants transparents, afin de rappeler aux amants le souvenirs des caresses.
FR. PICABIA

Λύνω τά μαλλιά της, βυθίζω τά χέρια μέσα στούς πλούσιους της πλοκάμους καί τό γέλιο μου ἀντηχεῖ σέ βουνά, κοιλάδες, ρεματιές, κορφές βουνῶν μέ χιόνια αἰώνια. Ἡ ἱκεσία τῶν ἄσπρων ματιῶν της μοῦ σπαράζει τήν καρδιά: πρέπει πάλι νά ξερριζώσω τά δέντρα, πρέπει πάλι ν᾽ ἀφήσω τ᾽ αὐλάκι νά τρέξῃ ἐλεύθερο, πρέπει ἐκ νέου οἱ μελαχρινές ὡραῖες κόρες νά᾽ρθουν νά ραντίζουν τούς μαστούς τους μέ τά νερά τοῦ ρόδινου σιντριβανιοῦ. Πρέπει, πρέπει, πρέπει...
Συνθλίβω ἀνάμεσα στίς εὐγενικές μου παλάμες τό ρόδι τῆς χαρᾶς.
Ἀνοίγω τό κλουβί τῶν πουλιῶν νά πετάξουν, ἐλεύθερα, μέσα στή νύχτα.
Ἀπό τό νεροχύτη ξεπετιέται ἕνας ἄγγελος.
Ἐγώ τόν καλωσορίζω, τοῦ προσφέρω γραμματόσημα, σύκα, δορές λεόντων, φιλιά.
Στέκομαι στό κατώφλι τῆς ἐπαύλεως. Ἐρευνῶ πέρα τόν ὁρίζοντα καί, σκύβοντας, προσπαθῶ μέ τά δάχτυλα νά καθαρίσω τήν πλάκα τοῦ τάφου, νά᾽ρθη ν᾽ ἀκουμπήση ἡ σελήνη.
Ξάφνου, φωνή:
«Νικόλαε Ἐγγονόπουλε, δέν ἔπρεπε νάν τό κάμης αὐτό!»
Καθόμαστε τότε ὅλοι, καί κλαῖμε γύρω στό τραπέζι μέ τό κόκκινο σκέπασμα, ὅπου μιά φρουτιέρα μέ μαραγκιασμένα φροῦτα μᾶς θυμίζει τή ματαιότητα κάθε ἀνθρώπινης προσδοκίας, ὅπως καί κάθε ἐλπίδος.

From: *IN THE FLOURISHING GREEK TONGUE* (1957)

Dichten ist zeugen
NOVALIS

THE MEMORY

… les croque-morts porterait des gants transparents, afin de rappeler aux amants le souvenirs des caresses.
FR. PICABIA

I loosen her hair, plunge my hands into her thick tresses and my laughter echoes in the mountains, the valleys, the riverbeds, the mountain peaks with their eternal snow. The entreaty in her white eyes breaks my heart: again I must uproot the trees, again I must let the brook run freely, the lovely dark-haired girls must come anew to sprinkle their breasts with the rosy fountain's waters. Must, must, must…

Between my gentle palms I crush joy's pomegranate. I open the cage that the birds may fly, freely, into the night.

An angel emerges from the sink.

I welcome him, offer him postage stamps, figs, lion skins, kisses.

I stand at the doorstep of the villa. I search the far horizon and, stooping, try with my fingers to wipe clean the tombstone, that the moon may come to rest upon it.

Suddenly, a voice:

"Nikolaos Engonopoulos, you should not have done that!"

Then we all sit down, and cry around the table with the red cover, on which a fruit bowl with wizened fruit reminds us of the vanity of all human expectation, as of all hope.

Ο ΕΡΑΣΤΗΣ

Μιλοῦσε μιάν ἄλλη γλῶσσα, τήν ἰδιάζουσα διάλεκτο μιᾶς λησμονημένης, τώρα πλέον, πόλεως, τῆς ὁποίας καί εἴτανε, ἄλλωστε, ὁ μόνος νοσταλγός.

THE LOVER

He spoke another language, the peculiar dialect of a now long forgotten city, for which in any case he alone felt nostalgia.

ΜΕΡΚΟΥΡΙΟΣ ΜΠΟΥΑΣ

Γονατίζει κι' ἀνοίγει τήν κασσέλα, κι' ἐνῶ μέ τόνα χέρι κρατᾶ τό καπάκι, μέ τ' ἄλλο κάτι ψαχουλεύει κι' ἀναδεύει κεῖ μέσα.
– Τί ἔχεις αὐτοῦ; τόν ρωτῶ.
Στρέφεται:
– Lettere d'amore, μοῦ κάνει.
Κι' ὕστερα:
– Δέν σ' ἐνδιαφέρουν;
– Μά φυσικά, ξέρεις, σάν πρόκειται γι' ἀγάπες..., ἀπαντῶ.
Τότες ἀρχίζει σιγά-σιγά, μέ προσεκτικώτατες κινήσεις, νά βγάζει ἔξω ἕνα-ἕνα διάφορα πράγματα καί νά μοῦ τά ἐπιδεικνύη.
Πρῶτα ἀνάσυρε, κι' ἔδειξε, διάφορα βελούδινα ὑφάσματα, σωρούς-κουβάρια, ἄλλα πλουμιστά κι' ἄλλα μονόχρωμα. Ὕστερα, ἕνα σάπιο στρῶμα, καί τελικά παρατᾶ τό καπάκι, βγάζει ὄξω ἕνα πτῶμα, καλῶς διατηρημένο, νεκροῦ ἀνδρός, καί τό ἀποθέτει χάμω. Ἐκεῖνο πού ἔκανε ὅλως ἰδιαιτέρα ἐντύπωση σ' αὐτό τό πτῶμα εἴταν τό στιλπνό κι' ἐκθαμβωτικά λευκό τῆς ἐπιδερμίδος, καθώς κι' ἡ ἀτίθαση κόμη καί τά ἀρειμάνια μακρυά μουστάκια.

MERCURIUS BOUAS

He kneels and opens the chest, and holding the lid with one hand, he gropes and rummages inside with the other.

"What have you got in there?" I ask him.

He turns round:

"Lettere d'amore," he tells me.

And then:

"Don't they interest you?"

"But of course, you know, when it's a question of loves…," I reply.

Then, with most careful movements, he slowly begins to take out various items one by one and show them to me.

First he pulled out and showed me various velvet fabrics, tangled piles, some brightly colored and others plain. Next a rotting mattress, and eventually letting go of the lid, he takes out the well-preserved corpse of a dead man, and lays it on the floor. What was most striking about this corpse was the glossy and dazzling whiteness of its skin, together with its unkempt hair and long bellicose moustache.

ΑΡΚΕΣΙΛΑΣ

...fuyard que je connais aux traces de tes larmes.
MARIE-JEANNE DURUY

ἔφυγε
καί τονέ βλέπω
ν' ἀπομακρύνεται
κατά μῆκος
τῆς ἐρήμου λεωφόρου
καί κάθε τόσο γυρνάει
καί μᾶς χαιρετᾶ
δι' ἀνεπαισθήτου κινήσεως τῶν βλεφάρων
ὡς ὅτου
– λίγο-λίγο –
τό καραντί του
νά χαθῆ
νά σβύση
στό βάθος τοῦ ὁρίζοντος

ἔγραψε

στό γράμμα του
ἔλεγε –ἀνάμεσα σ' ἄλλα –
πώς ἀγαπάει
τή
βροχή

«εἶμαι Ἕλλην
– εἶναι τά λόγια του –
πατρίς μου καί μητέρα μου
ἡ
βροχή»

ARCESILAUS

…fuyard que je connais aux traces de tes larmes.
MARIE-JEANNE DURUY

he left
and I watch him
moving away
along
the deserted street
every so often he turns
and bids us farewell
with a slight movement of his eyelids
till
– little by little –
his wake
vanishes
fades
in the depths of the horizon

he wrote

in his letter
he said – among other things –
that he likes
the
rain

"I'm Greek
– his exact words –
my mother and fatherland
is
the rain"

«σάν μέ προλάβη ή βροχή
–συνέχιζε –
σάν μέ προλάβη
ὁλόγυμνο
στούς δρόμους νά γυρνῶ
μέ ντύνει
–ή βροχή –
μ' ἀπίστευτης λαμπρότητος
καί ποικιλίας
φορεσιές
καί στήνει ἀέναα γύρω μου
ὡς προχωρῶ
μυθώδους πλούτου
σκηνικά
καί διακόσμους»

τώρα γυρνᾶ στά «τέρματα»
μέσ' στήν πολυκοσμία καί τίς μουσικές καί τή λαϊκή χαρά
κι' ἀνακατεύεται
– γίνεται ἕνα –
μέ τό πλῆθος

κι' αἰσθάνετ'
ἄλλοτε
σά βασιλιᾶς ἀναμεσίς στούς ὑπηκόους του
κι' ἄλλοτε πάλι
– ἴσως τήν ἴδια ἀκριβῶς στιγμή –
σάν
ἄρχοντας ἐξόριστος
ἀνάμεσα
σέ ξένους
–κι' ἄγνωστους –
λαούς

"when I'm caught in the rain
– he went on –
when I'm caught
stark naked
roaming the streets
I'm clothed
– by the rain –
in garments
of incredible resplendence
and variety
and as I proceed
it perpetually fashions a decor
and scenery
of mythical riches"

now he returns to the "termina"
amid the bustle and music and the populace's joy
and mixes
– becomes one –
with the crowd

and he feels
at times
like a king among his subjects
and at others
– perhaps at the very same moment –
like
an exiled ruler
among
foreign
– and unknown –
peoples

ΠΕΡΙ ΥΨΟΥΣ

*Certes, l'artiste désire s'élever,... mais
l'homme doit rester obscur.*
PAUL CÉZANNE

Ὁ ἰταλός πυροτεχνουργός ἔχει ἐγκαταστήσει τό λιτό κι' ἀπέριττο, τό φτωχικό ἐργαστήριό του, ἐπί τῆς κορυφῆς τοῦ ἀττικοῦ λόφου. Ἐκεῖ ἀσχολεῖται νυχθημερόν μέ τά ἄπειρα πειράματά του καί μέ τήν παρασκευή τῶν διάφορων προϊόντων τοῦ ἐπιτηδεύματός του: βαρελότα, χαλκούνια, καί ἄλλα «μαϊτάπια». Γιατί αὐτός εἶναι πού προμηθεύει τούς πανηγυριστάς τίς παραμονές τῶν μεγάλων ἑορτῶν τῆς Ὀρθοδοξίας, ἀλλά κι' αὐτός εἶναι, πάλι, πού, τίς νύχτες τῶν ἐθνικῶν ἐπετείων, διακοσμεῖ τούς οὐρανούς μας μέ λογῆς-λογῆς φανταχτερά λουλούδια, μ' ἐκθαμβωτικά πλουμιά καί μέ ταχύτατες ρουκέττες πού καταλήγουν σέ μυριόχρωμη βροχή ἀπό σπίθες. Σπανίως ἐγκαταλείπει τό ἔργον, ὅμως, τά βράδυα, ἐνίοτε, περιφέρει τή σακατεμένη κι' ἀλαμπουρνέζικη σιλουέττα του, ἀπό καπηλειό σέ καπηλειό, χρησιμοποιώντας, κατά προτίμηση, τά σκοτεινότερα στενά τῆς ἀγορᾶς. Τό ἐπάγγελμά του εἶναι ἄκρως ἐπικίνδυνο: πυρῖτις, κι' ἔσθ' ὅτε δυναμῖτις, εἶναι ἡ πρώτη ὕλη τῶν ἐργοχείρων του. Ἡ παραμικρή ἀπροσεξία ἀρκεῖ κι' ἐπέρχεται ἡ τρομερά καταστροφή: μέσα σέ ἐκκωφαντικό κρότο τινάζονται στό καθαρό πρωϊνό καί τό ἐργαστήρι κι' ὁ πυροτεχνουργός μαζύ, καί βλέπομε νά στριφογυρνοῦν ψηλά στόν ἀέρα, ὧρες, κι' ὁ Ἰταλός καί τά σανίδια τῆς μπαράγκας καί πηχτά σύγνεφα σκόνης, ἐνῶ μιάν ἔντονη μυρωδιά μπαρούτης ἁπλώνεται παντοῦ.

Ὅμως ποτέ δέν ἐπέρχεται τό μοιραῖον, γιατί ὑπάρχει κάτι. Ἕνα μυστικό. Κι' αὐτό τό μυστικό εἶναι ἁπλούστατα ἡ σύζυγος πού γρηγορεῖ. Πράγματι, ἡ γυναίκα του, δική μας: εὐλαβική κι' ὀρθόδοξος χριστιανή, ξημεροβραδυάζεται στίς ἐκκλησιές, καί κάνει βαθειές μετάνοιες, κι' ὅλο προσεύχεται γιά δαύτονε. Κι' ἔτσι τονέ κρατᾶ στή ζωή.

Μάλιστα, κάτω στήν χαράδρα πού περιβάλλει τόν ἀττικό λοφίσκο, ἐκεῖ, ἡ μαύρη, ἔχει σπείρει τόν κόσμο μ' ἀναρίθμητα προσκυνητάρια, τά περισσότερα μαρμάρινα, ἄλλα ταπεινότερα, ὅμως ὅλα μέ εἰκόνα

ON ELEVATION

Certes, l'artiste désire s'élever,... mais
l'homme doit rester obscur.
PAUL CÉZANNE

The Italian pyrotechnist has set up his frugal and modest, his humble workshop, atop the Attic hill. There he works night and day on his infinite experiments and on the manufacture of the various products of his craft: fireworks, crackers and other "shenanigans." For he it is who supplies the merry-makers on the eve of the major Orthodox feast days, and he it is again who on the evenings of the national anniversaries, decorates our skies with all kinds of spectacular flowers, with dazzling ornaments and soaring rockets that end in a kaleidoscopic shower of sparks. Rarely does he leave his work, yet sometimes, at night, he drags his weary and preposterous figure from tavern to tavern, using, as is his preference, the darker back streets of the marketplace. His profession is exceedingly dangerous: gunpowder, and on occasion dynamite, is the raw material of his handiwork. The slightest mistake is sufficient for a terrible disaster to ensue: in a deafening roar the workshop and the pyrotechnist with it are hurled into the clear morning, and we see whirling high in the air, for hours, the Italian and the boards of his hovel and dense clouds of dust, while a strong smell of gunpowder spreads everywhere.

Yet the inevitable never happens, for there is something. A secret. And this secret is most simply his ever vigilant wife. And indeed, his wife, one of us: a devout Orthodox Christian, spends all her days in church, prostrates herself, and constantly prays for him. And in this way she keeps him alive.

In fact, below in the ravine surrounding by the Attic hill, there, in that black place, she has sown the world with countless shrines, the majority of marble, others more humble, yet all with the

Θεοτόκου ἤ ἄλλου ἁγίου, κι' ὅλα μέ μιά θυρίδα, γιά τά λεφτά. Κάθε τόσο συλλέγει ὑπομονετικά τά χρήματα, καί τό μεγαλύτερο μέν μέρος διαθέτει γι' ἀγαθοεργούς σκοπούς, ἐνίσχυση ἀπόρων, ἀνακούφιση ἀσθενῶν, ἀποπεράτωση ἐκκλησιῶν, κι' ἕνα ἄλλο μέρος τό φυλᾶ προσεκτικά, καθώς σκοπεύει μ' αὐτό, ἐν καιρῷ, ν' ἀνεγείρη ἐκκλησία τιμωμένη μέ τ' ὄνομα τῆς Ἁγίας Αἰκατερίνης.

(Πιό πέρα, στή χαράδρα, κάποιος ἔχει ἐγκαταστήσει κυψέλες, μελισσιῶν, σ' ἕνα χωράφι, καί, πιό πέρα ἀκόμη, μέσα σέ περιβόλι, εἶναι τά ἐρείπια μισοχτισμένου ἀρχοντικοῦ).

Αὐτή ἡ ἱστορία τοῦ Ἰταλοῦ εἶναι κι' ἡ ἱστορία ἡ δικιά μας, Ἑλένη. Δέν εἶμαι ἐγώ ὁ πυροτεχνουργός; Τά ποιήματά μου δέν εἶναι Πασχαλινά χαλκούνια, κι' οἱ πίνακές μου καταπλήσσοντος κάλλους νυχτερινά ὑπέρλαμπρα μετέωρα τοῦ Ἀττικοῦ οὐρανοῦ; Κι' ὅμως, ἐάν ἀκόμη δέν μέ κατασπαράξανε ἀλύπητα, νά πετάξουνε τίς σάρκες μου στά σκυλιά, αὐτό δέν τό χρωστάω σ' ἐσένα, στή μεγάλη στοργή σου καί στήν ἀγάπη σου; Τό ξέρω, μή μοῦ τό κρύφτεις, τό ξέρω σοῦ λέω: προσεύχεσαι γιά μένα!

Μάζευε τά λεφτά τῶν προσκυνηταρίων μας καί σκόρπαε, μέ τ' ἅγια λευκά σου χέρια, τό καλό παντοῦ. Ὅμως κράτα ἕνα μέρος, νά συγκεντρώσωμε, κι' ἐμεῖς, λίγο-λίγο ἕνα ποσό, γιά ν' ἀνεγείρουμε μιάν ἐκκλησιά ἀφιερωμένη στήν Βασίλισσα πού εἶχε τ' ὄνομά σου. Ἐκεῖ μέσα, σ' αὐτήν τήν ἐκκλησία θέ νά σέ παντρευτῶ. Γιατί εἶσαι ὡραία, ἔχεις τήν πιό εὐγενική κι' ὑπερήφανη ψυχή, καί σ' ἀγαπῶ παράφορα.

image of the Virgin or some other saint, and all of them with a box, for the money. Every so often she patiently collects the money, the greater part of which she donates to charitable causes, help for the needy, relief for the sick, the upkeep of churches, while another part she carefully guards, since with this she plans, in time, to construct a church dedicated to Saint Catherine.

(A little further, in the ravine, someone has set up beehives, in a field, and, further still, surrounded by a garden are the ruins of a half-built mansion).

This tale of the Italian is also our tale, Eleni. Am I not the pyrotechnist? Are my poems not Easter firecrackers, and my paintings amazingly beautiful brilliant nocturnal meteors in the Attic sky? And yet, if they still haven't mercilessly torn me to pieces, thrown my flesh to the dogs, do I not owe this to you, to your great tenderness and to your love? I know, don't hide it from me, I'm telling you I know: you pray for me!

Gather the money from our shrines and, with your saintly white hands, spread good everywhere. But keep part of it so that we too might little by little put together a sum to erect a church dedicated to the Queen who bore your name. In there, in that church, I'll marry you. For you are beautiful, you have the most gracious and dignified soul, and I love you passionately.

ENOIKIAZETAI

μέσα σ' αὐτό τό δωμάτιο
παρέδωσε τό πνεῦμα
ἡ ὡραία ἀθηναία κόρη
ξαπλωμένη στά μεταξωτά χιράμια
– τά ξανθά μαλλιά ξέπλεκα γύρω στήν κερένια κεφαλή –
ἐνῶ ἀπ' τ' ἀνοιχτό παράθυρο
ἀκούγονταν
οἱ καμπάνες τῆς Ἁγια-Σωτήρας
πού βάραγαν
ἑσπερινό
ὡς τήν ἑπομένη ξημέρωνε
ἡ ἑορτή
τοῦ προφήτη Σαμουήλ

σ' αὐτό μέσα τό δωμάτιο
συνουσιάστηκαν τά δυό φοβερά τέρατα
κι' εὐφραίνονταν
μ' ἀγκομαχητά κι' ἄγρια γρυλίσματα
κι' ἀγριοφωνάρες
λές καί βουργάροι ὑλοτόμοι
τά βάλανε μέ θεώρατα ἐλάτια
ἤ μᾶλλον
(καλύτερο)
νά ἐγκρεμιζόντουσαν
βουνά

μέσα σ' αὐτό τό δωμάτιο
ἡ γηραιά δέσποινα
πέρασε χρόνια καί χρόνια
ἀνίας:
κουνοῦσε ἀνεπαίσθητα τά τρεμάμενα χέρια
προσπαθώντας στό σκοτεινιασμένο

TO LET

in this room
the fair Athenian maid
gave up her ghost
– lying on silken coverlets
her blonde hair loose round her waxen head –
while through the open window
could be heard
the bells of Saint Savior's
ringing
vespers
as the morrow was
the feast
of the Prophet Samuel

inside this room
the two terrible monsters had intercourse
and reveled
with wheezing and wild grunting
and ferocious cries
as if Bulgarian woodcutters
were wrestling with giant firs
or as if
(even better)
mountains
were crashing down

in this room
the aged miss
spent years and years
of boredom
barely moving her trembling hands
endeavoring in her dim

καί θολό μυαλό
νά ξαναφέρη εἰκόνας τῶν παλαιῶν της μεγαλείων
ἴσαμε τή μέρα
πού μέ βηματάκια ἀργά ἀργά
ξεκίνησε
– τήν ἐξεκίνησαν –
γιά τό γεροκομεῖο

μέσα ἐδῶ ἐγεννηθῆκαν τρία παιδιά
–γόνοι τιμίας κι' εὐυπολήπτου οἰκογενείας –
πού χάθηκαν
– τόπο δέν ἔπιασε κανένας τους –
ὁ ἕνας πῆγε στήν Ἀμερική
ὁ ἄλλος πέθανε κακήν κακῶς –μπεκρής –
κι' ὁ τρίτος
εἶναι κάπου ἀκόμη
φαροφύλακας

ἐδῶ –ναί ἐδῶ μέσα: σέ τοῦτο τό δωμάτιο –
σκότωσε χέρι ἄτιμο ἐκεῖνο
τόν παλληκαρᾶ
«νά τιμωρήση –λέει –ἐν τῷ προσώπῳ του τήν ἀναρχίαν»
κι' ἔγειρ' ἡ λεύκα καί σωριάστηκε χαμαί
καί κείνη ἡ μουντή κηλίδα
τοῦ πατώματος
κεῖ πέρα στή γωνιά
εἶναι τό αἷμα πού ποτάμι χύνονταν ἀπ' τήν πληγή
καί τίποτα ποτέ
δέν εἶταν δυνατό
νά τηνέ καθαρίση ἀπ' τά σανίδια

ὅμως ἀρκεῖ ὡς ἐδῶ: τί πάω νά κάμω;
πόσο δέ θᾶτανε κοπιαστικό
ἴσως κι' ἀδύνατο

and clouded mind
to bring back images of her former splendor
till the day
when with short steps slowly
she set out
– was led out –
for the old people's home

in here three children were born
– offspring of an honorable and respectable family –
who came to nothing
– none of them made good –
one went to America
one came to a bad end – a drunk –
and the third
is somewhere still
a lighthouse-keeper

here – yes in here, in this room –
an ignoble hand killed that
brave young lad
"to punish – so it goes – anarchy in his person"
and the fir-tree bent and toppled to the ground
and that dull stain
on the floor
over there in the corner
is the blood that streamed from the wound
and nothing ever
was able
to clean it from the boards

yet enough thus far: what am I trying to do?
how fatiguing it would be
perhaps also impossible

πάντως ἀτέλειωτο
καί μάταιο ἀκόμη κι' ἀνιαρό
νά σημειώσω τώρα μέ τόση λεπτομέρεια
τήν ἱστορία
τήν ἀτέλειωτη
αὐτοῦ τοῦ δωματίου

(ἄλλοτε ἔμπαζαν κρεββάτια
ἄλλοτε τἄβγαζαν
ἄλλοτε κεῖ ἤτανε σκρίνιο
ὕστερα ντουλάπα
ἔπειτα κασσέλα
ἄλλοτε στά παράθυρα εἴχανε βαρειά παραπετάσματα
ἄλλοτε τά τζάμια ἔμεναν γυμνά μέ μόνα τά παντζούρια
σέ κείνη τή γωνιά μιά εἴχανε τά εἰκονίσματα
ἄλλες φορές παντοῦ κρέμονταν κάντρα)

νά: ἄνθρωποι κι' ἄνθρωποι περάσανε καί φύγανε
κι' ἄλλοι –πολλοί –ἐδῶ μέσα γεννηθῆκαν
κι' ἄλλους πάλι ἐδῶ μέσα τούς βάλανε στήν κάσσα
καί τί δέν ἄκουσαν οἱ τοῖχοι αὐτοί
φωνές ὀδύνης
καί φωνές χαρᾶς
εἴδανε καί βαφτίσια
μουγγές ἀπελπισιές
καί στεφανώματα

(θά τό ξεχνοῦσα: καί πιάνο ἐδῶ μέσα ἀντήχησε παίζοντας ἁβρά
τή Romance du Mal-Aimé)

ἔζησα καί γώ –ὁ γράφων –μέσ' σέ τοῦτο τό δωμάτιο
χρόνια πολλά –φτωχά –κι' ὡς πάντα
κι' ἐδῶ γιομάτος πάθος ἀσχολήθηκα
μέ τή ζωγραφική τήν ποίηση

at any rate endless
and pointless even and boring
to note now in so much detail
the history
endless as it is
of this room

(sometimes they put in beds
sometimes took them out
sometimes there was a cabinet there
afterwards a cupboard
then a chest
sometimes heavy curtains covered the windows
sometimes the panes were bare with only the shutters
in that corner once they had icons
at other times frames hung everywhere)

so: people upon people passed through and left
and others – many – were born in here
while others again were put in their caskets in here
and how much these walls have heard
cries of grief
and cries of joy
they have also seen christenings
mute despondency
and wedding rites

(I almost forgot: a piano too resounded in here gently
        playing the Romance du Mal-Aimé)

I too – the writer – lived in this room
many years – in poverty – and as always
here too full of passion I concerned myself
with painting with poetry

τή γλυπτική
ἀλλά καί τή φιλοσοφία καί τόν ἔρωτα
κι' ἔμεινα ὧρες καθισμένος
– νά καπνίζω –
σέ κεῖ δά τό παράθυρο
κυττάζοντας
ἄλλοτε τόν οὐρανό
κι' ἄλλοτε τό δρόμο

καί τώρα πρέπει –φεῦ –κι' ἐγώ νά φεύγω
–δέν ἀποκλείεται ἄλλωστε νά μοῦ μέλλονται καλύτερα –

πάλι τό ἐνοικιάζουν τό δωμάτιο

Bruges, 1956

with sculpture
yet also with philosophy and love
and I spent hours sitting
– smoking –
at that very window
gazing sometimes at the sky
sometimes at the street

and now – alas – I too must leave
– besides it may well be that better things await me –

again the room is being let

Bruges, 1956

Η ΚΑΛΟΣΥΝΗ ΤΩΝ ΑΝΘΡΩΠΩΝ

σήκωσε τή λάμπα
κοιτάξου στόν καθρέφτη:
δυστυχισμένη
εἶν' οἱ κόγχες τῶν ματιῶν σου
ἄδειες!

(κι' ἀπό μακρυά
ἡ Ἠχώ
φωνάζει:
«Εὐρυδίκη!»)

THE KINDNESS OF PEOPLE

raise the lamp
regard yourself in the mirror
wretched woman
the sockets of your eyes are
empty!

(and from afar
the Echo
calls:
"Eurydice!")

ΝΕΑ ΠΕΡΙ ΤΟΥ ΘΑΝΑΤΟΥ ΤΟΥ ΙΣΠΑΝΟΥ ΠΟΙΗΤΟΥ
ΦΕΝΤΕΡΙΚΟ ΓΚΑΡΘΙΑ ΛΟΡΚΑ ΣΤΙΣ 19 ΑΥΓΟΥΣΤΟΥ
ΤΟΥ 1936 ΜΕΣΑ ΣΤΟ ΧΑΝΤΑΚΙ ΤΟΥ ΚΑΜΙΝΟ ΝΤΕ ΛΑ
ΦΟΥΕΝΤΕ

... una acción vil y disgraciado.

ἡ τέχνη κι' ἡ ποίηση δέν μᾶς βοηθοῦν νά ζήσουμε:
ἡ τέχνη καί ἡ ποίησις μᾶς βοηθοῦνε
νά πεθάνουμε

περιφρόνησις ἀπόλυτη
ἁρμόζει
σ' ὅλους αὐτούς τούς θόρυβους
τίς ἔρευνες
τά σχόλια ἐπί σχολίων
πού κάθε τόσο ξεφουρνίζουν
ἀργόσχολοι καί ματαιόδοξοι γραφιάδες
γύρω ἀπό τίς μυστηριώδικες κι' αἰσχρές συνθῆκες
τῆς ἐκτελέσεως τοῦ κακορρίζικου τοῦ Λόρκα
ὑπό τῶν φασιστῶν

μά ἐπί τέλους! πιά ὁ καθείς γνωρίζει
πώς
ἀπό καιρό τώρα
– καί πρό παντός στά χρόνια τά δικά μας τά σακάτικα –
εἴθισται
νά δολοφονοῦν
τούς ποιητάς

NEWS CONCERNING THE DEATH OF THE SPANISH POET FEDERICO GARCIA LORCA IN A DITCH AT CAMINO DE LA FUENTE ON 19 AUGUST 1936

... una acción vil y disgraciado.

art and poetry do not help us to live:
art and poetry help us
to die

total contempt
befits
all that fuss
the investigations
the views upon views
spouted every so often
by vain and idle penpushers
as to the mysterious and shameful circumstances
surrounding the execution of hapless Lorca
by the fascists

yet at last! everyone now knows
that
for some time now
– and above all in these crippling times of ours –
it has been customary
to murder
the poets

ΚΛΕΛΙΑ
ἤ μᾶλλον
ΤΟ ΕΙΔΥΛΛΙΟΝ ΤΗΣ ΛΙΜΝΟΘΑΛΑΣΣΑΣ

I

ἔχεις τά μάτια τῶν ἀνθρώπων
καί τή ζωή
τῶν παιδιῶν
ἡ λεπτή μέση σου
κλείει τό ἄπαν
τῶν ὀνείρων μου :
μοῦ δίνεις τή χαρά τῶν ἀητῶν

δέν μετανοιώνεις – δέν εἶν' ἔτσι; –
δέν μετανοιώνεις
πού ἐφύγαμε
πού καταφύγαμε στῆς λιμνοθάλασσας τήν πρασινογάλαζη εἰρήνη
κύττα – ἐν ὅσῳ εἶναι ἀκόμη καιρός –

στην ὁλονέν ἀπομακρυνόμενη
πλατεῖα
νά σεργιανίζουν
ὅλος τοῦτος ὁ συρφετός τῶν ἀνθρώπων μέ τή σκατωμένη βελάδα
– κύκλῳ οἱ ἀσεβεῖς περιπατοῦν –
μήν μετανοιώνεις – λέω –
δέν χάνουμε – δέν χάνεις – ἀπολύτως τίποτε
πού φεύγουμε
μακρυά

σ' ἀγαπῶ καί σέρνω τή μακρυά μου κόκκινη κόμη
στά λευκά λεπτά σου πόδια
μ' ἐμπνέουν οἱ ρῶγες τῶν μαστῶν σου

CLELIA
or rather
THE IDYLL ON THE LAGOON

I

you have the eyes of men
and the life
of children
your slender waist
encloses all
of my dreams:
you give me the joy of eagles

you don't regret – do you? –
you don't regret
that we left
and found refuge in the lagoon's green and blue tranquility
look – while there's still time –
as the square
grows ever distant
how they stroll
that mob of people their frock coats filthy
– the impious walk in circles –
don't regret it – I've told you –
we're losing – you're losing – nothing at all
by leaving
for afar

I love you and draw my long red hair
over your slender white legs
the nipples on your breasts are my inspiration

κι' ὀρθός
μέ χέρι σταθερό
ὁδηγῶ τήν ναῦν
πρός τά νησιά
ὅπου πετοῦν
σωρούς
τά κόκκαλα καί τίς καυκάλες τῶν νεκρῶν

στήν ἄμμο τήν ξανθή
τῆς ὄχθης
μᾶς περιμένει ἕνα ὑπέροχο κρεββάτι :
τό πλαισιώνουν τά
σπαθόχορτα
κι' οἱ καλαμιές

(καί πράγματι
ἐκεῖ ὑπήρξαμε ὁ ἕνας γιά τόν ἄλλονα κρήνη καλλίρειθρος
μόνο πού ἔγω ἐπι-
προσθέτως

εἴμουν
γι' αὐτήν
ταυτόχρονα
λάτρης
καί τιμωρός)

II

μήν κλαῖς – μήν κλαῖς καλή –
τίς μέρες πού πέρασαν :
εἴτανε – νά τό ξέρης – δῶρο τῶν θεῶν

and upright
with steady hand
I steer the boat
to the islands
where in piles
they cast
the bones and skulls of the dead

on the shore's
golden sand
a splendid bed awaits us:
swordgrass
and reeds
surround it

(and truly
there we were a wellspring for each other
except that I in
addition
was
for her
at the same time
both worshipper
and avenger)

II

Don't weep – don't weep my dear –
for the days that passed:
they were – be sure – a gift of the gods

ἡ γῆ σιγᾶ
καί πρίν ἀκόμη ὁ ἥλιος πού τόσο ἀγαπᾶμε σβήση
–καί δέν σκοπεύει πιά γιά μᾶς νά ξαναβγῆ –
θέ νά σέ πάρω
–γιά νά προχωρήσουμε –
ἀπ' τό λεπτό χεράκι

βλέπεις ἐκεῖνο τό μνημεῖο
ἐκεῖ πέρα
θ' ἀνοίξουμε τήν πόρτα

καί θά μποῦμε:
ἐκεῖ θέ νά σέ πάρω ἀγκαλιά
κι' ἀγκαλιασμένοι ἔτσι μιά γιά πάντα
θά χαθοῦμε
μέσ' στῆς Δευτέρας Παρουσίας
τά πολύχρωμα
γυαλιά

the earth falls silent
and before the sun that we so loved fades
– intent never to come out for us again –
I'll take you
– so we may move on –
by your slender hand

you see that monument
over there
we'll open the door
and enter:
there I'll take you in my arms
and arm in arm like that for ever
we'll vanish
into the Second Coming's
colorful
glass

ΜΑΡΣΙΝΕΛ

τώρα τά περιστέρια εἶναι κοιμισμένα

κι' ὁ οὐραγάν μαίνεται
τό τρελλό ἀναμάλλιασμα τῶν δέντρων
ἀκολουθεῖ τήν ὕποπτη σιωπή
μακρυά ἠχοῦνε βροντές θόρυβοι κανόνια
κι' ἐδῶ ἡ βροχή
ραβδίζει τά πάντα
οἱ φυλλωσιές οὐρλιάζουν
τά δέντρα ὀρθώνονται νά φύγουν
καί μέσ' στόν ἀγριεμένο βάτο π' ἄνοιξε
ἴδια ξεστηθιασμένη γριά
ἡ ἀπότομη λάμψη τῆς ἀστραπῆς
ἀποκαλύπτει
τούς δυό σάπιους κορμούς δέντρων
πού κοίτονται στή λάσπη
–τῶν δυό ἐραστῶν τά κορμιά –
μέ τά γυμνά κλαριά σά χέρια
νά κουνοῦν
φάσκελα
ἤ κραυγές:
«μάθε νά ζῆς!»;

στ' ἀπάγκιο
νά τό ψωμί πλάϊ ἡ γαβάθα π' ἀχνίζει
νά τό μαχαίρι
πάρε τό μαχαίρι νά κόψης ψωμί
πάρ' τό μαχαίρι
πάρ' τό μαχαίρι σοῦ λέω ἐργάτη:
ἀπόψε
νά προσέξης ἀπόψε:
τούτη ἡ νύχτα δέν εἶν' ὅμοια μέ τίς ἄλλες!

Marcinelle, 1956

236

MARCINELLE

now the doves are sleeping

and the hurricane is raging
the mad tousling of the trees
follows the suspicious silence
sounds afar of thunder clamor canon
and here the rain
lashes everything
the leaves howl
the trees straighten up to leave
and amid the frightened bush that opened
like an old woman baring her breast
the sudden flash of lightning
reveals
the two rotted tree-trunks
lying in the mud
– bodies of two lovers –
with bare branches like arms
hurling:
rude gestures
or cries of
"learn to live!"?

in the shelter
there's the bread and the steaming bowl beside
there's the knife
take the knife and cut bread
take the knife
take the knife worker I said:
tonight
be careful tonight:
this night is unlike any other!

Marcinelle, 1956

ΣΤΗΝ ΚΟΙΛΑΔΑ ΜΕ ΤΟΥΣ ΡΟΔΩΝΕΣ

...τοῦτο τό ἀσπαῖρον τριαντάφυλλον ροδῶνος ἀττικοῦ...
ΑΝΔΡΕΑΣ ΕΜΠΕΙΡΙΚΟΣ

ΣΤΟ ΘΑΝΑΤΟ ΤΟΥ ΑΝΘΟΛΟΓΟΥ ΤΗΣ «ΥΨΗΛΗΣ ΑΓΑΠΗΣ»

Et les seins mouraient.
B. PÉRET

Σέ τί κατεσπατάλησες πάλε τή νύχτα χτές πού μᾶς ἐπέρασε; Σέ τί
μετάνοιες ὑπεβλήθης, σέ τί πειρασμούς ὑπέκυψες; Σέ καταλαβαίνω,
τό βλέπω στά κλαϋμένα μάτια σου, στά κλάϋματα πού στεγνώσανε
τήν καρδιά σου καί τό πετσί σου, καί σ' τά κατάντησαν, δυστυχισμένε,
ὡσάν κελάϊδημα πουλιοῦ, ὡσάν τούς ξεραμένους μπακαλιάρους πού
ὀρτσάρουνε στό μεσιανό κατάρτι, νά ὑποκαταστήσουνε τίς σημαῖες τῶν
τόσο ἀνιαρῶν φανατισμῶν. Φέρε δῶ τά δυό μαῦρα διαμάντια πού κρατᾶς
στή φούχτα σου : αὐτά εἶναι ἡ ἀγάπη ! Κι' αὐτό πού κρατᾶς μέσα στήν
τζέπη τοῦ βρακιοῦ σου, πέταχ' το μακρυά : εἶναι τό περβάζι τῆς ἁμαρτίας,
εἶναι τό σαράκι πού τρώει τά σωθικά τῶν «ντερτιλήδων», εἶναι ἡ Ἀψίδα
τοῦ Θριάμβου ἀπ' ὅπου περάσανε τό λείψανό σου, Βενιαμίν Péret.

From: *IN THE VALE OF ROSERIES* (1978)

> *... this quivering rose from an Attic rosery...*
> ANDREAS EMBIRICOS

ON THE DEATH OF THE ANTHOLOGIST OF "SUBLIME LOVE"

> *Et les seins mouraient.*
> B. PÉRET

On what did you again squander the night just passed? To what penances did you subject yourself, to what temptations did you succumb? I can tell, I can see it in your tearful eyes, in the tears that dried your heart and skin, and left them, unhappy wretch, like a bird's warbling, like the dried cods luffing on the main mast, to replace the flags of such tiresome fanaticisms. Bring here the two black diamonds you have in your palm: for these are love! And what you have in your breeches' pocket, cast it far away: it is the verge of sin, it is the canker that devours the innards of the "lovelorn," it is the Arc de Triomphe through which they passed your remains, Benjamin Péret.

ΙΚΕΣΙΑ

Ἡ νύχτα διαδέχεται τήν ἡμέρα. Καί ὡς ἡ μέρα εἶναι ἡ περιοχή τῶν δέντρων καί τῶν λουλουδιῶν, ἔτσι κι' ἡ νύχτα εἶναι ἡ περιοχή τῶν φαντασμάτων καί τῶν κρουνῶν. Τοποθετεῖς τή σκάλα στόν τοῖχο, καί μέ πολλή πολλή προσοχή περνᾶς «ἀπό τήν ἄλλη μεριά». Ἀντιλαμβάνεσαι ψιθύρους, σάν θρόϊσμα νεκρῶν φύλλων, καί τό κελάρυσμα τῶν νερῶν, τόν σχεδόν ἀνεπαίσθητο θόρυβο πού κάμνει ἡ ρόδα τοῦ μύλου. Ἕνας τροχός, ἕνα ἀλέτρι, ἀστέρια, κι' ἀρχίζουν τά θαύματα καί τά μάγια τῆς νύχτας. Μέ τά χείλια κολλημένα στ' ἄσπρα της πόδια, στοχάσου καλά, λέγε μέσα σου πώς δέ θά πάψης ποτέ νά ἐλπίζης, πώς δέ θά πάψης ποτέ νά πιστεύης, πώς δέ θά πάψης ποτέ νά ἱκετεύης, πώς δέ θά πάψης ποτέ νά ἐπιστρατεύης ὅλη τήν ἀγάπη, πού ἔχεις μέσα σου κρυμμένη, ἐνάντια στίς δυνάμεις τοῦ κακοῦ.

SUPPLICATION

Night succeeds day. And just as day is the realm of trees and flowers, so night is the realm of ghosts and founts. You place the ladder against the wall and, very very carefully, you pass "to the other side." You perceive whispers, like the rustling of dead leaves and the babbling of the waters, the barely discernible noise made by the mill wheel. A wheel, a plough, stars, and the night's marvels and magic begin. With lips glued to her white feet, consider well, say to yourself that you will never stop hoping, that you will never stop believing, that you will never stop supplicating, that you will never stop mustering all the love that you have concealed within you against the forces of evil.

ΚΛΕΙΣΕ ΤΑ ΜΑΤΙΑ : ΤΟΤΕΣ ΜΠΡΟΣΤΑ ΣΟΥ
ΘΑ ΠΑΡΕΛΑΣΗ ΟΛΗ Η ΠΑΛΗΑ ΖΩΗ...

εἰς Μεμᾶν Μεσσήνην

Un homme au rêve habitué, vient ici parler
d'un autre qui est mort.

STÉPHANE MALLARMÉ

Περνοῦσα ἔτσι, ἀνύποπτος, μέσα στή γόνδολα, ὅταν μέ φώναξε :
– Ἕλληνα ! Ἔ, Ἕλληνα !...
Στέκονταν, ὄρθιος, πίσω ἀπ' τή σιδερένια καγκελόπορτα τοῦ
χορταριασμένου περίβολου, στόν Ἄη Γιώργη τῶν Γραικῶν, πάνω στό
κανάλι.
– Βρέ! τοῦ κάμω, τί ζητᾶς ἐδῶ;
– Εἶμαι νεκρός, μοῦ κάμει.
– Καλά, τοῦ λέω, εὐλογημένε! Σύ, ἕνας Ρωμαῖος, ἐδωπέρα βρῆκες
νά πεθάνης! Δέν ἐρχόσουνα ν' ἀναπαυθῆς κεῖ κάτω, στά χώματα τά δικά
μας, τά ἁπαλά!
– Θάν τὄθελα, μ' ἀπάντησε. Ἄλλωστω μοῦ τὄχε πεῖ μιά νύχτα κι'
ἡ Ναταλίνα τῆς Λιμνοθάλασσας, τήν ξέρεις, ἡ ἁπαλή κόρη μέ τούς
χρυσούς μαστούς. Μέ ξεμονάχιασε, παράμερα: «Πάρε με νά φύγουμε
ἀπό δῶ, μοῦ λέει. Εἶναι ἀδύνατο, δέν μπορῶ πιά νά ζήσω μέ "τσοί"
Μουρανέζοι». Ἡ μάννα της, βλέπεις, εἴταν Σμυρνιά. Ὅμως μέ κράτησε
ἐδῶ ἐκείνη ἡ ἄλλη, ἡ πουτάνα, ἡ ξανθιά ἡ ἔμορφη ἡ «Σ' Ἀγαπῶ», πού
ἐργαζότανε, θά τηνέ θυμᾶσαι, στά «πεννάκια» (;) στό γουναράδικο
τῆς Φρετσερίας. Ὡς κάθε βράδυ μοῦ ἐτραγούδαγε θερμά τό «μακρυά
κι' ἄν θᾶσαι», μοῦ γλύκαινε τ' ἀχεῖλι καί μοῦ σπάραζε τήν καρδιά.

CLOSE YOUR EYES: THEN ALL THE LIFE OF OLD
WILL PASS BEFORE YOU…

To Memas Messinis

Un homme au rêve habitué, vient ici parler
d'un autre qui est mort.
STÉPHANE MALLARMÉ

I was passing, unawares, in the gondola, when he called to me:

"Greek! Hey, Greek!…

He was standing erect behind the iron gate to the grassy yard of St. George of the Greeks, on the side of the canal.

"Son of a gun," I said, "What are you doing here?"

"I'm dead," he said to me.

"Well, for Heaven's sake," I told him, "Is this where you chose to die and you a Greek! Why didn't you come and go to your rest back home, in our own soft earth."

"I'd have liked to," he replied. "Besides, it's what I was told one night by Natalina from the Lagoon, you know her, the gentle girl with the golden breasts. She took me aside: "Let's get away from here," she said. "It's impossible, I can't live any more with 'zees' Muranese." Her mother, you see, was from Smyrna. But it was the other one who kept me here, the whore, the pretty blonde, the 'I'll always love you' one who worked, you'll recall her, at the 'quills' (?) at the fur store in Frezzeria. When every night she'd sensuously sing for me 'Though you're far away,' she'd sweeten my lips and break my heart."

Ο ΥΠΕΡΡΕΑΛΙΣΜΟΣ ΤΗΣ ΑΤΕΡΜΟΝΟΣ ΖΩΗΣ

είς Τριστάνο Tzara

ή σαρμανίτσα τοῦ ποιητοῦ
εἶναι τό νεκρικό κιβοῦρι
του
κι' ή κουδουνίστρα πού βάζουνε
στά βρεφικά του χέρια
εἶναι τό κυπαρίσσι
πού θά φυτρώση
πάνω στόν τάφο του

γιατί
– παρ' ὅλες τίς πικρίες πού τονέ ποτίζουνε –
ὁ ποιητής
τήν ἄρνηση τοῦ θανάτου φέρνει μαζύ του
κι' ἀκόμη
εἶν' αὐτός τοῦτος
τοῦ θάνατου ἡ ἄρνηση

κι' ἔτσι
τό νεκρικό κιβοῦρι τοῦ ποιητοῦ
θά γενῆ πάλε ἡ σαρμανίτσα του
τοῦ τάφου του τό κυπαρίσσι
πάλι ἡ κουδουνίστρα
πού θά κραδαίνη
στά φωτεινά τά χέρια
του

THE SURREALISM OF INTERMINABLE LIFE

to Tristan Tzara

the poet's cradle
is his
funeral casket
and the rattle placed
in his infant hands
is the cypress
that will grow
on his grave

for
– despite all the sorrows afflicting him –
the poet
brings with him death's negation
and still more
he is himself
death's negation

and so
the poet's funeral casket
will become again his cradle
the cypress on his grave
again the rattle
that he will shake
in his
shining hands

ΕΝΑ ΟΝΕΙΡΟ: Η ΖΩΗ

γύρω ἀπό τόν κορμό
τοῦ ὡραίου δέντρου
ἐλίσσεται
καί χορεύει
ἡ ὡραία
μιγάς

τό δέντρο εἶν' ὁλάνθιστο
ἀλλά καί τό κορμί
τῆς ὡραίας μιγάδος
ὡσαύτως:
ἀπ' τά λουλούδια –τίς ρῶγες –τῶν μαστῶν της
τή λαμπρότητα τῆς ἁπαλῆς κοιλιᾶς
τῶν σφαιρικῶν γλουτῶν
τῶν ἄψογων μηρῶν
στό φουντωτό σκοτεινό δάσος τῆς ἡβικῆς χώρας
τήν πλούσια κόμη
ὅπου σκορπάει τά βαρειά της μύρα
ὡς κυματίζει ξέπλεκη –ἐλεύθερα –
σπιθοβολώντας μέσα στή νύχτα

τό δέντρο εἶναι μιά μαγνόλια
κι' ἡ ὡραία μιγάς
εἶναι κι' ἐκείνη μιά μαγνόλια
χυμώδης
πλούσια
κι' ἡδονική

ποιό εἶναι ὡραιότερο
τοῦ ὡραίου δέντρου
τοῦ ὡραίου κορμιοῦ;

A DREAM: LIFE

round the trunk
of the beautiful tree
the beautiful
Creole
weaves
and dances

the tree is in full bloom
and the body
of the lovely Creole
likewise:
from the flowers – the nipples – of her breasts
the brilliance of the soft belly
of the rounded haunches
of the flawless thighs
to the pubic region's thick dark forests
the plentiful locks
where she sprinkles her heady scent
as they ripple loosely – freely –
glinting in the night

the tree is a magnolia
and the lovely Creole
is herself a magnolia
luscious
plentiful
and voluptuous

which is more beautiful
the beautiful tree
the beautiful body?

τ' ὡραῖο κορμί
γιατί τό δέντρο γιά πάντα του μνήσκει βουβό
– οὔτε κι' οἱ πιό τρελλοί ἀνέμοι δέν ἡμποροῦν
νά σείσουν τό βαρύ πυκνό φύλλωμα καί τά σαρκώδη ἄνθη –
ἐνῶ τ' ὡραῖο τό πλούσιο κορμί
πάει κι' ἔρχεται
μεθάει παράφορα
κλαδοκορμόριζα
δονεῖται
καί στόν
παραμικρό τόν ψίθυρο
τοῦ
«σέ ἀγαπῶ»

the beautiful body
for the tree remains forever silent
– not even the wildest of winds is able
to shake the thick profuse leafage and fleshy blossom –
whereas the beautiful and plentiful body
moves to and fro
becomes passionately drunk
shakes
root and branch
at even the
slightest whisper
of
"I love you"

ΣΤΟΥΣ ΔΡΟΜΟΥΣ ΤΟΥΣ ΒΙΟΤΙΚΟΥΣ

πρόσεξε: αὐτός ὁ οἰδίπους
πού πρόκειται νά συναντήσουμε
στή διχάλα τῶν βοιωτικῶν δρόμων
ὄχι: δέν εἶναι ὁ Οἰδίπους τῆς μυθολογίας

παρ᾽ ὅλη τήν οἰονεί ἐλεφαντίαση
τήν ποδάγρα – τήν ἀκρομεγαλία –
ἀπ᾽ τήν ὁποίαν πάσχει
σ᾽ τό λέω δέν ἔχει σχέση καμμιά μέ τόν Οἰδίποδα τόν παλαιό

οὔτε τόν πάτερα του ἔχει σκοτώσει
οὔτε – σύρε καί πρόλαβε καί πές το τῆς Ἰοκάστης –

οὔτε καί τήν μητέρα του πώς πρόκειται νά παντρευτῆ

ἄσ᾽ τόνε ἀκόμη λίγο καί θά προχωρήση
κι᾽ ὕστερα – σέ λίγο πάλε – μιά γιά πάντα θά χαθῆ

ὅμως κεῖνος ὁ μαῦρος σκύλος
πού κείτεται στή μέση τοῦ δρόμου τοῦ ἡλιόλουστου
– τοῦ «ἡλιόλουστου» ἀπ᾽ τόν ἥλιο πού πάει νά βασιλέψη –
κοιμισμένος ἤ νεκρός ἀνάμεσα στίς γκαβαλίνες
ἔ! λοιπόν αὐτός εἶναι
αὐτός εἶναι κάτι

μάθε το: εἶναι ἡ Σφίγγα τοῦ παραμυθιοῦ
ὡς ἔπεσε ἀπ᾽ τό βάθρο
σάν εἶδε
πώς «μυστικό»
δέν ὑπῆρχε πιά

ON LIFE'S PATHS

take heed: the swollen-footed man
that we're going to encounter
at the fork in Boeotian roads
is not, no, the Oedipus of myth

despite the so-called elephantiasis
the gout - the acromegaly -
afflicting him
he has I tell you no connection at all with the Oedipus of old

neither has he killed his father
nor - go, lose no time and tell Jocasta -
is he going to marry his mother

leave him a while longer and he'll be on his way
and then - in a while again - he'll disappear for good

yet that black dog
lying in the middle of the sunlit road
- "sunlit" by the sun about to set -
sleeping or dead amidst the dung
well! now this
this is something

listen then: it's the Sphinx of fairy tale
who fell from the pedestal
when she saw
there was no longer
any "riddle"

ΤΙΜΩΝ Ο ΑΘΗΝΑΙΟΣ

les délicats sont malheureux...
LA FONTAINE

ἐφανταζούντανε ἑαυτόν
σάν
ψωριασμένο λύκο
καθώς ὅλ' οἱ ἄνθρῶποι
ἀλυχτούσανε γύρω του
οἱ λυσσαγμένοι
σκύλοι

ἀλλ' ἐπί τέλους ἐκατάλαβε
– πόσον ἀργά Θεέ μου!
πόσο ἀργά –
πώς ἔτσι
πάντα
γίνεται:
νά ἐπιτίθενται οἱ ἄνθρῶποι
–ἄγρια κι' ἀλύπητα –
στόν κάθε μεμονωμένο τους συνάνθρωπο
ὅμοιοι
μέ
λυσσασμένα
σκυλιά

TIMON OF ATHENS

les délicats sont malheureux...
LA FONTAINE

he saw himself
as
a mangy wolf
since all the people
around him barked
the mad
dogs

but finally he realized
– so late dear God!
so late –
that this is
always
how it is:
with people attacking
any solitary fellow of theirs
– savagely and mercilessly –
just
like
mad
dogs

ΤΟ ΚΟΥΤΙ ΤΗΣ ΠΑΝΔΩΡΑΣ

Cogito, ergo sum.
ΚΑΡΤΕΣΙΟΣ

Ἡ Ἱστορία!
τί ἀβασάνιστες πληροφορίες συνεκράτησε
τί λανθασμένες φῆμες μᾶς μετέδωσε!
Πόσα χουνέρια καί τί πλεκτάνες!
Ἄ! ἡ Κλειώ! Μά βέβαιο
πώς ἐσημείωνε ὅ,τι κι᾽ ἄν ἄκουγε:
φαίνεται πώς πολύ λίγο θά τήν σκότιζε
ν᾽ ἀντιληφθῆ
τί εἴτανε ἀλήθεια
καί τί δέν εἴταν!
Μιά ὁλόκληρη ζωή σπουδῆς καί προσοχῆς καί ἔρευνας
μᾶς ἐπιτρέπει σήμερα
ν᾽ ἀποκαλύψουμε –νά ποῦμε –
πώς ὅλα τά περί Πανδώρας
καί τοῦ κουτιοῦ της
εἶναι ἀνάξια λόγου παραμύθια...
Οὔτε ἡ Πανδώρα οὔτε οἱ θεοί
βάλανε τίποτα μέσ᾽ στό κουτί
κι᾽ οὔτε μέ τ᾽ ἄνοιγμα
φύγαν τά δῶρα
(πού δέν ὑπῆρχαν).
Προσποιήσεις ψευτιές (φτηνές ψευτιές)
ἀνέντιμες ὑποσχέσεις καί προδοσίες
μᾶς κάναν νά
πιστέψουμε πώς κάτι ἔκλεινε μέσα τό
κουτί
πού εἶχε ἡ Πανδώρα!
Κι᾽ ἄν ὑπήρξαμε μωρόπιστοι
ἄνθρωποι καί κουτοί

PANDORA'S BOX

Cogito, ergo sum.
DESCARTES

History!
what desultory information it has retained
what misleading rumors it has conveyed to us!
So many mishaps and what machinations!
Ah! Clio! But no doubt
she recorded whatever she heard:
she had very little concern it seems
to grasp
what was true
and what not!
A whole life of study and observation and research
allows us today
to reveal – to state –
that everything concerning Pandora
and her box
is a fairytale unworthy of mention...
Neither Pandora nor the gods
placed anything in the box
nor when it was opened
did any gifts escape
(for none existed).
Pretenses lies (cheap lies)
insincere promises and betrayals
led us to
believe that something was shut inside the
box
that Pandora had!
And though we were gullible
people and foolish

(πρῶτος ἐγώ)
πάντως εἶμαι σέ θέση σήμερα
νά βεβαιώσω
πώς καί κουτί
(ν' ἀνήκη στήν Πανδώρα)
ἀκόμη δέν ὑπῆρχε!

(me more than anyone)
I am in a position today nonetheless
to confirm
that a box
(belonging to Pandora)
did not even exist!

ΤΑ ΒΑΣΑΝΑ ΤΗΣ ΑΓΑΠΗΣ

Du musst das Leben nicht verstehen,
dann wird es werden wie ein Fest.
R.M. RILKE

καθώς ἀνέμισαν
τά μαλλάκια της
ἔτσι μπροστά στά μάτια
μου
λές καί σάν ξαφνικά νά ξύπνησα
καί γιά πρώτη φορά
τήν εἶδα
– καί τήν ἐπρόσεξα –
τήν ὡραία
νεαρή
κόρη

μέ συνεκίνησε
ἡ ἁρμονία
τῶν κινήσεών της
ἡ ραδινότης τῶν μελῶν
τοῦ κορμιοῦ της
ἡ γοητεία τοῦ βλέμματός
της
ἡ ἁπαλή στρογγυλάδα
τῶν μαστῶν της
ἡ ὅλη χάρη τέλος
πού ἀνεδίδετο
ἀπό τό
κομψό
ὁλόδροσο
πλάσμα

THE TORMENTS OF LOVE

Du musst das Leben nicht verstehen,
dann wird es werden wie ein Fest.
R.M. RILKE

as her gentle hair
blew
before my
eyes
as though suddenly I had awoken
for the first time
I saw
– and observed –
that lovely
young
girl

I was taken
by the harmony
of her movements
the lissomness
of her limbs
the fascination
of her gaze
the gentle rotundity
of her breasts
and more by all the charm
emitted
by that
elegant
vernal
creature

κι᾽ ἀμέσως σκέφτηκα
–καί «φιλοσόφησα» –
ὁ νοῦς μου πῆγε
στόν ἀγαθό ἐκεῖνον
πού μπορεῖ κάποτε
–μά εἶμαι βέβαιος –
νά ὑποφέρη
μαρτυρικά
νά δυστυχήση
σά θά φαντάζεται
πώς ἔχει σκέψη
κι᾽ ἔχει ψυχή
τό τρυφερό
τό αἰθέριο
τό
πλασματάκι

καί νά ματώνη ἡ καρδιά του
ν᾽ ἀπελπίζεται
ὡς θ᾽ ἀποδίδη
ἔστω καί
κόκκο νοῦ
στ᾽ ὁλότελα
ἄδειο
μικρό
κρανίο

and I straightaway reflected
– and "philosophized" –
my mind turned
to that innocent
who may at times
– I'm quite sure –
suffer
torments
know misery
when he imagines that
the tender
the ethereal
the
little creature
has a mind
and soul

and his heart may bleed
despair
if he attributes
even
a grain of intelligence
to that completely
empty
little
head

ΕΙΣ ΚΩΝΣΤΑΝΤΙΝΟΝ ΜΠΑΚΕΑΝ

πού ἐνδιαφέρθηκε γιά «πρόσφατα» ποιήματά μου

πράγματι ἡ
«ποιητική» παραγωγή μου
τώρα τελευταῖα
εἶναι οὐσιαστικά
ἀνύπαρκτη

ὄχι βέβαια πώς ἔχω πιά πάψει
καί ποιήματα
καί στίχους
καί παραμύθια
ν' ἀραδιάζω
καί νά κρυφολέω στόν ἑαυτό μου

ὅμως ὡς παραλείπω
νάν τά σημειώσω στό χαρτί
τά λησμονῶ
καί φυσικά δέν
ἔχω πιά τίποτα νά παρουσιάσω

ἄλλωστε καί κανείς δέν μοῦ τά ζητᾶ:
εἶδα τί λίγη σημασία
γύρω μου
δῶσαν
καί δίνουνε στά ποιήματα

γιά ἕναν μελλοντικό σχολιαστή
θἄν' ὑπεραρκετά
τά ποιήματά μου τά παληά
καί πόσον εὔγλωττη
θά εἶναι
ἡ σιωπή ἡ τωρινή μου

TO CONSTANTINE BAKEAS

who showed interest in my "recent" poems

without doubt
my "poetic" production
of late
is essentially
non-existent

not that I've stopped
mumbling to myself
or churning out
poems
and verses
and fairytales

but as I omit
to note them on paper
I forget them
and naturally
have nothing left to show

besides no one asks me for them:
I saw what little significance
around me
they attached
and attach to poems

for some future critic
my past poems
will be more than enough
and how eloquent
my present silence
will be

Ο ΟΡΦΕΥΣ

les nuages, les merveilleux nuages…
CH. BAUDELAIRE

τόν Ὀρφέα ποτέ –μά ποτέ –τίποτα δέν τόν ἐπαρηγόρησε
γιά τήν διπλή ἀπώλεια
τῆς Εὐρυδίκης:
ἄλλοτε –γιά λίγο –ἔλεγε κανά τραγοῦδι μέσ' στό μαράζι του
ἄλλοτε –γιά λίγο πάλε –
τά χρώματα
τόν γοητεύανε
μέ τίς ἄπειρες ποικιλίες τους
καί τούς συμπτωματικούς
λογῆς λογῆς συνδυασμούς τους

μιά φορά –κατά τοῦ ἥλιου
τό βασίλεμα –
πρόσεξε μέσ' στό γαλάζιο τ' οὐρανοῦ
γοητευτικές ἀράδες
σύννεφα
–γι' αὐτά πού στό Καβοῦρι κάποτε ἕνας χωροφύλακας*
σά μεταμεληθείς ἐκραύγασε:
«Ἰδού τά σύννεφα τοῦ Ἐγγονόπουλου!» –

ἀλλά αὐτά –πραγματικά –
δέν εἴσανε τά σύννεφα τοῦ Ἐγγονόπουλου
εἴταν μαχαίρια
λεπίδες
ἀκονισμένες κάμες καί χατζάρια
πού πάνω στίς γαλάζιες τους ἐσθῆτες
ἐκρατάγανε

---

* Ἄραγες νά γνώριζε τόν συνάδελφό του--κατωτέρου ἄλλωστε βαθμοῦ--ἐν ὑπηρεσίᾳ στό Tinchebray (Orne);

ORPHEUS

les nuages, les merveilleux nuages…
CH. BAUDELAIRE

Orpheus never – but never – found any consolation
for the double loss
of Eurydice:
sometimes – for a while – he would sing a song in his languor
sometimes – again for a while –
colors
fascinated him
with their infinite varieties
and their accidental
combinations of all kinds

once – at the sun's
setting –
he noticed in the sky's blue
fascinating arrays of
clouds
– about which once in Kavouri a gendarme*
as if repentant had cried:
"Behold the clouds of Engonopoulos!" –

yet these – in truth –
were not the clouds of Engonopoulos
they were knives
blades
sharpened daggers and sabers
that upon their blue gowns
were worn

---

* I wonder if he knew his colleague – though of a lower rank – serving in Tinchebray (Orne)?

οἱ σκληρότατες τῆς Θράκης οἱ παρθένες

κι' αὐτά κραδαίνοντας
οἱ σκληρές παρθένες στ' ἄπονα τά χέρια τους
μ' αὐτά –λέω –πέσανε πάνω του:
τόν κατακρεουργήσανε
τόν κομματιάσαν
τόν Ὀρφέα

by Thrace's most cruel virgins

and brandishing these
in their heartless hands the cruel virgins
fell upon him – I repeat – with these:
butchering
hacking
Orpheus

ΠΕΡΙ ΑΝΕΜΩΝ, ΥΔΑΤΩΝ ΚΑΙ ΑΛΛΩΝ

...balançant le feston et l'ourlet...
CH. BAUDELAIRE

φυσάει ὁ ἄνεμος
τοῦ φθινοπώρου
καί σαρώνει
πάνω στό πλακόστρωτο τῆς αὐλῆς
τά ξερά φύλλα
πού ἐπέσαν ἀπ' τά δέντρα
σκισμένες ἐπιστολές
κουρέλια
πόθους
ἐλπίδες
ὄνειρα

ἄλλοτε ὁ ἄνεμος φυσᾶ
κι' ἀνοίγει τρύπες στό νερό
ἀπ' ὅπου ἀναβλύζουν
τά δάκρυα τῶν ψαριῶν
λουλούδια
φραντζόλες
πόθοι
ἐλπίδες
ὄνειρα

κι' ἄλλοτε ὁ ἄνεμος φυσᾶ
καί σέ ὄχι πολύ παρωχημένες ἐποχές
«μούντερνε» κάτω ἀπό τίς μακρυές τίς φοῦστες
τῶν ὡραίων γυναικῶν
κι' ἔφτανε μέχρι
τά εὐγενικά τους κάλλη
τά μυστικά

ON EVERYTHING UNDER THE SUN AND MORE

...balançant le feston et l'ourlet...
CH. BAUDELAIRE

the autumn wind
blows
and over the paved yard
sweeps
the dry leaves
fallen from the trees
torn-up letters
rags
desires
hopes
dreams

sometimes the wind blows
making holes in the water
from which spout
the fish's tears
flowers
loaves
desires
hopes
dreams

and sometimes the wind blows
and not in times long past
"diving" beneath the long skirts
of beautiful women
and reaching as far as
their secret
gentle charms

ΠΕΡΙ ΚΡΟΚΟΔΕΙΛΟΥ ΚΛΑΔΑ

ποιός εἴταν ὁ Κροκόδειλος Κλαδᾶς;
εἴταν πραγματικά κορκόδειλος
καί ψεύτικα κι' ἀπατηλά
τά κλάϋματά του
μέσ' στή νύχτα;
ὄχι: πραγματικά εἴταν ἀϊτός
πού ἔκλαιγε ἀληθινά
τή νύχτα

(δηλαδή κατά τῆς νύχτας τή διάρκεια
καί γιά τή νύχτα τῆς σκλαβιᾶς
πού ἔπνιγε ἄσπλαχνα – βαρειά –
ὁλόκληρη τή χώρα)

ἀλλά τά κλάϋματα γι' αὐτόν εἴσαν ἐκτόνωση
κάποτε τά δάκρυα στέρευαν
καί μέσα του ξύπναγε ὁ πόθος κι' ἡ ἐλπίδα τῆς αὐγῆς:
ὅλα νά τά βαρέση χάμου
καί ν' ἀνοίξη
τά φτερά του

καί μέσ' στή χαρά τοῦ ἥλιου μεγαλόπρεπ' ἀργοπέταγε
ἐτιμωροῦσε τούς δειλούς τούς ἄναντρους
κι' ἔσπερνε τῆς λευτεριᾶς μηνύματα
στίς ψυχές τίς καλογεννημένες

μέ τίς φονάρες του δέν ἐξεστόμιζε κοτσάνες – ὡσάν ἄλλους –
ἀλλά μόνε τή λέξη τήν ἱερή βροντολαλοῦσε:
Ἐλευθερία!

καί δέν τόν ἔγνοιαζε ἄν στό βασίλεμα
ψόφιο ἤ ζωντανό ὁ ἥλιος

ON CROCODILE CLADAS

who was Crocodile Cladas?
was he in fact a crocodile
and his crying
false and deceptive
in the night?
no: he was in fact an eagle
that genuinely cried
at night

(during that is the course of the night
and for the night of slavery
that was cruelly – deeply – stifling
the whole country)

yet crying was a relief for him
eventually the tears dried up
and within him woke the desire and hope of dawn:
to fling everything to the ground
and to open
his wings

and in the joy of the sun he majestically hovered
punishing the cowardly and craven
and sowing messages of freedom
in noble-born souls

in his loud voice it was not nonsense he uttered – as with others –
but rather he thundered the one sacred word:
Freedom!

and he cared not if at its setting
the sun would find him

τόν πετύχαινε:
πάντως θέ νά τόν ἔβρισκε ὁπωσδήποτε
ἀετό
μέσα στά δέντρα
χωρίς δεσμά
κι' ἐλεύθερο γιά πάντα!

dead or alive:
anyway it would certainly see him
as an eagle
amidst the trees
without fetters
and free forever!

Η ΑΔΕΛΑΪΣ* ΤΩΝ ΥΠΟΦΗΤΩΝ

Τό ἄκρον ἄωτον στήν ἐπιστήμη τῆς ὑπερευαισθησίας: ἡ ἀγάπη.
Τοῦ ἄκρου ἀώτου τῆς εὐαισθησίας; Πάλε ἡ ἀγάπη!
Βέβαια, κι᾽ ἡ ἀτέρμονη προσδοκία, στή ζωή, τῆς ἔρημης χαρᾶς.
Βάλε καί τά μάτια: μυριάδες μάτια,
σωροί ματιῶνε,
ἄπειρα ζεύγη ματιῶν,
μέ τή γοητεία τους, τό καθένα,
τό χρῶμα τους, τό βλέμμα τους, τή γλῶσσα τους
καί τό γλωσσάριό τους,
τό γέλιο τους, τά δάκρυα καί τή θλίψη τους, τόν ἔρωτά τους,
ἤ καί τήν ἀδιαφορία τους ἀκόμη.
Μάτια ὀρθάνοιχτα, σφαλιχτά, μάτια πού κρατοῦμε κρυφά, φανερά,
μυστικά, μέσα στά ἴδια μας τά μάτια, πάντα, πάντα.
Μάτια γυναικῶν, πουλιῶν, παιδιῶν,
μάτια ὅπου δέν εἴδαμε, κι᾽ ὅπου μᾶς εἴπανε πολλά γι᾽ αὐτά.
Μάτια γλαρά, νυσταγμένα, μάτια γιομάτα πόθους:
ἄστρα σπινθηροβόλα, ὑπέρλαμπρα, ἀτέλειωτα πάνω
στόν στοργικό ἀτέλειωτο νυχτερινό μας οὐρανό.

Κι᾽ ὅμως: φιλιά στά μάτια δέν εἶναι χωρισμός.

Ἡ ζωή, ἡ γνώση,
ἡ γνώση τῆς ζωῆς (τῶν ματιῶν πάντα)
νἄναι τροφή ὀνείρου ἁπαλοῦ,
ἤ μήπως παραλήρημα;

Λέω,
γιά τίς κληρομαντεῖες,
ὑπόλογοι
θἄν᾽ οἱ ὑποφῆται τοῦ Ναοῦ
τῆς ζωῆς (τῆς δόξας) τῶν ματιῶν.

---

* ἡ μεγάλη ἱέρεια τοῦ φετιχισμοῦ

ADELAÏS* OF THE HIEROPHANTS

The height of hypersensitivity's science: love.
The height of sensitivity? Again love!
And, of course, the endless expectation, in life, of desolate joy.
Add eyes too: myriads of eyes,
heaps of eyes,
infinite pairs of eyes,
each with their own charm,
their color, their look, their language
and their glossary,
their laughter, their tears and grief, their love,
or even their indifference.
Eyes wide open, shut, eyes holding hidden, overt,
secrets, in our very own eyes, always, always.
Eyes of women, of birds, of children,
eyes we haven't seen, but about which we've heard much.
Eyes bright, sleepy, eyes filled with desire:
radiant, brilliant stars, endless upon
our tender endless night sky.

Nonetheless: kisses on the eyes do not mean
separation

Is life, knowledge,
the knowledge of life (of eyes as always)
food for a gentle dream,
or perhaps delirium?

In my view,
accountable
for the priestly oracles
will be the hierophants of the Temple
of the life (the glory) of eyes.

* the great high-priestess of fetishism

Ο ΒΕΛΙΣΑΡΙΟΣ

...sous ses habits déchirés et poudreux,
effrangés par le temps, cardés par la misère...

CASIMIR DELAVIGNE

σά βόγγαε ή ἄγια αὐτοκρατορία
ἀπό τά δεινά
ὅταν τό ἔθνος λύγαε ἀπό
τίς ἐπιθέσεις τῶν Βαρβάρων
κι' ή ἐπικράτεια ὁλόκληρη γονάτιζε μέ τ' ἀλλεπάλληλα
τῶν ἐχτρῶν χτυπήματα
πάντα σ' αὐτόν προσφεῦγαν
γιά ν' ἀπαλλάξη τή χώρα ἀπό τά βάσανα
ἀπ' αὐτόν πάλι ἐπροσδοκοῦσαν
τήν ἀπολύτρωση
τή σωτηρία

κι' ἔπειτα;
ἔπειτα: ποῦ τόν ξέραν
ποῦ τόν εἴδανε;

ἔτσι
στούς τελευταίους ἀκριβῶς χρόνους τῆς φθίνουσας περιόδου «τοῦ
'30»
ἀναμεσίς
στούς φιλόδοξους μέ τ' ἀκαθόριστα σχέδια
τούς ἄγρια λυσσαγμένους –παρ' ὅλο τό ἰσχνότατο τῶν ἐφοδίων τους–
γιά μιάν ὅσο μποροῦσαν πλατύτερη ἐπικράτηση
τούς ἄγουρους –σαλιάρηδες –διακονιαρέους καί κλέφτες τῆς δόξας
ξεκίνησε νεώτατος ὁ Βελισάριος
παρέα μέ τόν Ἀνδρέα τόν Ἐμπειρῖκο
νά δημιουργήση
καί νά ζήση

BELISARIUS

...sous ses habits déchirés et poudreux,
effrangés par le temps, cardés par la misère...
CASIMIR DELAVIGNE

when the holy empire groaned
from its sufferings
when the nation reeled before
the barbarian assaults
and the whole realm crumpled beneath successive
enemy blows
it was always to him they turned
to free the land of its affliction
and it was from him again that they awaited
deliverance
salvation

and then?
then: no one
had ever heard of him

so
in the very last years of the waning "'30s"
amidst
the ambitious with their vague plans
those furiously thirsting – despite their meager talents –
for as great a prominence as possible
the green – driveling – beggars and stealers of fame
a youthful Belisarius set out
in the company of Andreas Embirikos
to create
and live

ΠΑΡΑΦΑΣΙΣ
ἤ
Η ΚΟΙΛΑΔΑ ΜΕ ΤΟΥΣ ΡΟΔΩΝΕΣ

τί εἶναι στή ζωή πού νά μήν εἶν' αἴνιγμα
                    γρῖφος;
μά κι' ἡ ζωή ἡ ἴδια δέν εἶναι γρῖφος
                   αἴνιγμα;

τί δυστυχία οἱ τεχνοκράτες
μέσα στήν τύφλα ἀπ' ὁλοῦθε πού τούς περιζώνει
νά παραμένουνε
στίς κοῦφες πεποιθήσεις (;) τους
ἰσχυρογνώμονες
πεισματωμένοι
γινατζῆδες

τοῦ ποιητῆ
πιά μόνη –θεόθεν –σωτηρία λύσις
παρηγόρηση
μένει ἡ κοιλάς μέ τίς τριανταφυλλιές
ὅ ἐστι
μεθερμηνευόμενο
ἡ κοιλάδα τῶν ροδώνων

PARAPHASIA
or
THE VALE OF ROSERIES

what in life is not an enigma
                         a riddle?
and is not life itself a riddle
                         an enigma?

how sad for technocrats
in the blindness surrounding them on all sides
to remain
with their hollow convictions (?)
opinionated
obstinate
pigheaded

the poet's
one – god-sent – saving solution
consolation
remains the valley with its roses
that is
to say
the vale of roseries

ΤΟ ΜΕΤΡΟΝ : Ο ΑΝΘΡΩΠΟΣ

ΤΟ ΜΕΤΡΟΝ: Ο ΑΝΘΡΩΠΟΣ

Ἡ ζωή, ὁ Θάνατος,
κι' ἀναμεσίς
ἡ Τέχνη (ἡ ποίηση)
ὅπου καταξιώνει τή ζωή,
τήν διαιωνίζει,
καί τό θάνατο καταργεῖ.

Γι' αὐτό, πρός τί, γιατί
ἡ «στράτευση», ἡ σάτιρα, τά πείσματα, τό μῖσος,
πού δέν τούς δίνει, πέρα ὥς πέρα, καμμιά σημασία ἡ ζωή,
κι' ὁ θάνατος δέν στέργει
ὅλως διόλου
νάν τά ξέρη.

From: *MAN: THE MEASURE* (2005)

MAN: THE MEASURE

Life, death,
and between
Art (poetry)
that appreciates life,
perpetuates it,
and abolishes death.

So, why, to what end
"militancy," satire, spitefulness, hate,
to which life gives no importance at all,
and which death does not deign
in any way
to accept.

ΕΞΟΜΟΛΟΓΗΣΕΙΣ ΤΗΣ ΣΤΕΡΙΑΣ, ΤΗΣ ΘΑΛΑΣΣΑΣ

ἡ πίπα ἀπό γιούσουρι
ὅπου θωπευτικά κρατῶ
στά δάχτυλα
ταυτόχρονα μέ τήν ἄφταστη τοῦ καπνίσματος
τήν ἡδονή
μοῦ φέρνει ἔντονα καί τῆς θάλασσας
τή γοητεία
μέ τ' ἀρμυρίκια καί τά φύκια
της
τούς ἄπατους βυθούς της
τούς βαθυγάλανους
καί τούς κρυφούς
τήν ἀπίθανη λαμπρότητα
τῶν ψαριῶν
καί τῶν φυτῶνε
της

ὅμως
ἀπ' τά σαρκώδη λούλουδα
τῆς θάλασσας
προτιμάω πολύ περισσότερο
τά ἄνθη τῆς στεριᾶς
τ' ἀέρινα

γιά τά λουλούδια τοῦ κάμπου καί τῶν περβολιῶν
παθαίνομαι
καί τά γνωρίζω καλά
ὡς τ' ἀγαπῶ:
ἡ ἀγάπη εἶναι ὁ μόνος τρόπος κάτι νά γνωρίσουμε

γνωρίζω
λοιπόν

CONFESSIONS OF THE LAND, OF THE SEA

the black coral pipe
that tenderly I hold
between my fingers
together with smoking's unrivalled
pleasure
also brings me the sea's
allure
with its tamarisk and
seaweed
its fathomless depths
deep blue
and secret
the amazing brilliance
of its fish
and
plants

yet
to the fleshy flowers
of the sea
I much prefer
the land's
ethereal flowers

I'm mad
about the flowers of plains and gardens
and I know them well
for I love them:
love is the only way for us to know something

I know
then

κάτι λουλούδια κόκκινα
πού δέν θυμᾶμαι πῶς τά λένε
καί φυσικά δέν μπορῶ καί νάν τά πῶ

καί κάτι ἄλλα λουλούδια
ὑπέροχα μυστηριώδη
καί κρυφά
γνωρίζω
ὅπου αὐτά τά ξέρω
τά ξέρω μάλιστα καλά
ἀλλά καί πού δέν κάνει διόλου νάν τά πῶ

certain red flowers
whose name I don't recall
and about which naturally I can't speak

and I know
certain other flowers
wonderful mysterious
and secret
which I recall
in fact I recall them well
but about which it's not right for me to speak

NOTES TO THE POEMS

I have chosen not to supply my own notes to the poems in this selection. Though I recognize that some of the culturally-specific references in the poems may be obscure to the non-Greek reader, I consider the bafflement this may cause totally in keeping with the aims of surrealist poetry. The notes which follow are those provided by Engonopoulos himself and I consider them an integral part of the poems. They are often characterized by the same irony and tongue-in-cheek humor as the poems themselves. According to one critic, with these notes, Engonopoulos is taking the reader into collusion with him (see Andreas Belezinis, "'Σχόλια ἐπὶ σχολίων': ὅπου ὁ Ἐγγονόπουλος μᾶς κλείνει τὸ μάτι," in *Diavazo* 478 (October 2007): 114–116). Consequently, they should not be seen as explanatory notes so much as glosses or comments on the poems by the poet. In any case, the notes are relatively few and did not originally accompany the poems but were added by Engonopoulos when his first two collections were republished by Ikaros in 1966, in other words almost thirty years after their first publication. The notes to *Bolivar*, which are considerably greater in number, were also added when the poem was republished in the first standard edition of his work and were, as I discussed in the introduction, probably written with the foreign reader in mind. Only in the case of *In the Vale of Roseries* were the notes published together with the poems in the first edition. Needless to say, I have translated and included only those notes relevant to the poems translated and included in this selection.

NOTES TO *DO NOT DISTRACT THE DRIVER* AND *THE CLAVICEMBALOS OF SILENCE*

Trams and Acropolis

The poem is very old indeed. One of my first poems. I don't know where it came from. Anyhow I didn't reject it: I included it in the collection [...].

Osiris

"Hippolýta" is what I wanted. The "Hippólyta" in the first edition is a mistake.

Eleonora

The poem resembles a somewhat similar one by André Breton. This was pointed out to me, in 1943, by my friend, the poet G. Likos, who showed me an anthology of surrealism containing the poem by M. Breton. I read it for the first time. An amusing coincidence! Quite simply I had taken the inspiration for my poem from the lines by Souris:

> ... like Aretinos
> sings of Lelia's
> hidden beauties.

I was also influenced by the recollection of the paintings by Goya, Gustave Courbet and others, who painted their beloveds in the same position always, sometimes clothed, sometimes naked, sometimes the front view, sometimes the rear view, etc.

Nocturnal Maria

Alexandros Karamanlakis. A Greek, and for this reason forgotten, pioneer of aviation. In my childhood, I heard a great deal of talk about him and his plane crash (in the bloom of his youth), a new Icarus, in the waters of the Corinthian Gulf.

Episode

Constantinople has never been the setting for any strong images in my life. However, I always recall its marvelous gardens with their magnolias.

Skala Oropos, July 1965

NOTES TO *BOLIVÁR*

The following notes contain either explanations concerning certain proper names or place names in the text, or are extracts from various readings, subsequent to the composition of the poem, that corroborate and strengthen, so to speak, certain images in *Bolivár*.

The first quote is from Plutarch. The second is from the book by Gabriele d'Annunzio: "Le dit du Sourd et Muet qui fut Miraculé en l'An de Grâce 1266." However, given that it is in quotation marks in the text, it is somewhat doubtful that it is by d'Annunzio, even though no source is cited.

Odysseus Androutsos is, for the poet, not only one of the most splendid figures of the 1821 Greek War of Independence, but also one of the most prominent figures in human history.

"they remained... always alone." Cf. "Se tu sarai solo, sara tutto tuo" (Leonardo da Vinci).

The line "Moistening their mattresses with tears" in the first edition instead of the correct "Moistening their pillows with tears" is due to a printing error.

"...on Hydra's seven shores...." Hydra, that stark symbol of Freedom! The recollection of this heroic and unconquered island was particularly welcome and comforting during the years of the Occupation.

"With a rifle hanging over your shoulder...." Cf.

> *What kind of chieftain are you,*
> *when you don't carry a rifle?*

(Folk song)

"With your chest bared, with your body covered in wounds...."
Cf.

Le fort... se trouvait contenir alors deux mille Albanais, qu'on désignait par le nom de Cimariotes. C'était pour moi un spectacle à la fois nouveau et suprenant de voir dix huit à vingt officiers, très vieux et tous bien portants, ayant la figure couverte de cicatrices ainsi que la poitrine que, par luxe guerrier, ils portaient toute découverte. (J. Cassanova : *Memoires*, tome I ch. VII.)

"...painted you... with wash, half white, half blue...." In many parts of the Greek domain, it is customary at times of religious festivals to paint the exterior of the church or the churchyard wall with whitewash and bluing.

"in the districts of the Tatavlians..." (nominative: Tatavla). A densely-populated district of Constantinople, first settled by Greeks from the Mani who worked in the Imperial Ottoman dockyards in the area known in Byzantine times as the *Tabula*. To the Greek visitor, it aroused similar but even stronger emotions than the Rio dei Greci in Venice and the Griechengasse in Vienna. It was, with its vibrant population, a living remnant of Turkish-occupied Greece, full of Orthodoxy's subtle charm and the elegance and pride of Hellenism. The younger elements of its populace maintained bloody accounts with the oppressor. The Turks succeeded in radically destroying the area to its very foundations during the interwar years, renaming the deserted district *Kourtoulous*, meaning, in their language, "redemption" or "deliverance." The ship used by the Turks to carry food supplies, by order of the International Red Cross, to the starving population of occupied Greece was also named "Kourtoulous."

"...deserted Macedonian town...." This does not refer, of course, to the towns that were distributed to the Slavs and that have today completely disappeared. It refers to those that remained Greek. What a contrast between the provincial quiet of the modern era and their tumultuous past! In other words from the time of their acme, with their trade and their schools during the Turkish Rule until the time of the Macedonian Struggle, with their superhuman sacrifices in order to escape the malice or the misconception of the Great Powers and the greed of their neighbors. And all this always against the same backdrop: the old palaces, the wealthy churches, the poplars, the rivers, the lakes, the waters.

"Naxos, Chios...." Reference to the cheerful and bright aspect of the towns in the Aegean islands in contrast to the dull and gloomy towns of the North.

"Misr." Egypt.

The enumeration of names of States in South and Central America. Apart from the charm and eurhythmy of the place names, their enunciation serves here as a screen for the unbridled expression of the poem's Hellenolatry.

"On the crown of your head ..." etc. Cf. the folksongs:

Like a rock is his back,
like a tower his head,
and his staunch breast
a mossy wall of stone.

and also:

O Xantinon, o Xantinon, ever renowned,
on the one nostril horses are standing.
on the other nostril the hand mill is turned,
and on your crown a pair of oxen are threshing.

(Xantinon)

"In Kastoria ...." See note to the "towns of Macedonia."

"you have the beauty of a Greek!" When one recalls the Socratic definition that to be a Greek is not a question of origin but of education, then one can understand just what heights of beauty can be attained by a Greek.

"Phanar, Mouchlio, Constantine Palaeologus." Many forget that the Phanar was, for many years, the Cradle of modern Hellenism. Mouchlio is a district in the Phanar that took its name from the Chapel "of the Mongols," the "Mongolio," situated there. "Mouchlio" is a corruption of the word. It is also true that the whole district, on the banks of the Golden Horn, is very humid [and so may also take its name from the Greek word "mouchla," meaning mold. Trans note].

The poet heard the descriptions of Constantinople from stories told by his father. His own experience of the city was brief and disappointing. It seems that Constantinople is a city located not only in space but also in time. In any case, its natural beauties are unquestionably incomparable and its historic remains and monuments unequalled.

There is a popular belief that Constantine Palaeologus was not killed, is not dead. He is in hiding somewhere and will reappear with the re-capture of his capital:

O Constantine, O King,
The one they call protector,
Tell me where it is you are.
Are you dead or in hiding?

(Folk Song)

Of course, support for unification or not is no longer an issue.

Boyaca, Ayacucho, Leskovik. As to the first two names, the same remark as for the names of the other South-American Republics. As to Leskovik, see immediately below.

"I was there ... etc." The poet's vivid recollections from the 1940–41 Albanian Campaign.

"...that Hormovo man." Kostas Lagoumtzis or Lagoumtzis Hormovitis, from Hormovo in Northern Epirus. He was an engineer at the time of the Revolution, renowned for his "lagoumia," the tunnels he dug under enemy camps in order to blow them up. He died in the heroic sortie from Mesolonghi in 1826.

"Vrass!" Albanian for "fire!" It was shouted by Ali Pasha at the massacre at Gardikio, something which is of not the slightest interest to us, but which does interest Valaoritis, because it was an internal family matter. The Gardikiots were Muslims. It was also shouted by the sailors in the 1821 War of Independence and by the unforgettable and renowned admiral Koundouriotis at the naval battle of Elli. I heard this from my late cousin, Athanassios Pinotsis, a native of Hydra.

"Pineapple" [Greek has "koumbaras," lit. "piggybank," Trans. note]. Military slang in the 1821 War of Independence for "hand grenade."

"traps" [Greek has "dolapia" Trans. note]. Military slang in the 1821 War of Independence.

"Aconcagua." The highest peak in the Cordilleras in the Andes (Chile). A volcano.

"Alabanda." Ancient town in Asia Minor (Caria). It produced marble that was used by ancient sculptors. I preferred it to Pentelikon because the phrase "of Pentelikon marble" has so often been linked to all kinds of profanities!

"Blachernae's holy water." Blachernae. Renowned Byzantine monastery, near to the palace of the same name, with an underground "holy spring," from which flows thaumaturgic water.

"Cyril Loukaris." The illustrious Patriarch. One of the most learned men of the Renaissance. Opponent of the Jesuits and the Uniates.

"Apollonius." Reference to Apollonius of Tyana.

"Rigas Ferraios." Antonios Kyriazis from Velestinon. The brave bard of Liberty.

"Antonios Economou." The pioneering and modest hero from Hydra.

"Pasvantzoglou." Semi-independent chief and later rebel in the region of Viddinio. A friend of Ferraios, who greatly admired him. Cf.:

Why stand there, Pasvantzoglou, so entranced?
Fly to the Balkans, like an eagle make your nest…

(Battle hymn)

"Maximilien de Robespierre." The great republican leader of France. In reality very different from what I had been taught at my school desk. Not only was he not the bloodthirsty tyrant described to me, but, on the contrary, he was a sincere ideologist, a virtuous politician of great stature, who never managed to neutralize the clandestine intrigues of the enemies of law and morality.

"that other great American, the one from Montevideo." Reference to Isidore Ducasse, comte de Lautréamont. Cf.:

"... C'est le Montevidéen qui passe!"

(Comte de Lautréamont: *Les Chants de Maldoror*).

"antistrophe." This is, in fact, a detailed description of the Liberian coat of arms.

"epode." Influenced by the popular song of Antonio Vargas-Heredia.

"Nauplion." The lovely township in the Argolid. Cf.: "To the popular mentality, Nauplion is the champion among all the lands and towns, just as Constantinople is the Queen, Venice the princess, Smyrna the beloved and Kalamata the housewife."

(F. Kontoglou, *Travels*).

Of course, the scandal referred to in the" Conclusion" was caused by the town's "peace-loving" bourgeois inhabitants.

"sardana." Catalonian song and dance rhythm particularly liked by the poet.

"general... Hydra?" "Général Engonopoulos – le grand-père du poète – aviez-vous donc abandonné votre natale Hydra pour sauter avec la poudrière de Larissa?"

(Robert Levesque: *Domaine Grec*).

NOTES TO *IN THE VALE OF ROSERIES*

The Surrealism of Interminable Life [together with On the Death of the Anthologist of "Sublime Love" and Close Your Eyes: Then

All the Life of Old Will Pass Before You]. Three poems published together in a literary magazine with the common title: "On the Death of Three Poets."

On Crocodile Cladas

Crocodile Cladas (1425–1490): the free, proud and ever victorious warlord of the Mani, who was, however, eventually defeated and flayed alive by the Turks.

Preveza, 15.9.77

NIKOS ENGONOPOULOS:
BIOGRAPHICAL DATA (1907–2007)*

1907 (21 October): Birth of N.E. in Athens, second son of Panayotis and Errietti.

1914 (Summer): Trip to Constantinople, where the family is obliged to settle following the outbreak of the War.

1923–1927: N.E. is enrolled as a boarder in a lycée in Paris. He spends his free days at the home of his uncle, Dr Liabeis.

1927 (November)–1928 (July): He spends his military service as a private in the 1st Infantry Regiment.

1928–1930: He works as a translator in a Bank and as a secretary at the University. At the same time, he attends night-school in Athens in order to obtain the Greek School-Leaving Certificate.

1930 (October)–1933 (March): He is employed on a daily basis as a designer in the Urban Planning Department of the Ministry of Public Works.

1932: He enrols in the Athens School of Fine Arts and studies under Konstantinos Parthenis. He also studies at the studio of Fotis

---

* Translated from the biographical data provided on Engonopoulos's website (www.engonopoulos.gr) and compiled by I.M. Vourtsis.

Kontoglou, where Yannis Tsarouchis had begun his studies a year earlier. The two students assist Kontoglou with the wall-paintings in his house.

1934: "Engonopoulos the Phanariot," portrait "by the hand of Fotios Kontoglou" (egg on wood 25.5 x 20 cm., R. Kopsidis Collection). **(May)**: He is appointed on a daily wage as an employee in the Topographical Service at the Ministry of Public Works. He is given tenure exactly six years later (Designer 1st Grade).

1937: His father dies in Constantinople.

1938 (January): For the first time, N.E. presents his works, temperas on paper depicting old houses from towns in W. Macedonia at the exhibition "Art of the Modern Greek Tradition," organised by the "Greek Popular Art" Association in the Stratigopoulou Exhibition Hall. He also assists with the models of the stately houses constructed by D. Pikionis and funded by the Ministry of Tourism. **(February)**: He translates poems by Tristan Tzara and publishes them in the volume *Sur(r)ealism I*. [The same poems were re-published in Tristan Tzara, *Surrealism and Post-war*, Ypsilon/Books, 1979]. He finishes his studies (receiving his diploma many years later, in January 1956). He publishes three poems – "There," "The Secret Poet," "Nocturnal Maria" – in the magazine *O Kyklos* (vol. 4), edited by Apostolos Melachrinos. **(June)**: He publishes his first collection of poetry: *Do Not Distract the Driver* (Athens, Kyklos, 64p.). He designs the sets and the costumes for Plautus' *Menaechmi* (directed by G. Sarandidis at the Kotopouli Theatre). **(December)**: Publication of *Apollonius* by Apostolos Melachrinou with pictures by the painter Nikos Engonopoulos (Athens: Kyklos).

1939 (September): Publication of his second collection: *The Clavicembalos of Silence* (Athens: Hippalektryon, 98p.) **(November)**: His first individual exhibition at the home of Nikos Kalamaris. Publication of the album *Greek Fashion* with cover and sketches by Nikos Engonopoulos. He fashions a medal for the Ministry of Press and Tourism. He designs the sets and costumes for Sophocles' *Electra* (directed by Karolos Koun at the Kotopouli Theatre). He participates in a group exhibition of Greek artists in New York.

1941 (January): He is called up to the Albanian Front.

1942: He participates in the "Professional" Painting Exhibition at the Zappeion Megaron. And again in the following year (1943). The "Greek Folk Art" Society enlists the architects N. Argyropoulos and A. Papayeoryiou together with N.E. to sketch old Athenian houses. He writes *Bolivar, a Greek Poem*. The poem initially circulated in manuscript form and was read at gatherings expressing resistance to the Nazi Occupation.

1944 (May): He publishes "Seven Poems" in the magazine *Ta Nea Grammata* (7, vol. 2). **(September)**: Publication of *Bolivar, a Greek Poem* (Athens: Ikaros).

1945 (Spring): He publishes three poems in the magazine *Tetradio* (vol. 1). **(May)**: He is seconded from the Ministry of Public Works to the National Technical University of Athens as an assistant lecturer in the Department of Architectural Design and Drawing, headed by D. Pikionis. He would remain in this post with continual renewals of the secondment until 1956. **(July)**: He publishes seven poems from *Return of the Birds* in the magazine *Ta Nea Grammata* (7, vol. 5–6). **(September)**: He writes the poem "Picasso the Poet" and the accompanying article (containing translations of poems by Picasso) for the magazine *Tetradio* (vol. 2). He designs the sets and costumes for Nikos Kazantzakis' play *Capodistria* (directed by Socrates Karantinos at the National Theatre). **(December)**: Publication of the magazine *Tetradio* (vol. 3) with the cover designed by N.E. and containing the text by Andreas Embirikos "Nikos Engonopoulos or the Marvel of Elbasan and of the Bosphorus."

1946 (May): Publication of his collection, *The Return of the Birds* (Athens: Ikaros).

1948 (January): A text by him is included in the special issue of the magazine Kyklos "devoted to the poet Apostolos Melachrinos for the 40 years since his Variations." **(December):** Publication of his collection, *Eleusis* (Athens: Ikaros). Paintings by N.E. of Kastoria ("The Picheos Residence") and of Zagora ("The School of Rigas") are published in albums in the series "Gallery of the Art of the Greek People. 1. Architecture of Secular Monuments." Vol. I Mansions of Kastoria (Athens, 1948), and Vol. II, Houses of Zagora in Pelion (Athens 1949), published by the "Greek Folk Art" Society.

1949: He participates in the Pan-Hellenic Exhibition at the Zappeion Megaron (and again in 1952, 1957, 1963, 1965, 1971, 1973 and 1975). He becomes a founding member of the art group "Armos," which has as its aim to promote a modern aesthetic movement in Greece (the members include Nikos Hatzikyriakos-Ghikas, Yannis Tsarouchis, Yannis Moralis, Nikos Nikolaou, Natalia Mela, Panayotis Tetsis and Yorgos Mavroidis). With the "Armos" group, he exhibits works in the same year, in 1950 (Athens and Thessaloniki) and in 1952. His paintings are also exhibited at the Greek pavilion in the International Exhibition in New York. **(September):** He works at the Ministry of Housing and Reconstruction with a group of architects led by D. Pikionis on the design of new buildings in districts that had been destroyed (Piraeus etc.). He designs the model for the Pan-Hellenic Folk Industry and Handicraft Fair.

1950 (March): Marriage to Nelli Andrikopoulou.

1951: He participates in a group exhibition of Stage Scenery in Oslo (and in those organised by the International Theatre Institute (I.T.I.) in Athens in 1957 and 1962, and in the one organised by the French Institute of Athens in December 1959). He also participates in the exhibition organised by the International Association of Architects (I.A.A.) in Athens (and again in 1954). Birth of his son Panos.

1952: He designs the scenery and costumes for Goldoni's *Il burbero di buon cuore* (directed by Socrates Karantinos at the National Theatre).

He assists in the painting of the frescoes in the church of St Spyridon in New York (undertaken by Fotis Kontoglou). N.E. does the images for the Twelve Days and the altar screen.

1953: He participates in a group exhibition of Greek painters in Rome and Ottawa (the exhibition moved on to Edmonton, Toronto and Vancouver in 1954 and São Paulo in 1955).

1954: He publishes his poem, "The Atlantic," in the magazine *Anglo-Elliniki Epitheorisi* (Vol. 6, no. 3) together with an oil-painting [Jason]. (**February**): Offprint: *The Atlantic*, Athens. (**Summer**): He represents Greece in the 27th International Biennale in Venice with 72 of his works [Catalogue La Biennale di Venezia (XXVII), Grecia, Nicos Engonopoulos, "Lombroso," Venezia, with an introduction by U. Paluchini and a text by D.E. Evanghelides]. Advertising sketch for the magazine *O Tachydromos*. He divorces his wife, Nelly Andrikopoulou.

1956 (May): ["Points of contact between Modern Art and the ideal of Greek Art"]. Reply to research by the magazine *Zygos* (vol. 7). (**June**): He is elected to the National Technical University of Athens as a tenured lecturer (proposed by D. Pikionis and N. Hatzikyriakos-Ghikas) and is appointed to the Department of Architectural Design and Drawing. He resigns from the Ministry of Public Works.

1957 (April): Publication of his collection, *In the Flourishing Greek Tongue* (Athens: Ikaros). (**May**): He is appointed as a lecturer to the Department of General Art History. He participates in a group exhibition of painting in Thessaloniki (and again in 1966 and 1973). He designs the scenery and costumes for *Girl, Aspects of a Woman, Medea* and *Ring and Trumpet* for Rallou Manou's "Greek Ballet." (**November**): Design for the brochure of the National Tourist Organisation of Greece: "Aigina. The Village Hotel."

1958 (December): He is awarded the First Prize for Poetry by the Ministry of National Education for his collection, *In the Flourishing Greek Tongue.*

1959: He participates in the group exhibition organized by "Zygos." He designs the scenery and costumes for Euripides' *Ion* and Aeschylus' *Prometheus Bound* (directed by Linos Karzis for the "Themelikos Theatre Company").

1960: Second marriage to Eleni Tsiokou. (**May**): He is appointed as supervisor to the Modelling Studio (directed by Professor K. Biris). (**August**): Journey to Switzerland, Germany and Austria.

1961: Birth of his daughter Errietti. (**August**): A text on Futurism in the magazine *Zygos* (vols. 68–69). "The Architecture of Athens Today" in the magazine *Techniki Epitheorisis* (vol. 5). Two texts: "The Ballet" and ["The Transfer of Greek Costumes onto the Stage"] in the volume *Greek Ballet*.

1962 (March): The poem "The Image" in the magazine *Pnevmatiki Kypros*. (**June**): ["On the single Cultural Centre"], reply to the magazine *Zygos* (vols. 78–79). He designs the scenery and costumes for Brecht's *The Threepenny Opera* (directed by N. Hatziskos), for Shaw's *Caesar and Cleopatra* (directed by Alexis Solomos) and for Molière's *Le Bourgeois Gentilhomme* (directed by Socrates Karantinos for the State Theatre of Northern Greece). (**December**): Second edition with notes and eight colour pictures of *Bolivar, a Greek Poem* (Athens: Ikaros).

1963 (February): Individual exhibition of painting at the Athens Technological Institute. His talk at the Official Opening, "A Few Things Concerning the Origin of my Work." His text, "A Few Things Concerning the Miracle of Cretan Theatre," is published in the magazine *Theatro* (vol. 7). (**March**): His talk at the opening of his exhibition at the A.T.I. is published under the title "Lecture" in the magazine *Epitheorisi Technis* (vol. 17, no. 99). His mother dies in Athens.

1964 (January): He participates in the Commemorative Exhibition for G. Bouzianis and D. Evanghelidis. (**February**): He resigns from the National Technical University. His text, "Two forms of a painting and three poems on the death of three poets," is published in the magazine *Pali* (vols. 2–3). He designs the scenery and costumes for Euripides' *Hippolytus* (directed by Socrates Karantinos for the State Theatre of Northern Greece). He participates in a group exhibition of Greek painters in Brussels. (**November**): Release of the record *Engonopoulos Reads Engonopoulos* on the "Dionysos" label.

1965: He designs the scenery and costumes for Aristophanes' *Lysistrata* (directed by Socrates Karantinos for the State Theatre of Northern Greece). (July): His statement ["Concerning Democracy"] is published in the special issue of the magazine *Epitheorisi Technis*.

1966 (May): For his work as a painter, he is awarded the Order of the Gold Cross of George I. (**June**): ["On Angelos Sikelianos"] published in the newspaper *Ta Nea* (22/6) (**October**): Second edition of *Do Not Distract the Driver* and *The Clavicembalos of Silence* in one volume with notes and an autobiographical note (Athens: Ikaros). (**December**): He publishes nine poems and two pictures in the magazine *Pali* (vol. 6).

1967 (October): He is elected non-tenured Professor at the National Technical University in the Department of Drawing.

1968 (May): His views on "The Parthenis Affair" published in the newspaper *Ethnos* (28/5). (**December**): He publishes "Short Biography of the Poet Constantine Cavafy" and "Essai sur l' inégalité des races humaines" in the magazine *Lotos* (vol. 3). Release of the record *Bolivar, a Greek Poem* on the Lyra label, in the form of a popular cantata, with music composed by Nikos Mamangakis and vocals by Yorgos Zografos.

1969 He publishes the poem "Of the Holy Jews" in the magazine *Philologiki Protochronia*. (**April**): He is elected tenured Professor at the National Technical University in the Department of Drawing and authorized Professor in the Department of General Art History. (**May**): He publishes the poem "Man Cannot Serve Two Masters" in the magazine *Lotos* (vols. 4–5). (December): A text on the Karaghiozis Shadow Puppet Theatre in the magazine *Lotos* (vol. 6).

1971: He participates in the exhibition "Modern Greek Art on the 1821 War of Independence. Painting–Sculpture–Engraving" at the Greek Chamber of Art. (**Autumn**): He publishes the poem "The Balad of Isidore-Sideri Steikovic" in the magazine *Prosanatolismi* (vol. 7, Larissa). (**November**): Publication of his article "The Sculptor Theodoros Vassileiou" in the newspaper *To Vima* (28/11). (**December**): He is awarded the Cross of the Commander of the Phoenix.

1972: Publication by the National Technical University of Athens Press of the album *Hellenic Houses*, containing 18 color paintings ["Psychographs of Houses" as they had once been characterized by D. Pikionis]. His poems "The Flag" and "A Dream: Life" are accepted for volume 6 of the magazine *Tram*, which, however, ceases publication in June.

1973 (August): Having reached the compulsory age for retirement, he resigns from the National Technical University. In 1976, he is named Professor Emeritus. "The Goalposts," "Pandora's Box" and "The Flag" are printed in the volume *Chroniko '73* (published by the art-gallery "Ora").

1974 (January): His poem "The Bugle-horn" is published in the magazine *Efthini* (vol. 25).

1975 (February): A text by him on Cobblers is published in the magazine *Zygos* (vol. 12). (**July**): His views ["Concerning Dionysios Solomos"] are published in the magazine *Ydria* (vol. 16). (October): Three poems "Orpheus" (together with the painting of the same name), "A Dream: Life" and "Associations" are published in the magazine *Speira* (vol. 3) and as an offprint. His text "On Kontoglou" is published in the collective volume *In Memory of F. Kontoglou* (Athens: Astir). (December): "On Everything Under the Sun," "On Hamadryads" and "Beroutian" are published in the anthology *Poetry '75*, edited by Th. Niarchos and A. Fostieris.

1976. (January): The poems "On Crocodile Cladas" and "Vitzentzos Kornaros" are published in the magazine *I Nea Poiesi* (vol. 7). Publication in Paris of *Bolivar, un poème grec*, translated by Franchita Gonzalez Batlle, bilingual edition "Voix Francois Maspero." **(November):** Exhibition of his paintings at the Moraitis School's Society for the Study of Modern Greek Culture and General Education. The poems "Readjustment" and "The Surprise," together with a picture, are published in the magazine *Tram* (2nd series, vol. 3).

1977 (November): "Ikaros" publishes the second volume of his *Poems*, containing the collections: "Bolivar," "The Return of the Birds," "Eleusis," "The Atlantic" and "In the Flourishing Greek Tongue." (December): "Dioni," "A Somewhat Elderly Brave General" are published in the anthology *Poetry '77*, edited by Th. Niarchos and A. Fostieris.

1978 (October): "On Fotis Kontoglou," text published in the magazine *Zygos* (vol. 31). **(November):** Publication by Ikaros of his collection, *In the Vale of Roseries* (With 20 Colour Paintings and One Sketch). "Poems of a twenty-year period, together with some others" (From N.E.'s "Notes").

1979: For the second time, he is awarded the National Prize for Poetry. His text "Herakleion, Crete and the 3rd Christian Girls' School" is published in the book *Elli Alexiou. A Small Dedication* (Athens: Kastaniotis).

1980 (November): His essay, *Karaghiozis. Greek Shadow Theatre*, is published by Ypsilon/Books.

1981 (January): "The Betrothed," poem published in the magazine *I lexi* (vol. 1) (special feature on Nikos Engonopoulos with an interview, sketches and a text by K. Yeorgousopoulos).

1983 (March): Retrospective exhibition of his work with 105 paintings at the National Gallery / Alexandros Soutsos Museum. **(April):** His text "Cavafy, Simply Perfect" is published in the special issue on

Cavafy of the magazine *I lexi* (vol. 23). (**December**): His poem "The Carnations" is published in the magazine *I lexi* (vols. 29–30). *Bolivar. Un poema Griego*, translated by Miguel Castillo Didier, is published by Juventud Griega de Venezuela and Editorial Arcadia in Caracas.

1984 (November): Individual exhibition of water-colours, sketches and temperas in the "Zoumboulaki" Art Gallery.

1985 (31 October): N.E. dies of a heart attack. He is buried in the First Cemetery of Athens at public expense. (**November**): Individual exhibition "Nikos Engonopoulos. Painting 1975–1985" at the "Gallery 3" Art Gallery, Athens.

1987 (August): Individual exhibition of engravings at the "Aigina" Art Gallery, Aigina. (**November**): Ypsilon/Books publishes his *Prose Texts* (With Two Colour Paintings). The French Institute of Athens stages the exhibition "Nikos Engonopoulos, Painter and Poet. Oils, Temperas and Books from Private Collections."

1988 (November): Special double issue of the magazine *Hartis* is devoted to N.E.

1991 (June–September): His works are included in the exhibition entitled "Surréalistes Grecs" at the Centre Georges Pompidou, Paris.

1993 (November): Publication of N.E.'s Letters to his wife Eleni 1959–1967, ... *And I Love You Passionately* (with fifteen colour paintings).

1994 (December): Works by Engonopoulos are included in the exhibition "The Masters," "Skoufa" Gallery, Athens. Conference at the Goulandris-Horn Foundation on the topic "Nikos Engonopoulos. The Beauty of a Greek. 50th Anniversary of the First Edition of *Bolivar.*"

1995 (December): His works are included in an exhibition entitled "Surrealism. The Greek Dimension" at the "Titanium" Gallery,

Athens. Individual exhibition entitled "10 Years Since the Death of Nikos Engonopoulos" at the "Skoufa" Gallery, Athens.

1996 (February): Publication of the volume: *Nikos Engonopoulos: The Beauty of a Greek (Nine Studies)*, Goulandris-Horn Foundation. **(November)**: Publication of *Sketches and Colours* in a bilingual edition (Athens: Ypsilon/Books). **(December)**: Individual exhibition of sketches, bozzetti and oils at the "Zoumboulaki" Art Gallery, Athens on the occasion of the presentation of the book *Sketches and Colours*. Re-publication in a smaller format of *Hellenic Houses* by the National Technical University of Athens Press.

1997 (February): A retrospective exhibition of his work at the Municipal Gallery, Thessaloniki as part of the events organized for "Thessaloniki. Cultural Capital of Europe." **(May)**: A special issue of "Epta Imeres" (Sunday Supplement of the newspaper *Kathimerini*) entitled "Nikos Engonopoulos. Painter and Poet" is devoted to his work. **(Summer)**: His work is included in the exhibition entitled "Greek Painters and Ancient Greek Drama: Scenery Variations" at the European Cultural Centre of Delphi, Delphi.

1998 (January): A special issue of the literary magazine *Diavazo* is devoted to his work. **(May–June)**: His works are included in the exhibition "The Portraits from Faiyûm and the Generation of the '30s in the search for Greekness" at the Benaki Museum, Athens.

1999 (March): His works are included in the exhibition "Great Painters in Small Paintings" at the "Zita-Mi" Gallery, Thessaloniki. Individual exhibition of his works entitled "Nikos Engonopoulos. Mythology, Byzantium, Revolution" at the "Astrolavos" Gallery, Athens. **(June)**: His *Poems I* and *Poems II* are re-published by Ikaros in one volume.

1999 (November): A collection of interviews and articles by Engonopoulos covering the period from 1938 to 1985 is published by Ypsilon/Books in the volume *The Angels in Paradise Speak Greek ... Interviews, Comments and Views*.

2001: Publication of the album: *Nikos Engonopoulos the Byzantine.* Forty-one Egg Temperas / Eight Sketches / Twenty Poems / and One Ink on Paper.

2003: The magazine *i lexi*, devotes a special issue to his work (vol. 179).

2005: Publication of *Man: The Measure.* Five Poems and Ten Paintings, Ypsilon/Books [containing three previously unpublished poems and paintings from private collections]. Special issue of the book supplement *Eleftherotypia/Vivliothiki*, (12/8) "Nikos Engonopoulos, Hellenocentric and Ecumenical."

2006: On the occasion of the upcoming centenary of his birth, *The Poet Nikos Engonopoulos, Diary 2007* (an anthology of his poetry and painting, together with critiques of his work), and *Nikos Engonopoulos, Mythology* (an album) are published by Ypsilon/Books.

2007: Numerous events are organized by the National Book Centre of Greece to mark the centenary of his birth. (**February**): The National Book Centre of Greece publishes the album *"Love is the only way...."* (**February–April**): Exhibition "Engonopoulos 2007... The Beauty of a Greek" at Athens International Airport. (**March**): Show dedicated to his work is performed at the Athens Music Megaro (director: Yannis Kakleas). (**March–April**): As part of the campaign for International Poetry Day 2007, posters designed by students at the Athens School of Fine Arts based on Engonopoulos' verses are carried by Athens public transport. (**May–June**): Exhibition "Topos: Engonopoulos" at the Macedonian Museum of Modern Art, Thessaloniki. (**November**): International Conference "Engonopoulos 2007: Poet and Painter" at the Benaki Museum, Athens. (**November – January 2008**): Major retrospective exhibition of his painting at the Benaki Museum, Athens.

INDEX OF GREEK POEMS